P9-BYS-702

CELTIC WOMEN

CELTIC WOMEN

Women in Celtic Society and Literature

Peter Berresford Ellis

WILLIAM B. EERDMANS PUBLISHING COMPANY
GRAND RAPIDS, MICHIGAN

© 1995 Peter Berresford Ellis
First published 1995 in Great Britain by
Constable and Company Ltd
3 The Lanchesters, 162 Fulham Palace Road,
London W6 9ER

This edition published 1996 in the United States of America
through special arrangement with Constable by
Wm. B. Eerdmans Publishing Co.
255 Jefferson Ave. S.E., Grand Rapids, Michigan 49503
All rights reserved

Printed in the United States of America

01 00 99 98 97 96   7 6 5 4 3 2 1

Library of Congress Cataloging-in-Publication Data

Ellis, Peter Berresford.
Celtic women : women in Celtic society and
literature / Peter Berresford Ellis.
p.   cm.
Includes bibliographical references and index.
ISBN 0-8028-3808-1 (hardcover : alk. paper)
1. Women, Celtic — History. 2. Women, Celtic — Folklore.
3. Civilization, Celtic. 4. Women in literature.
5. Mythology, Celtic. I. Title.
HQ1137.C45E45   1996
305.48′8916 — dc20   95-50651
                                                         CIP

Contents

Illustrations

Women were by no means excluded from positions of authority.

Cornelius Tacitus (*c.*AD56–117)
on Celtic women in *Agricola*.

It is a truism that there has never been born bishop, king nor saintly prophet but from the womb of a woman; therefore, woe to him who speaks ill of women.

Gearóid Iarla
*c.*AD1335–98

Introduction

D URING the 1690s a piece of subversive literature was being circulated in Ireland, copied and distributed by an 'underground' in much the same way as dissident literature was copied and circulated in the former Soviet Union during the 1970s and 1980s. It was a book entitled *Párliament na mBan* – The Parliament of Women.

At the time, Ireland was a defeated country once again. King William's victorious armies were 'mopping up' after the collapse of the Irish parliament and the rump of the vastly depleted Irish army, some 12,000 soldiers, had surrendered at Limerick and been allowed to follow their generals into exile. They were to join the Irish Brigades of France and Spain. The losses to Ireland during the war were almost incalculable. During one disastrous battle alone, the clash at Aughrim, in July 1691, Ireland had lost 400 officers and 7000 men.

In victory, William was not merciful. After the remnants of the Irish army were deported some 1,500,000 acres of land were confiscated for English colonisation. Ignoring his promises of religious toleration, made to the Irish in the articles of the 'Treaty of Limerick', the document by which his generals had negotiated the Irish surrender, William approved a series of draconian 'Penal Laws' whereby the only religion allowed by law in Ireland was that of the Church of England. Catholics and all Dissenting Protestants, especially the radical Presbyterians of Ulster, were the subject of debilitating laws making them 'non-citizens'.

The 'Penal Laws', said one commentator, presumed that no such being as an Irish Catholic even existed, while Presbyterian ministers were treated as outlaws and harassed. They received three months in gaol for delivering a sermon, £100 fines for performing religious services, three months in gaol for teaching children, and all marriages performed by them were declared illegal. Civil and religious liberty, guaranteed under Acts XIII and XV of James II's Dublin parliament, were suppressed in the wake of the Williamite Conquest and the Irish language was subjected to another attempt at total eradication. Education for Irish Catholics and Dissenting Protestants was banned, leading to the rise of secret 'hedge-schools' as an attempt was made to keep learning alive among the Irish. This was not a haphazard English policy but, as with most conquests, a deliberate attempt to eradicate the Irish intelligentsia and thus Irish culture. Most of the Irish intellectual classes were either destroyed or driven into exile.

In such circumstances as these, the Irish, denied printing presses, would either circulate manuscript literature or else have books printed abroad, at Louvain, Paris, Antwerp and Rome, and these would then be smuggled back into the country. It was at Louvain that the first printed Irish dictionary (Micheál Ó Cléirigh's *Foclóir no Sanasan Nua*) had to be printed and taken surreptitiously into Ireland. Literacy in Irish had become a forbidden fruit and manuscripts and books had to be kept hidden. It was during this period also that the native law system, popularly called the Brehon laws, was finally eradicated. The Brehon families (the hereditary lawyers) tried to hide the old law books, burying them, even attempting to hide the ancient vellum texts in lakes. Possession of such texts meant death or transportation. Much was destroyed.

The scholar, Dr W.K. Sullivan, in the introduction to Eugene O'Curry's *On the Manners and Customs of the Ancient Irish*, recounts:

During the first part of the eighteenth century the possession of an Irish book made the owner a suspect person, and was often the cause of his ruin. In some parts of the country the tradition of the danger incurred by having Irish manuscripts lived down to within my own memory; and I have seen Irish manuscripts which had been buried until the writing had almost faded, and the margins rotted away, to avoid the danger their discovery would entail at the visit of the local yeomanry.

Yet some forty-odd copies of the book *Párliament na mBan*, circulating in the 1690s, have survived, showing just how popular this work

was. The work was written in an Irish judged to be that current in
Co. Cork during the period.

The story of the *Párliament na mBan* is that the women of Ireland,
fed up with the mess that men have plunged their world into, have
decided to seize political power themselves, set up their own parliament and enact their own laws. One woman, opening the parliament,
deprecates the former inactivity of women in political and public life
– 'remaining always at home attending to our distaffs and spindles,
even though many of us are no good about the house'. Other speakers
point out how the eternal quarrelling and fighting of men had ruined
the country. 'If women had control of all affairs it is certain that
things would be more settled and peaceful than they are.'

The debates and acts of the parliament follow with the women
deciding that girls should be educated equally with men in the seven
liberal arts and should be qualified in divinity, law and medicine
and, indeed, that men's conduct should be kept under close scrutiny.

Was such a pro-feminist concept a mere literary aberration of the
time? Or was it simply symptomatic of an ancient cultural tradition
of female rights within Celtic society?

Let me play devil's advocate for a moment.

Can we read anything into the fact that one of the earliest revolutionary feminist tracts, *An Appeal of One Half of the Human Race,
Women, against the Pretensions of the Other Half, Men, to Retain
them in Political and thence in Civil and Domestic Slavery*, was
written by Anna Wheeler and William Thompson of Cork in 1825
– a work which became a landmark in the struggle for women's
emancipation? Can anything also be read into the fact that when
the Welsh made their attempt to establish an independent Welsh-
speaking state, Y Wladfa, at the mouth of the River Chubut in Pata-
gonia in the 1860s, women had the voting franchise, being able to
elect, and be elected, as delegates to Y Senedd (Senate) which governed the colony until it was annexed by Argentina? Between 1867
and 1869 this tiny independent Welsh 'state', flying its Red Dragon
flag and using Welsh in all its affairs, was the only place in the world
where women could vote in political elections. It was in 1869 that
the territory of Wyoming, not yet a state, gave women the right to
vote.

Can anything be read into the fact that another small Celtic
country, the Isle of Man, passed a Women's Suffrage Act in 1881,
granting the vote to women some thirty-seven years in advance of

the United Kingdom? Of course, it must be mentioned that, in spite of this early according of political rights to women on the Island, the first female member of the House of Keys, Marion Shimmon, was not elected until 1933. She served until 1942. Curiously, no history of women's suffrage ever seems to mention Y Wladfa or the Isle of Man, which is constitutionally a self-governing Crown Dependency outside the jurisdiction of the United Kingdom. The generally accepted history is that New Zealand in 1893 was the first country to enfranchise women, followed by Australia in 1903. Of course, women won the right to vote and stand for office in South Australia in 1894. When the Australian Mint produced a $5 commemorative coin in 1994 it rightly featured the image of Irish-born Mary Lee who left Ireland at the age of fifty-eight to live in Australia and work for social reform, founding the Women's Suffrage League of South Australia in 1888.

Can anything be read into the fact that the first woman to be elected to the United Kingdom Parliament was Constance Markiewicz (1868–1927) by the people of the St Patrick's constituency of Dublin? She stood on a Sinn Féin ticket and therefore refused to take that seat, joining the revolutionary Dáil, the Irish parliament which then declared Irish independence in Dublin in 1919. Connie Markiewicz was one of the Gore-Booths of Lissadell, Co. Sligo. She became Minister for Labour in the Irish government of 1919–21, the first woman to become a government minister in any modern democracy. Or is there some significance in the fact that twenty-one-year-old Bernadette Devlin, in April 1969, also made history by becoming the youngest Member of Parliament ever to be elected to the United Kingdom Parliament at Westminster? She stood for the Mid-Ulster constituency, a socialist and republican.

Are these just isolated matters or is there a connecting theme which has its roots in a particular cultural background?

For years the image of 'Celtic women' has been conjured as the totem of the emancipated female. The very phrase 'Celtic women' has evoked all sorts of imagery. There is the fearsome warrior as personified by Connie Markiewicz, the beautiful 'Red Countess', in her 'rebel' uniform and carrying her Mauser pistol, on the barricades of Dublin during the 1916 uprising, with her historic antecedents such as Boudicca of the Iceni, Gwenllian of Dyfed or Gráinne Ní Máille of Connacht or such literary figures as Scáthach, at whose military academy all the warriors of Ireland were sent to learn their skill at arms, or the tumultuous warrior-queen Medb of Connacht. There is the ambitious female as personified by Nest of Dyfed in history and Ness of Ulster in mythology. There are the beautiful, romantic heroines such as Étain, Rhiannon, Emer, Gráinne, Deirdre, Aranrhod and countless others. There are the tragic, wronged queens, such as Der Bhfhorgaill of Breifne. There are goddesses by the score from old hags and screaming harpies to stately and beautiful goddesses of sovranty, fertility, healing and love; the wise women, the learned Druidesses and the great female *religieuses* and saints of the early Celtic Church. The Celtic culture encompasses them all.

Over the years there has arisen a debate as to whether the women in Celtic history and culture were possessed of a more privileged position than their sisters in other European cultures. But is the very idea of women's equality in the ancient Celtic world a myth in itself? Writing in the Summer 1979 issue of *Carn* (No. 26) Margaret O'Hara and Bernadette Bulfin, in a carefully studied piece, 'Descent into Civilisation', suggested that the laws of ancient Ireland and Wales proved the point. 'They gave more rights and protection to women than any other western law code at that time or since. Equal pay for work of equal value, "wages for housework", protection from violence, equitable separation laws, enforcement during marriage of the right of both spouses to respect and fidelity – before the English conquests, Celtic women enjoyed all this and more.' The thesis was that 'in the area of women's rights much of the long struggle is only to regain what was once enjoyed by Celtic women fifteen hundred years ago.'

This brought a reply in the Spring 1980 issue on 'The Social Status of Women in Wales' from barrister and Welsh law expert Ifan Lloyd who, while admitting that 'the status of Welsh women in the eighteenth century was far lower than under the native Law of Hywel in the twelfth century', felt that what the Welsh law had to say was not really an important criterion for establishing social status.

Margaret O'Hara made a lengthier argument in *Carn* (No. 34), Summer 1981, 'Women of Equal Dignity', relying on the Irish law rather than Welsh law to prove her point and also relying on references to some of the great historical Celtic female leaders to demonstrate their dominance in early society.

One of the most famous of these historical female personalities of the Celtic world is undoubtedly the first-century AD figure of Boudicca, better known in this day and age by the textually incorrect form of Boadicea. She was a ruler of her people in her own right, and accepted as a war leader against the Roman occupation forces not only by her own tribe, the Iceni, but by the Trinovantes and other neighbouring tribes who joined her, such as the Coritani. As she stood in her war chariot facing the Roman army of Gaius Suetonius Paulinus, the military governor of the newly annexed lands of southern Britain, she had her two young teenage daughters by her side. 'This is not the first time that the Britons have been led to battle by a woman.' It is the Roman historian Tacitus, whose father-in-law Agricola was a witness to the battle, acting as an aide-de-camp to Suetonius, who significantly puts these words into her mouth. 'I do not come to boast the pride of my ancestry, nor even to recover the plundered wealth of my family. I take the field like the ordinary citizen among you, to assert the cause of liberty; to seek justice for my body, scarred with the Roman lash, and to avenge my raped daughters. From the pride and arrogance of Rome, nothing is sacred; all are subject to violation; the old endure the whip and the young girls are raped.'

Boudicca, the 'Victorious', went on her way to meet her fate and take her place in the history books.

A woman. A female ruler and general? Was she some aberration of her day? Was she merely an individualist, a powerful personality, able to throw off the constraints of the time to achieve her position? Or was she simply part of a culture in which women could and did achieve an equality with men?

'It is indeed impossible to have any true understanding of either Celtic history or Celtic literature without realising the high status of Celtic women, and something of the nature of their place in society, in both Gaul and Britain,' say Celtic scholars Myles Dillon and Nora Chadwick in *The Celtic Realms*. But Professor Fergus Kelly, in *A Guide to Early Irish Law*, responds: 'Exaggerated claims have sometimes been made about the degree of power and freedom enjoyed by women in early Irish society.' Does Professor Kelly simply mean that the Irish Celts were less better off than their Celtic cousins in Gaul and Britain? Or does he imply that the 'exaggerated claims' apply to women in all Celtic societies? He apparently means the latter.

Gilbert Márkus OP, in his paper on 'Early Irish "Feminism"', also makes clear that he believes the 'exaggerated claims' are made for all Celtic societies. 'The claim that women had a high place in traditional

Celtic society seems to be unsubstantiated by the evidence.' However, Father Márkus also makes the point: 'It seems, in fact, that they had a higher place following the introduction of Christianity.' But then, perhaps, we might allow that a member of the Dominican *Ordinis Praedicatorum* would attempt to argue that the Christian institutions had improved the lot of women in pagan Ireland.

The example of the actions of Rome against clerical wives, with Pope Urban II issuing a decree that such wives could be rounded up by nobles and used as slaves and chattels, is hardly in keeping with the rosy view of the lot of Christian women which Father Márkus would have us envisage.

In contradiction to Father Márkus's views, Mary Condren's thesis, expressed in *The Serpent and the Goddess: Women, Religion and Power in Celtic Ireland*, is that it was the very introduction of Christianity which accelerated the already altering coequal role of women in Celtic society; that it was after the introduction of Christianity that Celtic women rapidly began to lose their prestige and status. The teaching of St Augustine of Hippo, that 'the woman herself alone is not the image of God: whereas the man alone is the image of God as fully and completely . . .', certainly is hardly an attitude conducive to any improvement of women's lot in society. J.P. Mackey's conclusion in *An Introduction to Celtic Christianity* is that pre-Christian Celtic women did occupy a 'superior place' in their society than fell to the lot of their Christian descendants.

In 1390 Maghnus Ó Duibhgeánnáin supervised the compilation of a large folio volume of 501 pages at Ballymote, in Co. Sligo. It contained copies of several older books such as the *Leabhar na gCeart* (Book of Rights). Among the works included was a history of the most remarkable women of Ireland from early times down to the Anglo-Norman invasion. That *The Book of Ballymote* should contain this work is fascinating for it allows one to make the claim for Irish that it contains Europe's oldest women's history.

In spite of this, however, Donnchadh Ó Corráin and Fidelma Maguire, in *Irish Names* (1990), have pointed out that there are over 12,000 personal names recorded in early Irish sources. Of these only just over 4000 are the names of women. This reflects the fact that the historical records generally concern themselves with the deeds of men rather than women. One interesting aspect of Irish names is that although, as in other cultures, Irish usually distinguishes between male and female names, there are an unusual number of names in Irish which are found to be common to both sexes and some obvious male names that are also applied to women. This is an interesting phenomenon for even when a name is the same there is usually a masculine and a feminine form of that name. It has been suggested that the androgynous names are another aspect of equality of the sexes.

This volume is concerned with sketching the role of women in early Celtic society and attempting to explain the changes in that role during the encounter and conflict with the alien values of Roman and then Germanic cultures which today have all but subsumed it. Certainly we can argue that this role was by no means a passive or subservient one as emerges in other European cultures. On the other hand, we cannot go to the other extreme and argue that Celtic women lived in some kind of socially liberated feminist paradise. It is true that they had a position which was not paralleled in the majority of other contemporary societies. They could govern, took prominent roles in political, religious and artistic life, even becoming judges and law-givers; they could own property which marriage could not deprive them of; they chose when they wanted to marry and, more often than not, who they wanted to marry; they could divorce and, if they were deserted, molested or maltreated, they had the right to claim considerable damages.

Nevertheless, what we see in the early period is a society in flux and change. The role of women was diminishing as firstly encounters with the Roman empire and then the conquests of the Saxons, Franks and Normans, together with the influence of western Christianity, with its Greek and Roman moral codes, exerted pressure on Celtic society.

Professor Jean Markle, in *La Femme Celte*, observes:

It would appear that the Celts had been forced to keep some aspects of former social structures, because women's moral influence had remained strong. It is difficult to discard old customs, and the Celts very likely took longer than other peoples to rid themselves of social practices inherited from earlier gynaecocratic societies. Women did enjoy a liberal sphere of influence; it was conceived and drawn up by male legislators who had the greatest possible respect for their customs in theory, but organised affairs so as to diminish their practical importance. There are a number of historical examples within Celtic societies, Welsh, Breton and

Irish, that show that the laws favourable to women were not auto-matically applied; under the influence of Christianity they were gradually abandoned completely.

However, in the early period of recorded history, Celtic society was undoubtedly attempting to retain an order in which women were harmoniously balanced in relation to men. It was a different concept from the repressive male dominance of classic Mediterranean society. The position of women in Celtic myth, law and early history now seems to constitute an ideal. Before we can appreciate this we must examine how women appeared in Celtic myth, early history and under the law.

[1]

The Mother Goddess

THE earliest recorded native origin myths of the Celts are to be found in the *Leabhar Gabhála* (The Book of Invasions), the earliest surviving sections of which occur in the twelfth-century *Leabhar na Nuachonghbhala*, compiled by Fionn Mac Gormain of Glendalough. The book is therefore sometimes known as the *Book of Glendalough* but more popularly as the *Book of Leinster*. Now when the stories of the *Leabhar Gabhála* came to be written in this form, they were written by Christian monks who immediately weaved the Hebrew creation myth around them. However, it is my contention that the basis of the original Celtic creation myth can be rescued by a careful examination of the stories and a comparison with other Indo-European creation myths, in particular, Hindu mythology. In these myths, the Celtic peoples ascribed their creation to a mother goddess.

In the *Leabhar Gabhála* it is told how Bith, the son of the Hebrew Noah, with his wife Birren, were denied a place in the Ark. Bith's daughter Cesair advised her father to build an idol. This he did with companions called Fintan and Ladra. The idol, in turn, advised them to build a ship and take refuge in it as the idol was unable to tell them exactly when the Deluge would occur. They built the ship and, with three men and fifty women on board, they sailed off and after seven years came to the shore of Inisfáil, the Island of Destiny, or Ireland. Cesair became the wife of Fintan. But Bith and Ladra died and Fintan had to become the husband of all fifty women. He eventually fled. The Deluge suddenly came and Cesair and her women were drowned. Only Fintan survived by turning himself into a salmon.

In the Welsh myths there is an echo of the Deluge myth which tells of the overflowing of Llyon-Llion, the Lake of Waves, from which Dwyfan and Dwyfach escaped in a ship built by Nefyed Naf Nefion. This is undoubtedly the basis for the Arthurian tale of Lyonesse. The Welsh Deluge was caused by a monster called Addanc. His relationship to the Deluge is reminiscent of Haya-Griva in Hindu myth. Where Haya-Griva is defeated by Vishnu, Addanc is slain by Peredur. The builder of the ship, Nefyed Naf Nefion, appears to be the same person as the Irish Nemed, leader of the third invasion of Ireland. Nemed is claimed by the Christian scribes as a descendant of Magog, son of Japhet, one of the three sons of Noah, who went to occupy the 'Isles of the Gentiles'. Nefyed's ship contained Dwyfan and Dwyfach who are progenitors of the 'Cymry'.

Now it is clear, as I have said, that the Christian monks were liberally mixing Hebrew myths, gained from the new religion, with some older stories which have their basis in Indo-European traditions. But we can look through the Hebraic superstructure to the original Celtic core. The first two men, Bith and Ladra, die because they are drained of their life force by an excess of sexual liaisons with their women. R.A.S. MacAlister translates from the *Leabhar na gCeart*:

> Lightly they lay and pleasured
> In the green grass of that guileless place.
> Ladra was the first to die;
> He perished of an embrace.
>
> Bith was buried in a stone heap,
> Riot of mind, all passion spent.
> Fintan fled from the ferocious women
> Lest he, too, by love be rent.

The women die, frustrated by their inability to realise the promise of fertility. 'To make the land prosper,' says Peter R. Cherici in his study *Celtic Sexuality*, 'union between male and female was necessary. But the sexual requirements of the female were great and potentially deadly. The myth of Cesair warned men to be wary of women.'

It is my belief that the myth of Cesair is predated by an even more potent creation myth; that the original Celtic creation myth lies in the story of Danu, the true mother goddess of the Celts. Her children, the Tuatha Dé Danaan, appear in Irish myth as the gods and goddesses of the Celtic world. This pantheon of deities is paralleled by the Children of Dôn in Welsh mythology. Danu and Dôn are, of course, the same mother goddess entity.

Firstly, let us extrapolate this creation myth. In doing so we should bear in mind that the Celtic peoples are said to have evolved at the headwaters of the Danube, still bearing its Celtic name and that name being Danu, the mother goddess. The earliest known Celtic society developed here before the expansion of the Celts through Europe at the start of the first millennium.

In the beginning Danu or Dana, whose name we can make cognate with Sanskrit (the nearest we can come to our hypothesised common Indo-European), as 'Waters from Heaven', flooded from the sky to form the river named after her – Danuvius, in its earliest known form. These 'waters from heaven' fell and nurtured a sacred oak tree, Bíle. Danu and Bíle then gave birth to the being who became known as the 'father of the gods'. In Irish myth this was The Dagda, the 'Good God'. His children, the descendants of Danu and Bíle, became the gods and goddesses of goodness but, significantly, they are identified as the Tuatha Dé Danaan, the children of Danu, rather than the children of Bíle or, indeed, of her son, The Dagda. The creator deity was therefore a *mother goddess*.

Conversely, as with all good, there must also be evil. We find that Danu, 'Waters from Heaven', has an evil counterpart in the goddess Domnu, meaning both 'The World' and 'Deeps of the Sea'. When the Children of Danu reached Ireland, they had to struggle against their enemies, who were already in Ireland, the evil Children of Domnu who are also known as the Fomorii or 'under-sea dwellers'. The Irish epics contain many episodes of the struggle between the Children of Danu and the Children of Domnu, the eternal struggle of light and good over darkness and evil. But the Children of Domnu are never completely overcome or eradicated from the world. The fact that Domnu means 'the world' takes on a new significance, while Danu can only mean the 'heavenly' or spiritual aspiration of mankind.

Danu's name is to be found in many river names not only within Britain and Ireland but through those parts of Europe where the Celts once dwelt. The worship of rivers and 'divine waters' is prominent in pagan Celtic religion. Was there religious symbolism when, in 222BC, the great Celtic king, Viridomar, boasted that he was a 'son of the Rhine'? The Rhine still clearly bears its Celtic name, Renos, cognate with the Irish *rian*, a poetic and archaic name for the oceans but one which, like the majority of other Celtic river names, would have applied to a sea goddess. The same name appears in the River Reno in northern Italy, once part of Cisalpine Gaul.

The ancient Irish bards believed that the river's edge, the brink of the water, was the only place where *éisce* – wisdom, knowledge and poetry – was revealed. It was also a word that meant divination. In one version of the story of the birth of the great Ulster king, Conchobhar Mac Nessa, we find that the Druid, Cathbad, demands that Nessa brings him a drink from a river. There are two worms in the cup and, as punishment, he forces her to drink it instead. She becomes pregnant and gives birth to Conchobhar who is thereby named 'Son of the River' which bears the same name as Nessa. Has the goddess of the river taken the form of worms to be reborn as Conchobhar? Whatever the reason, it is significant that Conchobhar (this name means 'Wolf-lover') does not carry the usual patrynomic; he is Conchobhar Mac Nessa – Conchobhar son of his mother Nessa.

In the *Leabhar Gabhála* we have a minor story of a female, clearly a goddess, who had a magic cask which she opened and water from it flowed for so long that it eventually covered the earth. Can this be a faint echo of our original Danu creation myth?

To make comparisons with our Celtic creation myth, bearing in mind that we are dealing with an Indo-European people, we can turn to Hindu mythology. We find a very comfortable parallel in the story of Ganga, a mother goddess who, in later Hindu tradition, became one of the wives of Shiva. The waters of the Ganges, named after her, flow from heaven, according to the *Rigveda*. Joseph Campbell remarks on 'the idea of the sacred river, the Jordan, the waters that pour from heaven, flowing inexhaustibly out of some source. In India the very source of the Ganges, up in the Himalayan area, is a very sacred place.' Also in the *Rigveda*, Aditya appears not only as a mother goddess but as the name of a mythical river which is the source of all the waters of the world.

In fact, the combination of divine water and earth is the very essence of most creation myths, even those outside the Indo-European ambit. According to Genesis: 'In the beginning God created the heaven and earth. And the earth was without form, and void; and darkness was upon the face of the deep. And the spirit of God moved upon the face of the waters.' In this version we find the male has taken the place of the instigator moving on the face of the waters (female). In the Hebrew Bible the sentence is 'And Eloihim moved upon the face of the waters.' In the Finnish *Kalevala*, the Finns, a non-Indo-European people, have a virgin descending from heaven on to the waters of the earth and becoming Ilmatar, 'Mother of the Waters'. The Greek Aphrodite was 'born of the sea'.

According to Professor Jean Markle:

The belief in the sea as mother of all life has survived into our own times. Its mystery and depth made it the supreme feminine symbol and as patriarchal ideas gained predominance its secret and forbidden aspects were increasingly stressed. It contained strange creatures, hidden palaces and hoarded treasures; only exceptional divine beings were able to live in it. But endless taboos came between the sea and man. It was dangerous to probe its depths and only in particular cases were faultless heroes allowed to travel through the marvellous universe of that lost paradise.

In Brittany we have the story of a young man named Guengualc'h (White Falcon) who fell into a river and disappeared. His friends found St Tugdual and asked for help. Tugdual prayed and Guengualc'h rose to the surface but he had a silk sash tied to his right foot. He told how he had been persuaded under the waters by beautiful young women who had fled when Tugdual began to pray. In the panic, one of them forgot to untie her sash. The story has been Christianised and given a new moral, debasing and banishing the old goddesses. The same story remains more in its original form in the Irish tale of Condle Ruadh, son of Conn. He beheld a vision of a young and beautiful woman. He set out to find her and she led him away under the sea in a 'glass boat' to the 'Land of Promise' inhabited only by women in which he found true wisdom.

Indeed, the waters, which were of such importance to the ancient Celts as sources of food, for transportation and even, in terms of practicality, as clan boundaries, were the domain of the mother goddess and her various personifications. Brigid, whom we shall examine in detail shortly, and who is often made interchangeable with Danu, gave her name to many rivers such as Brigid (Bride in Munster, Ireland), Braint (Anglesey, Wales) and Brent (England). Danu not only gave her name to the Danube but to rivers in England, Wales, Scotland and France. In Ireland, the rivers Liffey, Boyne and Shannon are also named after goddesses who seem to appear as aspects of the mother goddess. The Severn in England is but a corrupt form of

Sabrina, a name noted by Tacitus. But that, in itself, is also a corruption of the original Celtic Sabrann, claimed as another goddess. Not only was the Lee in Ireland once anciently called Sabrann but the name was once applied to what is now a stream in Bedford.

Danu appears, as we have said, in Welsh mythology as Dôn while Bilé becomes Beli. Like the Irish myth, we are introduced to her children, rather than the children of Beli. The children of Dôn are clearly gods and goddesses with special responsibilities but they need disentangling from the coy interpretations of the Christian scribes who set down the tales. There is Gwydion (science and light), Aranrhod (dawn goddess), Gilfaethwy, Amaethon (agriculture), Gofannon (smith-craft), Nudd or Lludd (sky god), Penardun (wife to Llyr, the sea god), Nynniaw and Peibaw. Aranrhod, in turn, gives birth to Nwyfre (space), Lleu Llaw (sun god), and Dylan (sea god) while Nudd's son Gwyn is the keeper of Annwn (the Otherworld). There are still traces of the relationship of these gods and goddesses to the Irish pantheon but with the Welsh texts they have been transcribed into mortal guise. For example, Manawydan fab Llyr (Manánnan Mac Lir) becomes a mortal hero, presumably to appease the sensibilities of the Christians.

The Celtic myths are replete with powerful goddesses. J.A. Mac-Culloch has observed:

> Irish mythology points to the early preeminence of goddesses. As agriculture and many of the arts were first in the hands of women, goddesses of fertility and culture preceded gods, and still held their place when gods were evolved. Even war goddesses are prominent in Ireland. Celtic gods and heroes are often called after their mothers, not their fathers, and women loom largely in the tales of Irish colonisation, while in many legends they play a most important part. Goddesses give their name to divine groups, and even where gods are prominent, their actions are free, their personalities still clearly defined. The supremacy of the divine women of Irish tradition is once more seen in the fact that they themselves woo and win heroes; while their capacity for love, their passion, their eternal youthfulness and beauty are suggestive of their early character as goddesses of every springing fertility.

The Children of Danu serve to define the sexual roles in ancient Celtic society. They are all sexually active; some more so than others.

Sexuality was a pleasurable and necessary activity in Celtic myth, entered into on equal grounds by male and female.

From the mother goddess, Danu or Dôn, there are also descended several goddesses of fertility who carried on the process of pro-creation and who may also be deemed as aspects of the mother goddess. Of all these goddesses, or aspects, there is none so prominent and popular as the triune goddess Brigid. A ninth-century glossographer wrongly observed that all the goddesses of the pagan Irish were called Brigid. While wrong, the statement confirms Brigid's exalted position. In fact, the very name means 'Exalted One', which seems to confirm that it was probably an epithet for the mother goddess.

Confusingly, the texts generally make Brigid the daughter of The Dagda, the father of the gods. Yet Brigid appears in some texts as an aspect of Danu, the mother goddess of the Celts. She certainly appears not only as The Dagda's daughter but also as his mother and his wife. Brigid was known among the British Celts as Brigantu which, it has been argued, became known to the Roman occupation forces of Britain as Britannia, goddess of sovranty. The female figure sitting on a globe and learning with one arm on a shield, grasping a spear, first appeared on a British coin issued during the Roman occupation at the time of Antoninus Pius (c.AD161). But many Romans seemed to equate Brigantu with the Roman Minerva and gave her symbols associated with Minerva or Isis, such as the vulture, serpent and cow. She was also known among the Continental Celts. A tribe taking their name from her, the Brigantii, had their capital at Brigantion, now Bregenz, on Lake Konstanz, in Austria. And it has also been suggested that the north British tribal confederation took their name, the Brigantes, from her.

In Ireland this triune goddess has three differing functions. She was a goddess of healing, a goddess of smiths and, most importantly, a goddess of fertility and poetry. In this form, her festival became one of the four most important festivals of the pagan Celts – the feast of Imbolg or parturition, when ewes came into lamb, on 1 February. Significantly, the saint Brigid took this festival over for her feastday and much of the goddess's symbolism has been subsumed into that of the Christian saint.

Medieval writers made Brigid into the wife of Bres, the half-Fomorian ruler of the Children of Danu, by whom she had a son Ruadhan who was to wound the smith-god Goibhniu at the second battle of Magh Tuireadh but who was himself slain in the combat. Brigid is reported to have come to the battlefield to mourn her son with what is said to be the first *caoine* (keening), or lament, heard in Ireland. In other stories Brigid became the wife of Tuireann and had three sons, Brían, Iuchar and Iucharbam who slew the god Cian, father of Lugh Lámhfhada. A fascinating link to the traditions of the saint Brigid is the fact that a woman called Darlughdacha appears in St Brigid's community of Kildare as her close companion, sharing Brigid's bed. Darlughdacha, who became abbess of Kildare on Brigid's death, means 'daughter of Lugh' and the 'saints' lists' also give her feastday as 1 February. We will return to Brigid of Kildare and Darlughdacha later. Mary Condren thinks that Darlughdacha might even be the original name for the goddess Brigid, presumably as Brigid (Exalted One) is a title rather than a name. Mostly, Brigid appears as a goddess of fertility and procreation. She has two oxen, Fea and Feimhean, as well as Triath, the king of pigs. A mythical boar named Torc Triath often appears in the myths. The animals were said to cry out a warning and thus make Brigid into a guardian of domesticated animals.

When the civil law of Ireland was set down it retained its old name, the *Senchus Mór*, being named after the legendary chief judge or Brehon, Sencha Mac Ailella, who was supposed to have lived in the time of Conchobhar Mac Nessa. According to Mary Condren:

> Although Brigid was clearly one of the major powers behind the early Irish laws, the laws eventually were said to have been called after Sencha, the supreme wise old man in Irish tradition. Later writers have not managed to eliminate Brigid who constantly appears behind Sencha as his mother, or daughter, or even his wife.

Mary Condren quotes her references, in this regard, from the *Ancient Laws of Ireland*. She sees the goddess Brigid as being regarded as the 'Lawmaker'. However, the lady who is famous for correcting her husband Sencha's judgement on the rights of women is given as Bríg Briugaid, a female Brehon who has none of the attributes of the goddess Brigid. In my opinion she is a very real, human figure and not a representation of a deity, although it is important that the name she bears is cognate with that of the goddess; perhaps it is as significant as the fact that the later Christian saints bore the same goddess's name. Her second name, Briugaid, indicates that this Bríg was a woman of property and high standing. The legal tract, the *Uraicecht Becc*, says that the *briugaid* has the same grade as a *flaith* or ruling noble for the *briugaid* has twice the wealth of the *flaith*'s grade. So Bríg Briugaid was, indeed, a powerful lady in her own right.

We should also note that while Brigid was a goddess of healing there was another goddess who was a physician. This was Airmid, daughter of Dian Cécht, the Irish god of medicine. She helped her father guard a sacred well which restored the dead to life. Also she and her brother Miach sewed a cat's eye into the socket of the one-eyed porter of Nuada's palace giving him sight again. When Miach proved a better physician than his father, Dian Cécht slew him in jealousy. Airmid gathered the herbs which grew from Miach's grave and laid them out on her cloak in order of their various healing properties. Dian Cécht, still jealous, overturned the cloak, confusing the herbs so that no human would learn the secret of immortality.

As previously mentioned, the great Celtic chieftain, Viridomar, who led his warriors against Rome in 222BC, called himself 'a son of the Rhine'. As the Rhine, named after a sea goddess, must also have been an aspect of the mother goddess, it was natural for him to hail her and describe himself as her son. Certainly, we can interpret from the evidence that the Celts, spread throughout Europe at this time, considered themselves all children of a Great Mother Goddess.

Mary Condren correctly points out that the concept of the matri-centred society did survive for a surprisingly long time among the Celts.

> Throughout Irish mythology, relationships to the mother are emphasised. The Tuatha Dé Danaan were 'children of the goddess Dana'. Even the famous heroes were called after their mothers; Buanann was 'mother of heroes' while the Goddess Anu was known as 'mother of the gods'. In some cases men were even called, not alone after their mothers, but after their wives.

Anu, incidentally, was merely another form of Danu.

But something had started to occur in Celtic culture in the centuries before the birth of Christ. A *father* of the gods was replacing the *mother* of the gods in Celtic perceptions. Patriarchy was beginning to replace matriarchy in society while the society remained matrifocal. Sir John Rhŷs, in order to explain this change from feminine deities to masculine ones, claimed that the supremacy of the goddess was a pre-Celtic conception, a notion which 'the masculine orientated' Celts incorporated. But MacCulloch has rightly dismissed this as nonsense. 'It is too deeply impressed on the fabric of Celtic tradition to be other than native, and we have no reason to suppose that the Celts had not passed through a stage in which such a state of things was normal. Their innate conservatism caused them to preserve it more than other races who had long outgrown such a state of things.' MacCulloch speaks unfortunately with the complacency of masculine arrogance, implying that a female orientated society was primitive and a masculine one was a more mature state of affairs. Nonetheless, I believe he is right in his observation but for the wrong reasons. Early Celtic society was matriarchal but was turning into a patriarchal one long before the arrival of Christianity. The change was certainly not made because it was the natural order of things, as MacCulloch states. Why then was there a change at all? The most likely explanation was the clash of Celtic cultures with those of Greece and Rome from the middle of the first millennium BC. The Celtic world, spread from Ireland in the west to the central plain of Turkey (Galatia) in the east, and from Belgium in the north to southern Spain and northern Italy, was a close-knit one, as I have pointed out in *The Celtic Empire*. Ideas spread swiftly through the lands of the Celts even to the insular Celtic cultures of Britain and Ireland.

In Ireland perhaps the symbolic beginning of 'male dominance' can be seen in the naming of the great centres and festival sites. Each one of them is named after a goddess who has been raped and/or dies in childbirth. There appears a surprising number of stories which result in the defiling of the goddess by rape, beginning with the principal goddess of love and fertility, Áine, meaning 'Radiance' or 'Splendour'. The name of this goddess became a popular name for girls in medieval Ireland. Significantly, Áine has been presented as an aspect of Anu, which again is simply a corruption of Danu. In stories about her, Áine is constantly falling in love with mortals, but this could be interpreted as the symbolism of procreation and fertility. However, in one story the goddess is raped by the king of Munster, Ailill Olom, or 'Bare Ear', because she cut off his ear and slew him in vengeance. Surprisingly, Áine's cult survived to some extent down to the last century when, at Cnoc Áine (Knockainey, or Áine's

Hill in Co. Kerry) people gathered on St John's Eve (Midsummer Eve) and went to the hill to invoke the spirit of Áine na gClair (Áine of the Wisps) to guard them against sickness and ensure fertility.

The rape of the goddess occurs in the legends of the sites of Tailltinn, Tlachtga, Teamhair, Macha, Carmán and Culi. Mary Condren implies that the status of these goddesses was destroyed by the symbolism of rape in which the goddess gave birth to children who became famous warriors. Thus the warrior society triumphed over the culture of the wise women.

Tailtu, who gave her name to Tailltinn (Anglicised as Teltown, between Navan and Kells), was a daughter of a Firbolg king who became foster mother to Lugh Lámhfada. Tailltinn became the site of one of the most famous gatherings in Ireland, held on the feast of Lughnasadh, which was originally the feast of the goddess Tailtu. The last such gathering was in August 1169, just on the eve of the Anglo-Norman invasion. Teamhair or Tea, was a Dé Danaan goddess of sovranty who married the first Milesian king, Eremon, thus giving official blessing to his rule. She gave her name to Tara. Tlachtga was a goddess, daughter of a solar deity, who was, significantly, as the story is set down by Christian scribes, raped by the sons of Simon Magus. She produced three sons by the three different fathers at one birth and then died. She was buried on the Hill of Tlachtga, now the Hill of Ward, near Athboy, Co. Meath, where the annual Samhain festival was held. Her three sons became famous warriors. Carmán, remembered in the Leinster festival also on 1 August, gave birth to three ferocious warriors, Calma (Valiant), Dubh (Black) and Olc (Evil). It is recorded that death 'came upon her in an ungentle shape'.

Is it coincidence that the deities representing war, death and battles among the ancient Celts are personified in female form?

Mary Condren says:

The idea of a 'war goddess' is itself an interesting reflection of the distorted perspective of patriarchal scholarship. Scholars are agreed that the so-called goddesses of war do not 'themselves participate in battle'. Instead they usually try to undermine the male armies, to demoralise them or otherwise trick them into fulfilling their will. In some cases they will even confuse the armies into killing their own people rather than inflicting hurt on the opposition. Unlike the male gods who delight in the descriptions of their

weapons, the 'war goddesses' use magical means to undermine the
armies; weapons are not their province.

This would be a good argument if we did not have the evidence of
the numerous female warriors who taught males the use of weapons.
Scáthach, for example, who gives Cúchulainn the terrible spear called
the Gae Bolga, or 'Belly Ripper'. We will consider these mythical
female warriors in the next chapter and their historical counterparts
in the subsequent one. Mary Condren's argument is that the role of
the war goddess was to confuse male warriors in an attempt to turn
them from the futility of war. But the major goddess of war, death
and slaughter, The Mórrígán, whose name means 'Great Queen',
does not represent the type of image Mary Condren conjures. She
embodies all that is perverse and horrible among the supernatural
powers. Moyra Caldecott points out: 'Her twin appetites for sexual
gratification and for bringing about violent death are a travesty of
the very necessary and natural forces of creation and destruction that
keep the universe functioning, any imbalance of which brings about
disaster.' She might well be a sister of the Hindu goddess Kali. Any
male who sought her assistance had to sleep with her beforehand.
The Dagda accepted sex with her in return for the destruction of his
enemy Indech, son of the Fomorii goddess Domnu. But if any male
rejected her sexual advances, she was a terrible enemy.

She tried to entice Cúchulainn to make love to her and, when he
spurned her, she attacked him in various forms as an eel, a wolf and
a heifer. When he was eventually killed, she appeared on his shoulder
in the form of a gloating crow. The raven or crow was her most
popular symbol. She watched while a beaver drank Cúchulainn's
blood. She appeared to many warriors, such as Conaire Mór, to
gloat before their deaths, which does not accord with Mary Condren's image of the peace-making goddess. Nor is The Mórrígán
kind to her own sex. When the young girl, Odras, tried to stop The
Mórrígán's magic bull making off with the cow of Buchat Buasach,
the unfortunate mortal woman was changed into a pool of water.

In one source The Mórrígán is glossed in Latin as *lamia*, a Latin
borrowing from Greek meaning a witch or vampire who sucks children's blood. Near Hadrian's Wall, at Benwell in Northumbria, is a
representation of a triune goddess which bears the inscription *Lamiis
Tribus* showing that at one period the British Celts also had their
equivalent of The Mórrígán.

Her son Mechi had three hearts; in each heart lived a serpent. When Mac Cécht, husband of Fótla, the goddess of sovranty, slew Mechi, he had to burn the hearts and throw the ashes into a stream which promptly boiled to nothing.

In Welsh mythology Agrona seems to be the equivalent of The Mórrígán around which 'Washer at the Ford' legends are told. The River Aeron is named after her. There is, however, no equivalent in Irish myth to the lady known as Cymidei Cymeinfoll. She is another goddess of war, as well as of healing and procreation. Cymidei, 'Big-bellied Battler', was wife to Llasar Laesgynfnewid. She had a magic cauldron and when a warrior was slain, he was cast into it and came forth alive and ready for battle but lacking the power of speech. Cymidei also gave birth to a fully armed warrior every six weeks, indicating her status as a goddess of war.

However, The Mórrígán of Ireland seems to be a collective form and is usually represented as a triune goddess, interchangeable with Macha, Badb and Nemain. Of the three, Macha is the more humane. But she must not be confused with the historical/legendary queen Macha Mong Ruadh, nor does she entirely equate with the wife of Nemed. More likely she is the same Macha as the wife of the god Nuada of the Silver Hand who was killed by Balor of the Evil Eye at the second battle of Magh Tuireadh. There is also a good argument for placing this Macha as the mysterious wife of Crunniuc Mac Agnomain of Ulster who cursed the warriors of Ulster.

Crunniuc's wife had just died and a beautiful woman appeared at his fort and took on the role of his wife. She called herself Macha. She became pregnant by Crunniuc. One day, at a royal gathering, with the king's horses and chariot winning all the races, Crunniuc, in a vain and boastful mood, claimed that his wife, as pregnant as she was, could run faster than the king's horses.

The pregnant Macha was summoned and told she must race against the king's chariot and best team of horses. The king added that Crunniuc would be executed if she refused. It was in answer to the king's direct question that Macha revealed her name. She pleaded with the king to allow her to have her babies before she was forced to race. 'Help me,' she cried to the assembly, 'for a mother bore each one of you.' She then turned to the king and made a personal plea. 'Give me, my king, but a short delay, until I am delivered.' But he and the people were oblivious to her plight.

The race began. Pregnant as she was, Macha raced the chariot and reached the winning post first. As she reached it, she gave birth to twins, a son and daughter. Then all the men of Ulster fell weak with women's birth pangs. Macha pronounced her curse:

> From this hour the ignominy that you have inflicted upon me will redound to the shame of each one of you. When a time of oppression falls upon you, each one of you who dwells in this province will be overcome with weakness, as the weakness of a woman in childbirth, and this will remain upon you for five days and four nights; to the ninth generation.

Macha's appeal for humanity to the people, 'Help me, for a mother bore each one of you,' which fell on deaf ears, has been seen as an appeal on the grounds of participation in the eternal chain of creation and procreation. Mary Condren's interpretation is both refreshing and one for which sympathy can be felt. But in view of their actions, I cannot subscribe to the triune war goddesses as being caring, peaceful aspects of the mother goddess. If one divorced Macha from her sisters Nemhain and Badb, indeed, from The Mórrígán, and saw her simply as a 'horse goddess' and aspect of Danu, then I would accept Mary Condren's final analysis:

> Her cry was possibly the last symbolic attempt to appeal to true motherhood as the basis for public social ethics. That her people ignored her meant that the values of relationship and affiliations were effete; violence, death, and the threat of death became the dominant grammar of political relationships.
>
> Just before her death, the Goddess Macha cursed the patriarchal age that had dawned. The Goddess was effectively saying: Although you may develop sophisticated doctrines of rebirth; although you have taken on yourselves the right of life and death; although your efforts might seem logical and plausible in the light of patriarchal culture, your efforts cannot but be doomed to failure so long as they are based on the subordination of women. Speaking the language of peace and the common good with one hand, with the other, you are calling the troops to war against women and the earth.

We could argue, perhaps, that Macha was not a war goddess at this time and that, as Mary Condren has implied, she was reinvented in the role by the later patriarchal society. With Macha, in the story of her famous curse, Mary Condren has a strong case. But the case seems weak when she argues that The Mórrígán, Nemhain and Badb are really good, caring goddesses who only spread confusion on the battlefield to stop the male warfare.

Nemhain (Frenzy) was certainly at battlefields to spread panic among warriors. In Medb's war against Ulster, during the last battle, she raised such a howl of horror over the armies that a hundred Connacht warriors fell dead from terror before the battle began.

Badb (Rage, Fury, Violence) is the third of the triune goddess, who appears in the form of a raven or crow. In Gaul there is reference to a goddess Cathubodua (Badb Catha, Badb of the Battles), showing that the same basic deities were found throughout the Celtic world. Badb is the harbinger of doom whenever she appears as an ugly, black crow. Sometimes she appears as an old woman, who, like the Welsh Agrona, washes the arms of warriors at a ford before a battle. Those she has washed are about to die. There is, like The Mórrígán, no trace of human charity or goodness in either of them. They wax healthy on the blood of the slain – be it men, women or children.

The final group of goddesses connected with the mother goddess image represent sovranty. The theme goes right through Celtic myth, that a rightful king must be recognised by the goddess of sovranty before he can be hailed as a just and legitimate ruler. Often, he will meet an old hag who demands a kiss, or that he make love to her. If he is the rightful king, he will do so and she will turn into a beautiful young maiden. This certainly seems to be an acknowledgement of the role of women as the symbol of knowledge and freedom and the moral pivot of Celtic society. The union between the king and the goddess of the land was essential. In this act, the ancient Celtic society was not unique; the concept was used by other early Indo-European civilisations, such as that of Mesopotamia, where Sumerian kings married symbolically with the goddess Innan. Or among the Hindus where the goddess Laksmi, Indra's consort, appears as the personification of sovranty. Laksmi prepares 'the drink of which none tastes who dwells on earth'. It is called *soma*. Indra drinks this from the goddess's own mouth. In a poem about Medb Lethderg, not to be confused with the queen of Connacht, it is said that no one can be king in Ireland unless they drink the mead of Cuala. Medb is the daughter of Conan of Cuala and her very name means 'intoxication' (the English word 'mead' derives from Medb).

When the goddess of sovranty gave Niall of the Nine Hostages a drink, she said: 'Smooth shall be the drink from your royal horn, it will be mead, it will be honey, it will be strong ale.'

Ireland, over the centuries, has been known by the names of the three main goddesses of sovranty, Éire, Banba and Fótla. They were three sisters, goddesses of the Children of Dana. Éire was the wife of Mac Gréine (Son of the Sun), a son of Ogma and grandson of The Dagda. Banba was the wife of Mac Cuill, another son of Ogma. Fótla was the wife of the third son Mac Cécht. All three gods were slain in the Milesian invasion. And when the Milesians were victorious, Éire and her sisters greeted them and hailed their victory. Amairgen, the chief Druid of the Milesians, promised that the country's principal name would be Éire while the names of Banba and Fótla would also be used. In fact, Banba and Fótla are still used in poetic reference to Ireland, but Éire remains its principal name.

But Éire, Banba and Fótla are not the only goddesses of sovranty in Irish myth. Medb and Macha have also been conjured to that task while Fliathius (Royalty), who appeared to Niall of the Nine Hostages and foretold his kingship, is also a sovranty symbol. Perhaps well known through the poem '*Mise Éire*' (I am Ireland) is the Cailleach Beara, the Old Woman, or Hag, of Beara (the peninsula in southwest Ireland). Known as both Buí (Yellow) and Duineach (Strong), she appeared as a triune goddess with her sisters Cailleach Bolus and Cailleach Corca Dhuibhne. She was acclaimed not only as a wife of the god Lugh Lámhfada but as having married seven husbands and having fifty foster children who founded many tribes and nations.

It is an interesting comment on continuing perceptions that Pádraig Pearse's poem 'The Old Woman of Beara' appeared as part of the graffiti on a house in Chamberlain Street, Derry, in 1985, and then in the Monagh Road, Belfast, in 1988.

> *Mise Éire*
> *Sine mé na an Chailleach Bheara*
> *Mór mo ghlóire*
> *Mé do rug Cúchulainn cródha*
> *Mór mo náir*
> *Mo chlann féin do díol máthair*
> *Mise Éire*
> *Uaigní mé na an Chailleach Bheara.*

I am Ireland
I am older than the Old Woman of Beara
Great my glory
I that bore Cúchulainn the valiant
Great my shame
My own children have sold their mother
I am Ireland
I am lonelier than the Old Woman of Beara.

It is interesting that Falga, the ancient poetical name for the Isle of Man, a form of Fótla, became a popular female first name on the Island, as Eubonia did during the eighteenth century. Eubonia was also a name given to represent the Island's sovranty. Significantly, a third name, Mona, by which the Isle of Man was referred to in poetical terms, became a popular feminine name.

The attitude of nations to the gender accorded to the deity representing sovranty, demonstrated by the split between 'motherland' and 'fatherland', marks certain martial attitudes. Most empires seem to emanate from 'fatherlands'. Ireland's perception of a 'motherland', represented by sovranty goddesses, was countered by the English perception of a 'fatherland'. During the nineteenth century England conceived of Ireland as a female, a 'recalcitrant harlot' who needed England's male 'John Bull' to tame and civilise her. The resurrection in the eighteenth century of the female image of Britannia, which was a British Celtic 'motherland' image, to serve the English purpose in uniting the nations of the British Isles, under English domination, to act as the nucleus of a 'British empire', has never expunged the dominant masculine aspect of England represented by John Bull and the male bulldog. The character of John Bull was first identified by a Scottish writer, John Arbuthnot (1667–1735), who wrote *The Art of Political Lying* in 1712. If the female personification of Ireland was a harlot, then the introduction of 'The Grand Old Dame Britannia' has served as a 'Judas Goat' for the rapacious John Bull.

For the pagan Celt, the essence of the universe and all its creativity was female. The mother goddess, and all her personifications of fertility, sovranty, love and healing, was an essential basis of their very role in the world. Therefore, when the Christian movement, at the Council of Ephesus in AD431, made Mary officially the 'Mother of God', the Celts turned to her enthusiastically as the replacement 'mother goddess', seeing in her the goddesses of fertility, love and healing. The early Celtic Christians pictured Mary as the eternal mother figure, encouraging men and women to turn to her in times of trouble.

For a while, during the early period, other Celtic goddesses vied with Mary in the perceptions of the people; for example, the fertility goddess Brigid, whose cult had been absorbed into that of Brigid of Kildare. Brigid then became 'Mary of the Gael'. By the eighth century, the cult of Mary had become widespread in the Celtic world, and nowhere more so than in Ireland. Poets chanted her praise. Blathmac mac Cú Brettan (*fl.* AD750–70), a monk who wrote a two-part poem on Mary concerned with her sufferings, accused the Jews of the Irish crime of *fingal*, or kin-slaying. Oengus the Culdee (*fl.* AD800–50), Pilib Bocht Ó hÚiginn of Sligo and other poets sang paeans to Mary, establishing her in the role of the mother goddess.

Of the stories relating to the miracle of Jesus' birth, one particularly interesting Celtic one was current in the tenth century. It was claimed that Jesus was born from the skull of Mary. The pagan Celts believed that the soul dwelt in the head. It is obvious that this belief was not overturned immediately. Eventually, however, the image of Mary had been changed in Celtic perception from the mother goddess to an untouchable ideal, an image of frigidity rather than fertility. Now statues of Mary appeared with her crushing a snake under one foot.

In Hebraic-Christian myth, the snake or serpent was the main Devil which tempted Eve in the Garden of Eden. It has been suggested that the Hebrew identification of the serpent as the Devil was an attempt to stamp out remnants of the earlier pre-diluvial religion. There are many traces of earlier serpent worship such as Uadjit, a mother goddess of Egypt whose form was a serpent, and serpent worship also appears in the Zoroastrian creation myths of Persia as well as in Hindu culture. Even in the Pelasgian creation myth of Greece we find Ophion, the great serpent. Also in Celtic myth, the serpent was a feminine symbol, an aspect of the mother goddess. It was not, of course, an evil symbol. But, by accepting the Hebrew symbolism, and having Mary, as the Mother of God, stepping on the snake, the Christians were demonstrating their victory over the competing liberated feminine attitudes of pagan times.

Only after the Celtic Church was entirely subsumed by Rome did the veneration of Mary as Virgin, Mother of Christ, present a new role model for women – wife, mother and faithful follower but completely asexual. In other words, in recent centuries the Roman image of Mary turned into a positive barrier to feminine fulfilment: women were forced to stifle their sexuality and their independence, and become simply slaves to men. Mary was no longer the mother goddess but a passive, eternally suffering vehicle through which the male God could enter the world.

[2]

Women in Myth

WOMEN feature prominently in Celtic mythology. We not only have a pantheon of goddesses but numerous mortal women who display a range of characters and positions in society. There are powerful women, weak women, serious women, capricious women, vengeful women and ambitious women. They all have a part to play in the sagas and tales. But whatever part they play, and whether goddess or mortal, they are all fully developed human characters. One of the most fascinating aspects of the Celtic myths is that there are no empty-headed beauties. As Moyra Caldecott, in *Women in Celtic Myth*, remarked: 'One of the things I find refreshing in the Celtic myths is that women are honoured as much for their minds as for their bodies. The dumb blonde would not stand much of a chance in ancient Celtic society.' Indeed, neither would the women who denigrated her femaleness. Mind and body were not separate issues in the myths but complementary sides of the whole person.

Peter R. Cherici points out, in *Celtic Sexuality*:

Generally, women in Celtic myth enjoyed full control of their sexuality, dispensing their favours as they saw fit. Men, however, frequently attempted to harness female sexuality through the forceful subjugation of passion by reason. In part, this reflected the position of women in Celtic society. They did not enjoy full equality with men. But neither was Celtic society a patriarchy. Women could contract, bear arms, become Druids, and engage in politics. If they tired of a husband, they could divorce. And for some men, particularly those enmeshed by the male ethics of a warrior solidarity, the sexual and reproductive freedom for women was an intolerable situation.

It could be argued that the women of Celtic mythology are highly idealised and that, as is the case with women in Greek myth and early literature, their status is not representative of the reality. In the world of Homer and other Greek writers, the female characters were governed by literary convention and thus enjoyed a moderately free position in society, as befitted a heroine. Greek reality, as we will discuss later, was entirely different. Do the women who appear in Celtic mythology simply occupy positions idealised by the early story-tellers or do they represent the women of practical, everyday Celtic life? It is my contention that the women of Celtic myth, unlike their Greek sisters, were indeed representative of the realities of early Celtic society.

One of the reasons why I believe that we may take the mythological figures as representative of people in historical Celtic society is that their actions and positions are not contradicted by the early Celtic laws and the strictures placed on them. Even female warriors existed into historical times and it was not until AD590, when Colmcille introduced a law exempting women from military service, that an attempt was made to exclude women from warrior society. Even so, the change in status did not immediately happen; in AD697 Adomnán had to revive the law and incorporate it with his famous *Lex Inno-centum* which was enacted at the Synod of Birr and which forbade women to take up the profession of arms.

Medb (Anglicised as Maeve) is perhaps the best known of Celtic mythological heroines. She is certainly the most written-about Irish heroine and most quoted by those arguing for the equality of women in early Celtic society. The name, and its variants such as Meadhbh, Meadhbha and Méabh, means 'She Who Makes Men Drunk' or 'Intoxicating One'. It became one of the twenty most popular names in medieval Ireland. There is, however, confusion between the heroic Medb, queen of Connacht, and a Medb who seems to be a goddess of sovranty. But a careful reading of the texts shows that two distinct Medbs existed. The goddess of sovranty is Medb Lethderg (Red Side) whom it is necessary for a king to ritually marry in order to reign legitimately. It is recorded that this Medb was wife to nine High Kings of Ireland, including the father of Conn Cétchathach (of the Hundred Battles), Conn himself, Conn's son Art and Art's son

Cormac. Medb has been conjured not only as a goddess of sovranty but also as a goddess of war. I think this is pushing interpretation too far, for there is no reference to her in this function.

Some scholars have seen the more famous Medb, queen of Connacht, as a literary reincarnation of the sovranty goddess. She appears as the daughter of a High King named Eochaid Féidhleach. She seemed to be a 'man-eater' and is credited with numerous husbands and lovers before settling on Ailill Mac Máta. Ailill was a common name, indeed, it was the fourth most popular name in ancient Ireland, meaning 'Spirit of an Elf'. Because of the many Ailills in the myths, there is confusion about which Ailill we are talking about when we speak of Medb's husband. Some settle for Ailill being the son of Ross Ruadh of Leinster. Some stories have it that he was the commander of Medb's bodyguard, the Gamhanrhide. My argument is that as Medb came from Leinster, so Ailill was clearly a king of Connacht and is recognised as such in most of the sagas, although he plays a secondary role to Medb. They ruled from their palace at Cruachain.

Medb, in her dominant relationship with Ailill, certainly has some specific ideas on marriage.

My husband must be free from cowardice, and free from avarice, and free from jealousy; for I am brave in battles and combats, and it would be a discredit to my husband if I were braver than he. I am generous and a great giver of gifts, and it would be a disgrace to my husband if he were less generous than I am. And it would not suit me at all if he were jealous, for I have never denied myself the man I took a fancy to . . . and I never shall whatever husband I have now or may have hereafter.

There has been an ongoing argument among scholars as to whether Medb was purely myth or whether she was based on an historical personage. The argument will probably continue until the end of time. Doubtless 'myths' are created from realities, from moral tales and actual events lost in the recesses of history. Whatever the outcome of such debates, Medb's literary role is secure. She features in many of the tales of the Ulster Cycle (or Red Branch Cycle) of the myths.

In the famous epic of the *Táin Bó Cuailgne* (The Cattle Raid of Cuailgne) she appears as a very determined, forceful, strong, devious and oftimes bloodthirsty queen. At the start of the epic Medb finds that her possessions, which are considerable, are not as extensive as her husband's. The White Horned Bull of Connacht was born into her herd but has taken itself to Ailill's herd. Medb, however, hears about the fabulous Brown Bull of Cuailgne, in the kingdom of Ulaidh (Ulster), and, after attempts to buy it, she raises an army from the other kingdoms of Ireland to invade and seize it by war. She personally leads her warriors into battle, standing in her chariot in a way that foreshadows Boudicca of the Iceni.

Medb appears in several other tales which demonstrate her power and her devious attitude. When the king of Ulaidh, Conchobhar Mac Nessa, sends three warriors to Ailill – Conall, Laoghaire and Cúchulainn – and asks him, as an unbiased judge, to assess which warrior should be champion of Ulaidh, it is Medb who advises her husband how to answer. There are dangerous consequences in the judgement for the two losers will doubtless turn on Ailill in enmity. It is Medb who comes up with a clever piece of subterfuge to save Ailill. She advises him to tell each warrior that he is the champion and, swearing them to secrecy, gives each one a champion's symbol wrapped in cloth which, when given to the king Conchobhar Mac Nessa, will demonstrate his right to be champion. Laoghaire has a drinking cup of bronze with a silver bird at the bottom; Conall has a cup of silver with a bird of gold; but Cúchulainn has a cup of gold with a bird of precious stones. Thus Ailill's judgement is made at a distance and he is protected from the immediate wrath of the losers.

Medb and Ailill had seven sons, each named Maine. But it is their daughter Findbhair (Fair Eyebrows) who plays the most prominent part in the myths. It should be pointed out that there is some argument that the derivatives of the name, Finnabair, Fionnabhair and Fionnúir, could indicate a meaning of 'Sprite'. The Welsh equivalent of this name is Gwenhwyfar, the wife of King Arthur, which is better recognised by English speakers in the form of Guinevere.

Findbhair first appears in the *Táin Bó Cuailgne* as a Druidess, one who has been trained among the Druids of Britain. She has prophetic vision and warns her mother of the bloody outcome of her war against Ulaidh. Medb lets loose the war. But she demonstrates that she is a superb strategist and military commander, and in one battle she fights a single combat and wounds the hero Cethern with a cast of her *slegh* or light spear.

In this and other stories, Medb appears as a dominant mother figure who, while asserting her own rights in aggressive fashion, ignores the rights of her daughter. When Medb realises that her daughter is in love with Fráech (sometimes given as Fraoch, meaning 'Fury'), a handsome warrior, it is Medb who conceives several intricate tasks for Fráech to solve to prove his worthiness. In one of these, recounted in the *Táin Bó Fráech*, he has to fetch rowan berries from an island surrounded by water in which dwells a terrible monster. With Findbhair's help, Fráech kills the monster but he is badly wounded and has to be tended by the gods and goddesses before he is healed. Findbhair is all that which Medb is not. She is a soft personality, tender, loving and loyal; not devious but open-hearted.

In the second part of the story, Fráech returns to his fortress to find Findbhair, his three children and his cattle herds have all been carried off. He sets out to find them, meeting the champion Conall Cearnach on the way; after numerous adventures, which take them as far as the European Alps, they are successful in rescuing her, the children and the cattle, and they return to Ireland.

There are other versions in which Findbhair loses Fráech, who is killed in single combat with Cúchulainn, and, after mourning, she marries Rochad Mac Faethman, an honourable warrior of the Red Branch, the élite guard of the kings of Ulster. He is someone of whom her mother Medb approves, unlike Fráech, of whom she had disapproved. Finally, Findbhair realises just how much she has been dominated by her mother and the realisation destroys her. She drowns in a river and her ring is found in the body of a salmon, the Celtic symbol for wisdom.

Indeed, the Celtic tradition is that one received wisdom at the water's edge, so we may wonder whether there is another implied symbolism in the fact that when Medb meets her own end, she is killed by a cast of a spear from Forbaí, the son of Conchobhar Mac Nessa of Ulaidh, while bathing at the water's edge in a lake, Loch Ria (Lough Rea, Galway) at the point named Inis Clothrand. Ailill is also said to have been killed by a spear cast by Conall at the same time. In other versions, Medb's ending is more dramatic for she is killed by a slingshot cast by Furbaide, the son of her own sister Ethné, as an act of vengeance.

Ethné was drowned by Medb's other sister, Clothra, while she was pregnant. Clothra is less well known than Medb, but is equally determined and ambitious: she drowned Ethné because of jealousy. After death, Ethné's child was cut from her womb and was found alive, showing that the Caesarean operation was known and practised among the ancient Celts. He was named Furbaide. Clothra proceeded to have affairs with each of her three brothers and gave birth to a son who became High King. He was named Lugaid Riab nDerg, 'of the Red Stripes', because he had two red stripes which divided his body into three sections, each section resembling one of Clothra's three brothers, thereby proclaiming him the son of all three. When Lugaid grew up he begot a son by his own mother who was called Crimthann Nía Náir, 'Modest Warrior', who also became High King.

A verse in the myths runs as follows:

> Lugaid Riab nDerg to fair Crimthann
> Was father and was brother,
> And Clothra of the comely form
> Was Grandmother to her son.

Medb is reported to have been buried under a large cairn which still exists on Knocknarea (Hill of Executions) in Co. Sligo where, for centuries, it has been a custom to place a stone on the cairn whenever one passes it. The place received its name, Cnoc na Riaghadh, when four persons were executed there in the seventh century having murdered Cellach, bishop of Kilmore-Moy.

Of the many fascinating women who feature in the Irish romantic tales let us examine some of the best known – Emer, Étain, Deirdre, Gráinne and Créd. All have very different characters, so they are representative of the many types we find in the myths.

Emer was the daughter of Forgall Manach, lord of Musca, whom Cúchulainn desired to marry. He falls in love with her at first sight. Glancing at her breasts, he says: 'I see a sweet country. I could rest my weapon there.' But her father tries to prevent the marriage. The young hero is set a number of tasks to perform. He does so but finds more constrictions placed in his way. Finally, frustrated by the delays, Emer and Cúchulainn elope, to the fury of Emer's family. We find that the Celtic custom of female choice of sexual partners is observed here and that Emer has control over her future sexual union.

But Cúchulainn, in fact, has to fight with Emer's warrior sister, Scenmed. She has to be defeated before they can establish themselves at Cúchulainn's fortress of Dún Dealgan. But all is not smooth in their future relationship. There is no 'and they lived happily ever after' in the Celtic world. Cúchulainn spends most of his career falling in and out of love with numerous women. Emer patiently bears all his philandering until Cúchulainn falls in love with Fand (the Pearl of Beauty), wife to Manannán Mac Lir. At that point, Emer, like others before and after her, feels enough is enough. She decides to kill Fand.

She discovers the spot where Cúchulainn and Fand are having an assignation. She and Fand argue over him but then she sees that Fand really loves him and she demonstrates her own love by saying that she will give him up for the greater good. It is then that Fand realises the depths of Emer's own love, and realises, too, the fickleness of Cúchulainn's emotions. She tells Emer, in a moving poem which comes from a twelfth-century manuscript and which has best been translated by Seán O Faoláin:

> Pity the woman who loves a man
> when no love invites her.
> Better for her to fly from love
> if, unloved, love bites her.

Fand decides that she should return to her own husband. As he is Manannán Mac Lir, the sea god, he is able to help them by shaking his cloak between Fand and Cúchulainn to ensure they will never meet again. Cúchulainn falls sick and the Druids of Ulster give him and Emer a drink of forgetfulness. The affair is forgotten. Emer comes over in the myths as almost a martyr, content for love's sake to put up with Cúchulainn's numerous affairs and always waiting for his return. In my view, she is the epitome of the unliberated woman.

Moyra Caldecott, in *Women in Celtic Myth*, is more generous to Emer.

I find Emer's attitude to Cuchulain admirable. She loves him beyond life itself, yet she does not waste their time together fretting about the other women in his life. She knows him. She knows him well. He is pursued by women wherever he goes, like all handsome and glamorous heroes. She is secure in her own estimation of herself and understanding of him. There is no one who can jeopardise his love for her. He plays. He boasts. He fights. But the home he comes to is always hers. She lives at Dundealgan a rich and respected woman, with herds of cattle and a host of servants. She goes to court when she feels like it, or she entertains the court in her own house. She rules her own domain. She makes her own decisions — and often those of her husband.

Yet Moyra Caldecott admits that he does fail to return to her after the experience with Fand. In fact, afterwards, when he is ill, he insists on being taken to Emain Macha where he has another lover, Eithne Inguba. It is Eithne who takes care of him during this illness. Another mistress of Cúchulainn was Niamh, the wife of Conall Cearnach, who also tended him in his sickness. All these affairs poor Emer suffered with resignation. In fact, it is only in her encounter with Fand that Emer stands up for herself. I could agree with Moyra Caldecott that 'Emer is not an abstract concept. She is very much a woman of flesh and blood, who changes, strengthens and grows through the trials of her own life.' We have doubtless all encountered her 'type', passive in the face of her husband's 'wenching'. She reminds me of the narrator of the poem 'John-John', written by poet and playwright Thomas MacDonagh, executed for his part in the 1916 insurrection in Ireland. The last verse shows how the woman is content to put up with her wandering husband.

> Oh, you're my husband right enough,
> But what's the good of that?
> You know you never were the stuff
> To be the cottage cat,
> To watch the fire and hear me lock
> The door and put out Shep . . .

The previous verse says it all when the narrator says of her neighbours' attitude to her:

> Tis pity me they do,
> And that I'd rather have, John-John,
> Than that they'd pity you . . .

So Emer puts up with Cúchulainn. Among Cúchulainn's various lovers and mistresses are some rather sad ladies, such as Buan, daughter of Samera, who, desperate to be with him, tries to leap on to his chariot, falls, strikes her head on a rock and dies. She is not to be confused with the Buan who was wife of Mesgora Mac Da Thó, whom we will deal with later. There is also the tragic Blathnát (Little Flower), daughter of Mend. The Munster king and warrior Cú Roí fell in love with her and married her. His fortress at Sleemish (Slieve Mis) was so constructed that no one could find an entrance. When Cúchulainn, with whom Blathnát has fallen in love, besieges the castle, she gives him a signal by emptying milk into a stream which runs through the fortress. Cúchulainn's attack is therefore successful. Cú Roí is slain and Blathnát is going happily off with Cúchulainn when Fer Cherdne, Cú Roí's bard, seizes the opportunity to avenge his king. As Cúchulainn's prisoners are being led along some cliffs, Fer Cherdne leaps forward, seizes Blathnát around the waist, and jumps over the cliffs killing them both.

Is this a moral tale about treachery? Or does its meaning go much deeper; is it telling us that things should not be taken for granted? It seems connected with a tale which appears in Welsh myth and features Blodeuwydd (Flower Aspect) – the name is remarkably similar to Blathnát. She is a beautiful woman, created by the gods to be the perfect wife for Lleu Llaw Gyffes, the Welsh equivalent of the Irish god Lugh Lámhfada. But she is unfaithful with Gronwy Pedbyr, lord of Penllyn. Together they plan to murder Lleu but Lleu discovers the plot and kills Gronwy; Blodeuwydd is turned into an owl, outcast even among the birds. There is another message here, for Blodeuwydd was created by the gods to be a perfect docile wife. Moyra Caldecott compares the story to American novelist Ira Levin's horror tale *The Stepford Wives*. Instead, Blodeuwydd, the perfectly created wife, rebels and turns on her husband.

Deirdre is not a martyr but she is certainly a victim of her attractiveness to men. Deirdre of the Sorrows was the daughter of Felim Mac Dall, an Ulster chieftain. At her birth, Cathbad the Druid prophesied that she would be the fairest of all the women in Ireland but that only death and ruin would come upon the land because of it. We are, at once, presented with the powerlessness of people in the face of inexorable predestination. Conchobhar Mac Nessa, the king, now an old man, decides that she must be his wife. He has to wait, of course, until she is at the age of choice. Her foster mother makes a last-minute attempt to avert fate by telling Conchobhar that she has grown unattractive. But Conchobhar is determined. Before the wedding, however, Deirdre sees a young warrior, Naoise, son of Usna, a hero of the Red Branch warriors. Deirdre is not shy and it is she who engineers a meeting. It is she who chooses Naoise while he is unsure of himself, feeling himself unworthy of her love for she has, indeed, fallen in love with him. She gives him courage. Naoise and Deirdre, accompanied by his two brothers, Ainlé and Ardan, elope and flee to Alba. For some years they live happily there. They even have a daughter, Aígréne, 'Ray of Sunshine'.

Revenge is a cornerstone of the tale. Conchobhar pretends that he has forgiven Naoise and Deirdre. He sends Fergus Mac Roth, an honourable warrior, to invite them to return to Ulaidh with assurances of forgiveness and peace. Deirdre sees beyond these appearances to Conchobhar's bitterness and knows vengeance broods in his heart. But Naoise insists on returning. Fergus Mac Roth is purposely distracted, and forced to leave the party, while they go on to the Red Branch hostel at Emain Macha. With Fergus out of the way, Conchobhar orders his warriors to attack. Naoise and his brothers are killed and Deirdre is forced to wed Conchobhar.

Deirdre is his wife in body. She is unsmiling, non-participating, and thus driving Conchobhar mad. He possesses her body but that is all. The only emotion he can stir in her is hatred. Conchobhar, that vengeful man, hits on the ultimate insult. He gives her to Eoghan Mac Durthacht, the warrior who actually killed her husband Naoise, to do with as he wills. To prevent her escape, her hands are bound, and she is placed in Eoghan's chariot. But Deirdre is no martyr; she contrives to throw herself from the chariot, head foremost, and kills herself. From her grave grows a pine, and from Naoise's grave grows a second tree. The two full-grown trees meet and intertwine above the graves so that nothing can part them. Her ending, the solution to the terrible fate which pursues her, is as surprising as it is abrupt for we are not really prepared for it. Here is a woman who is fully in control of her own destiny.

Gráinne is another heroine who is not a placid martyr like Emer. But she is certainly no loyal lover, like Deirdre. She is a shallow person, wilful, ruthless, sexually passionate and somewhat neurotic. She is the daughter of Cormac Mac Art, the High King. She is promised in marriage to Fionn Mac Cumhail, the commander of the king's élite warriors, the Fianna. On the night before the wedding Gráinne decides to 'play the field' because she is not really interested in the elderly Fionn. She makes a proposition to Fionn's son, Oisín, who rejects her proposal indignantly. Then she turns to a young man, Diarmuid Ua Duibhne, whom she persuades to elope with her.

Being an honourable young man, he at first refuses, but she tricks him with a *geis*, a sacred taboo, which gives him no choice.

'The Pursuit of Diarmuid and Gráinne' begins. The symbolism in the story is obvious. Diarmuid does his best to reassure his chieftain Fionn, to whom he is loyal, that he has not made sexual advances to Gráinne by leaving behind symbolic pieces of unbroken bread or uncooked salmon. Gráinne tries her best to seduce him, finally resorting to mockery. Inevitably, in spite of everything, Diarmuid grows to love this capricious and wilful woman. Fionn grows even more angry and the pursuit continues for sixteen years until Aonghus Óg, the love god, intercedes.

A peace is made and Fionn comes to dine with Diarmuid and Gráinne at their fortress, Ráth Gráinne. The next day Fionn and Diarmuid go out on a hunt. Diarmuid is wounded by a boar in the hunt. Fionn can save his life but does not choose to do so. Gráinne at first demands that her sons seek vengeance on Fionn. But eventually she gives way to a new passion that has grown in her for Fionn. Are hate and love two sides of the same coin? It seems so. She accompanies Fionn back to the Hill of Allen. Fionn's men, while respecting him, do not respect Gráinne for her capricious change of lovers, declaring they would 'not have given one of Diarmuid's fingers for twenty such as Gráinne'.

Étain is an entirely different personality from the other heroines. The name seems to mean 'Jealousy' and there are many Étains in the early literature of Ireland, including the goddess, daughter of Dian Cécht, god of medicine, who is also a healer in her own right and wife to Ogma, god of eloquence. As well as the many distinctive Étains in the myths there is a reference to a St Étain of Connacht, patroness of Tumna, Co. Roscommon, whose feastday is 5 July. Étain was the name of a warrior daughter of Fínghin Mór Mac Carthaigh (d. 1262). Of another Étain, one poet, perhaps bitterly, wrote in around the twelfth century:

> I can't tell
> Who will sleep with Étain;
> But this I know
> Fair Étain will not sleep alone.

'The Wooing of Étain' in Irish mythology seems to involve several Étains, passing from the goddess to a semi-mortal to a mortal, from grandmother to granddaughter and finally a great-granddaughter simply known as Mess Buachalla (the cowherd's foster child). The goddess Étain consorts with Ailill of Echraidhe and they have a daughter Étain Echraidhe. This is where the story really starts and this Étain seems to have no control over the situations in which she finds herself. The god, Midir the Proud, falls in love with her and, through the intercession of the love god, Aonghus Óg, he makes arrangements to wed her. She goes to live with him in Brí Leith as Midir's second wife. But his first wife, Fuamnach, is jealous of the new wife and with the help of her father, a sorcerer named Etarlann (sometimes given as Bresal), she turns Étain into a pool of water. The pool is then turned into a worm, then a fly, in order to confuse Midir who is searching for her. He finally finds her in the guise of the fly but Fuamnach, still jealous, gets Etarlann to create a strong wind which blows the fly away.

Seven years later it is blown to Bruigh na Boinne, the dwelling of Aonghus Óg, who immediately reports to Midir. But Fuamnach overhears and Etarlann has to cause another wind to blow the fly away before Midir can go to reclaim her. Another seven years pass and the fly is blown through the roof of the house of Etar, a Red Branch warrior. His wife is drinking at the time and the fly falls into her cup and is swallowed. Etar's wife becomes pregnant and gives birth to a fully mortal daughter, naturally called Étain. This Étain has no knowledge of her previous existence.

She grows into a great beauty. The High King, Eochaidh Airemh, hears of Étain's beauty and decides to woo her. She comes to love him and they marry. She accompanies him to Tara, the seat of the High Kings. But Eochaidh has a brother, Ailill, who also falls in love with her and who succumbs to a wasting sickness because she does not return his love. Étain is a sensitive and caring person and, rather than let Ailill die, she promises to meet him in secret. It is then that the god Midir appears on the scene. He has finally tracked Étain and he makes Ailill fall into a deep sleep from which, on waking, he is cured of his passion. But Midir, in the guise of Ailill, keeps the assignation with Étain. Midir finds out that Étain has no remembrance of him and is happy in her mortal life in which she is truly in love with Eochaidh. Midir takes matters into his own hands and drugs Étain, carrying her back by force to Brí Leith, in the Otherworld. Eochaidh discovers she has been kidnapped, follows Midir to the Otherworld itself and forces him to release her. She returns to live with Eochaidh for ten happy years and gives birth to their daughter, Étain Óig.

In spite of their central position in the tales, we learn nothing of any of the Étains' own desires, simply the desires of the men about them and the jealousy of Fuamnach. Étain, in each persona, is almost a passive doll-like figure, at times literally (as a fly) blown where destiny takes her. But not so her granddaughter Mess Buachalla, the daughter of Étain Oig and Cormac of Ulster. Cormac, desiring a son, decides to get rid of his daughter as soon as she is born and her sex discovered. The servants ordered to perform the deed are so captivated by the child's smile that they leave her in the care of the cowherd of the High King Eterscél. The cowherd fosters the child – hence Mess Buachalla, the cowherd's daughter. She also becomes a great beauty and the High King falls in love with her.

She agrees to marry him but on the evening before the wedding she is visited by Nemglan, the bird-god. She makes love with him and from their union is born Conaire Mór. Conaire is raised by Eterscél, who thinks the child is his own, and in adulthood he becomes one of the greatest of Irish High Kings.

The main Étain, Eochaidh's wife, is regarded by the story-tellers as the ideal of Celtic feminine beauty. 'Every lovely form must be tested by Étain, every beauty by the standard of Étain,' says the text. We shall be discussing this further when we consider the personal adornment and dress of the Celts. The character and symbolism of Étain seem to have some similarities in Welsh myth to Olwen, 'She of the White Track', so named because four white trefoils sprang up wherever she trod. She is the beautiful daughter of Yspaddaden Pencawr. The hero Culhwch has to overcome many difficulties before he can finally declare his love for her. A tenth-century version of her story describes her thus:

She came wearing a flame-red silken tunic, and a great collar of red gold with precious pearls and rubies in it. Her hair was more yellow-gold than the flowers of the broom; her skin was whiter than the foam of the wave; her palms and fingers were more white than the flowers of melilot among the tiny pebbles washed by a gushing spring. No eye was fairer than hers, not even the eye of the mewing hawk nor the thrice-mewed falcon. Whiter than the breast of a white swan were her breasts; redder than the foxglove were her cheeks. All who saw her became filled with love for her.

Four white trefoils would grow up in her footprints when she walked and hence she was named Olwen.

Olwen is thus seen in Welsh terms as the personification of beauty in the same way as Étain is in Irish myth. The melilot is, incidentally, a sweet kind of clover.

We have mentioned Buan, the unfortunate who loved Cúchulainn. Her better known namesake is the wife of Mesgora Mac Da Thó, the king of Leinster. One day, the Ulster poet and Druid, Athairne the Importunate, comes on a visit. He is a bitter man. Fergus Mac Roth says that even 'the lakes and rivers receded before him when he satirised them'. He had previously stayed with Luain, the one-eyed king of Connacht, and demanded his eye under the laws of hospitality by which no host could refuse a guest. As soon as he sees the beautiful Buan he demands that Mac Da Thó give her to him. The king of Leinster refuses point blank. Athairne hastens back to Ulster and persuades the Red Branch champions to make war on Leinster because of Mac Da Thó's refusal to abide by the laws of hospitality. Conall of the Victories slays Mac Da Thó and orders Buan to go with him. The girl refuses and dies of grief for her husband. Here is a determined and loyal lady.

Another interesting woman, who has passion but believes in honour and obedience to law, is Créd, sometimes given as Creide. There are a number of famous women in Irish history and literature who bear this name but the outstanding one is the daughter of Guaire Aidne, king of Connacht. She married Marcán, an elderly chieftain of Uí Maine, but she did not love him. It was a political marriage and he already had a wife and a grown-up stepson named Colcú. The annals record that during the reign of the High King Aedh Slaine (d. c.604) a prince from Skye, Cano Mac Garnait, came to Ireland. At Guaire's court he met Créd and fell in love with her and she with him.

She refused to make love with him while he was under the laws of hospitality. But he gave her a stone which he said contained his life. He would leave Ireland and return home, thus removing himself from the obligation of the laws of hospitality. But before he did so he arranged an assignation at the lake which later became Loch Créd. Her stepson, Colcú, whose sexual advances had been rejected by Créd, thwarted the plans. In anguish, Créd dropped the stone which Cano had given her and it fragmented. Cano died three days later. Professor Kuno Meyer, in *Stories and Songs from Irish Mss* (1899),

found and translated one lament attributed to Créd but dating from
the tenth century.

These are arrows that murder sleep
At every hour in the bitter-cold night:
Pangs of love through the day
For the company of the man from Roiny.

Great love of a man from another land
Has come to me beyond all else:
It has taken my bloom, no colour is left,
It does not let me rest.

Sweeter than songs was his speech,
Save holy adoration of Heaven's King;
He was a glorious flame, no boastful word fell from his lips,
A slender mate for a maid's side.

When I was a child I was bashful,
I was not given to going to trysts:
Since I have come to a wayward age,
My wantonness has beguiled me.

I have every good life with Guaire,
The king of cold Aidne:
But my mind has fallen away from my people
To the meadow at Iruachair.

There is chanting in the meadow of glorious Aidne
Around the sides of Colmán's church:
Glorious flame, now sunk in the grave
Dinertach was his name.

It wrings my pitiable heart, O Chaste Christ,
What has fallen to my lot;
These are arrows that murder the sleep
At every hour in the bitter-cold night.

In this version of the tragic love story, Créd's husband becomes
Guaire. But Dinertach Mac Guaire was actually her brother who

became king of the Uí Fidgente (of Limerick) and who is recorded as slain in the battle of Aidne in AD649. So is the poem confused? Is she lamenting Cano, 'a man from another land', or is she lamenting her slain brother Dinertach? Perhaps there is simply a confusion of transcription of the name. Professor Meyer, however, believes that the Dinertach of the poem was unrelated to Guaire and was another man with whom Créd fell in love.

Créd is certainly the subject of a cycle of romantic tales, surviving mostly in fragmentary form. She is the prototype Iseult with Cano in the Tristan role and Marcán taking the same name role as Mark (Marc'h of Cornwall). Like Marc'h, Marcán mac Tomaini, king of Uí Maine, was an historical ruler and is recorded as falling in battle against the Uí Briúin kings Cend Fáelad mac Colgan and Máenach mac Baíthín in AD653. It is also interesting that Marcán and Marc'h of Cornwall have a similar name, which means 'horse'.

A rather evil and ambitious lady emerges in the person of the daughter of Fidach of Munster, called Mongfhinn. She became the first wife of the High King Eochaidh Muigemedon and stepmother to Niall, who became Niall of the Nine Hostages. Niall's mother was Cairenn Chasdubh, Eochaidh's second wife. Mongfhinn forced her to do every menial task in the palace even while she was in late pregnancy. In fact, Cairenn gave birth to Niall while she was working. In the story of Mongfhinn, the evil-minded lady makes several attempts to kill the boy but finally succeeds in killing herself by accidentally taking the poison that she had prepared for him. A poetic retribution? She became the personification of evil in Irish folklore and, in Munster, old women in the nineteenth century used to say prayers to ward off her evil presence.

Another lady who did not believe in taking a passive role in her love affairs was Moriath, daughter of the king of the Fir Morca, the lover and wife of Móen. When Móen was courting her, it was said that her mother's two eyes never slept at once. One eye was always watching her daughter so that she would know no man. Moriath told Móen's harpist, Craiftine, how to play special music which would put her mother and father to sleep so that she and Móen could meet and make love undisturbed. She was also instrumental in curing Móen's dumbness, which had been caused by the shock of his parents' death when he was a child and by being made to eat their flesh by his evil uncle.

A steadfast wife, not often mentioned in any examination of the

Irish myths, is the beautiful Eórann, the wife of Suibhne, king of Dál nAraide, who was cursed by St Ronán and went mad with terror at the battle of Magh Ráith. Magh Ráith (Moyra) is recorded as an historic battle taking place near Lisburn, in June AD637, when the High King, Domhnall, is said to have tried to assert his authority over the Dàl Riada kingdom. In a tale called *Buile Shuibhne* (Frenzy of Sweeny) we are told that he was so badly injured he went mad (*geilt*) in such a way that he returned to animal familiarity with Nature, wandering the woods. It became a popular tale during the eighth century and many poems were composed in the name of Suibhne. Interestingly, Suibhne Geilt has a Welsh counterpart in the person of Myrddin Wyllt, Merlin himself, who also took himself to the woods and leapt from tree to tree in impersonation of a bird.

Suibhne's beautiful wife Eórann despairs for her mad husband, who is now living the life of a hermit in the woods. She has to remarry for political reasons. But when, wandering the woods, she comes across her insane former husband, she sings to him:

> Blessings on you, my dear splendid madman:
> Although sleep overtakes it
> My body has been ravaged since the day
> When I learned that you were destroyed.
> Now, although a king's son leads me
> Into the splendid banqueting halls,
> I would prefer to sleep in a tree's small hollow,
> With you, my only man, if only I could.
> If the choice were only mine,
> I would live on cress and water
> And be with you, without sin.
> Sad it is, to see you blind and distressed,
> Grief to me, that you are so weather-worn,
> That briars and thorns tear your once white flesh.
> I wish that we could lie together now
> In light and in darkness
> And wander with you, day and night . . .

There is another story in Irish myth of a person possessed by madness. This time it is a young woman and she is cured by her lover. The girl's name is Mis, who features in the twelfth-century

Dinnsenchus. She is claimed as a sister of the fictional character Eochaidh Mac Maireadha who fell in love with his father's second wife Eibhliu; when they eloped they were eventually drowned together. Mis was married to Coemgen who gave her the mountain Sliabh Mis (Slemish, Co. Kerry) as a present, according to one source, and thus the mountain received its name. In most texts, however, it is also recorded that *meisi* means 'phantoms' and these phantoms were created by the goddess Banba and sent to dwell on the mountain.

The tale of the madness of Mis survives from fifteenth-century fragments and is seen in its completed form from an eighteenth-century retelling. Mis was the daughter of Dáire Dóidgheal, a warrior who went into battle against Fionn Mac Cumhail and his Fianna at Fionn Tráigh (Ventry, Co. Kerry). Finding her father's body after the battle, Mis becomes demented, even trying to drink the blood from his wounds to heal them. Insane, she then runs off to Sliabh Mis where she kills every human being that comes near her. 'Fur and hair grew on her, so long that it trailed on the ground behind.' Curiously, the story now takes a plunge from the mythical world of Fionn Mac Cumhail into the historical world of Fedilimid Mac Crimthainn (d. 847), the king of Munster. It is he who offers a great reward to anybody who can capture Mis alive.

No warrior or hero dares to accept the challenge. Finally, a gentle harpist named Dubh Ruis, described as the son of Raghnall, dating the story to after the Viking period, takes up the challenge for a handful of gold and a handful of silver. Dubh Ruis sets off for the mountain. Reaching it he lies down and plays music on his harp. Mis appears and, hearing the music, recalls that her father had a harp. Dubh Ruis shows her the gold and silver and she recalls that her father had such things. Dubh Ruis then displays his genitals and invites her to have sexual intercourse. Her curiosity is piqued for she cannot recall her father doing this. The love-making calms her wildness.

Then Dubh Ruis stays with her, teaching her the forgotten art of cooking and preparing food and then preparing a bath for her and washing away the dirt of the forest so that she becomes beautiful again. They then lie down, make love and fall asleep. In the morning, leaving her sleeping, Dubh Ruis goes off to build a proper house. On returning, he finds her awake and weeping over his disappearance:

It is not the gold I weep for,
the sweet harp or the food,
It is for the penis of Dubh Ruis, son of Raghnall,
that I am longing.

Dubh Ruis stays with her for two months, calming her wildness and helping her regain her reason. Then he takes her to his home and marries her. But, as in reality, no one lives 'happily ever after'. Dubh Ruis is killed by hostile warriors angered by his actions which, because they were too frightened to take up the challenge, have made them look small. This time, faced with death, the memory of her lover helps Mis keep her reason and she laments him only in passionate verse. The story of Mis is an unusual one but in it there seem to be echoes of the story-motif relating to the goddess of sovranty — the ugly hag who becomes a beautiful woman after sexual intercourse with a hero who will one day be king. But in this story, the hero is no warrior but a gentle harpist who is eventually slain.

A few other ladies from the Irish myths deserve a passing mention. The two daughters of the High King Tuathal Teachtmhair are symbols of honourable behaviour. When Eochaidh of Leinster comes to Tara and tells Tuathal that his wife, Fithir, Tuathal's eldest daughter, has died, Tuathal allows him to marry Dairine, his second daughter. When Dairine arrives at Eochaidh's fortress in Leinster, she finds, to her indignation, that her sister is still alive. Eochaidh has lied. Rather than face the future sharing Eochaidh by this deceit, the two girls die of shame. When Tuathal hears the news he goes to war with Eochaidh and Leinster and, after victory, exacts an annual tribute. This is to consist of the payment of cows, the origin of the Bóramha (Boru) or the 'cattle counting'. One of the most famous historical kings of Ireland was Brían Bóramha (AD941–1014) who won the nickname by successfully imposing the tribute for the last time on Leinster.

The sensuous wife of the Ulster champion Celtchair, son of Uthecar Hornskin, a lady called Bríg Bretach, has a passionate affair with Blaí Bruige, son of Fiachne, a fellow warrior. When Celtchair learns of the affair, he slays Blaí in Emain Macha and violates the laws of hospitality. He is ordered to make reparation by performing three deeds, including the slaying of Conganchas Mac Daire, brother of Cú Roí, who is laying waste the country. Celtchair initially comes out of the deal with a new wife, the daughter of Conganchas named

Niamh. But he dies in the same manner as that in which he killed Blaí, so completing the circle of fate.

The Welsh myths also possess some fascinating women. Rhiannon, 'Great Queen', is one of the most interesting. Rhiannon's story is a journey through womanhood. She starts as a beautiful young maiden who marries and has a son. Unjustly accused by her husband, she becomes wise in the ways of men. Then, with a mother's love blinding her to danger, she stumbles, forgetting her wisdom, but is rescued through the support of her second husband, who is prepared to sacrifice himself for her.

Pwyll, lord of Dyfed, sees Rhiannon as a beautiful maiden. He wants her but she has been betrothed to Gwawl. By a trick, he obtains her from Gwawl. There is a similarity in this tale to the Irish tale of Brandubh, king of Leinster, who wins Mongán's wife from him by a similar trick; Mongán then recovers her in like fashion.

Rhiannon is happy with Pwyll and bears him a son. But the son is abducted in mysterious circumstances. Rhiannon's maidservant, who has fallen asleep during the crucial period, awakes to find the child gone. She does not want to be blamed, so she kills a puppy dog and smears the blood on the still sleeping Rhiannon before raising the alarm. The conclusion is obvious. Rhiannon is unjustly accused of killing her own child. For years, Pwyll punishes her by ostracising her and having his servants treat her harshly. Then much later she discovers that her child is alive and has been raised by Teyrnon, lord of Gwent-Is-Coed. The child's name is now Pryderi. It is a comment on Rhiannon's nature that she can forgive Pwyll the years of ill-treatment at the joy of finding her child again.

Manawydan fab Llyr becomes her second husband. He is a wise and patient counsellor and, in the Welsh tales, bears no sign of having been a god of the oceans. The Welsh Christian scribes had a firmer censorial hold over the retelling of the tales than did their Irish cousins. Pryderi, Rhiannon's son, is now an adult with a wife of his own in the very human person of Cigfa. She is the only one of the four of these characters, in their subsequent adventures together, who is frightened by what transpires. They all live at the palace at Arbeth, in Dyfed. One day there is a peal of thunder and a mist sweeps the landscape. When it lifts, all the people have vanished except the four of them. The land is desolate; there are no cattle herds nor crops. After a while, they set out to discover what has happened.

Pryderi, in spite of a warning from Manawydan, follows a magic boar to a castle where he finds a fountain and golden bowl on a marble slab. It is an early motif of the magic cauldron tale which, under Christian scribes, became the basis of the Holy Grail legend. He tries to take hold of it, is struck dumb and is unable to let go. This is when Rhiannon, forgetting her wisdom and Manawydan's warnings, rushes forward and tries to rescue him but suffers a similar fate. A mist envelops them and they disappear.

Manawydan and Cigfa search in vain and continue to have adventures until they are finally able to rescue them. It appears that the whole saga has been started off as an act of revenge on Rhiannon by Llwyd, son of Cilcoed, who was a friend of Gwawl, son of Clud, which takes us back to Rhiannon and Pwyll's first meeting and wedding. In other words, one never escapes the results of one's actions; old debts have to be paid.

A debt certainly has to be paid when Gilfaethwy decides to rape Goewin, daughter of Pebin, the virginal foot-holder to Math, son of Mathonwy. Gilfaethwy 'fancies' Goewin and confides in his brother Gwydion. The brothers form an intricate plot to get Math out of the way so that Goewin is left on her own. While Gwydion cheers on the sidelines, Gilfaethwy rapes Goewin. She might be a self-effacing woman, content with her place in life and doing her duty, but she does not crawl off as a 'disgraced woman'. She speaks up and denounces both men to Math. The result is that she ends up as Math's wife while Gwydion and Gilfaethwy are punished and have to go through a whole series of incarnations, from deer to swine to wolves, before they complete their full penance.

It is Gwydion who also features in a tale involving Aranrhod (sometimes Arianrod). In fact, he is her brother. Aranrhod is a free spirit: wild, elemental, self-assertive and restless. Gwydion has proposed her as Math's virginal foot-holder to replace Goewin. She is brought before Math and asked to step over his magic wand as a test of her virginity. As she does so, male twins drop from her womb. Gwydion takes one baby, who becomes Lleu, and manages to conceal it. The other, yellow-haired, leaps into the sea and takes on its nature; he is known as Dylan Eil Ton, 'Son of the Wave'. The story of Lleu and Dylan seems very similar to that of Krishna and Balarama in Hindu myth in which it is Balarama who disappears into the sea.

We must remember that Aranrhod is a daughter of Dôn, the

equivalent of Danu, the mother goddess. Indeed, when Dylan is slain by the Welsh equivalent of the smith-god, Gofannon, it is cognate with the killing of Ruadán by Goibhniu in Irish myth. It seems that the two children are, in fact, Gwydion's own sons by his sister. He certainly takes responsibility for the boy Lleu who grows up as Lleu Llaw Gyffes, the equivalent of Lugh Lámhfada, and it is Gwydion who creates Blodeuwydd, mentioned earlier, as the ideal, docile wife for Lleu. But, as we have seen, that scheme backfires. While the Christian scribes depict Aranrhod as a self-willed woman, the pagan goddess still shows through the veneer. Her name, 'Silver Wheel', is still used as a name for the constellation of the Corona Borealis – Caer Arianrod – and is connected with the great wheel of fate. She is no ordinary woman and in Lleu Llaw Gyffes she has given birth to no ordinary son.

Perhaps one of the most famous Celtic women of myth in terms of popular world culture is Gwenhwyfar, who has become better known as Guinevere, the wife of Arthur. Her beauty and abduction bring betrayal, war and ultimate disaster, placing her as a counterpart to Helen of Troy or Persephone. The basis of the medieval Arthurian tales, which have found new interpretations and developments in England, France and Germany, are clearly rooted in Celtic myth. Based on a fifth-century historical Celtic warrior, the tales of Arthur were worked and reworked in the years after his death, with considerable borrowings from the earlier Irish tales of Fionn Mac Cumhail, as I have demonstrated in *Celt and Saxon*.

It has been argued by Catlín Matthews, in *Arthur and the Sovereignty of Britain* (London, 1989), that Gwenhwyfar was a triune goddess of sovranty like Éire, Fótla and Banba. Certainly, there is evidence of three different Guineveres married to Arthur which might support this contention. But there is much in the story to suggest a comparison with Étain rather than with Éire.

One cannot pass the story of Arthur without saying something of his mother Eigr, sometimes known in English by the form Ingraine, who, according to *Brut y Brenhinedd*, was the daughter of Anlawdd Wledig and married to Gwrlais of Cornwall. Uthr Pendragon desired her and demanded that Myrddin (Merlin) transform him into the shape of Gwrlais, in which Uthr seduced her. Arthur was born as a result of this. Eigr is pictured as a hapless victim of Uthr's lust, thinking that she is making love to her husband but in reality being raped. Does Christian morality enter the story when we find Gwrlais conveniently being killed later on with Eigr marrying Uthr?

As queens go, Branwen, daughter of Llyr, proves herself to be a sensitive and intelligent young woman. She is married to Matholwch of Ireland but because her half-brother, Efnisien, insults him, Matholwch decides to make her suffer for his behaviour. She is forced to do menial tasks in the kitchen. She rears a starling and teaches it to talk, sending it with news of her plight to her brother Bran, ruler of the Island of the Mighty. Bran invades Matholwch's land to seek redress for the insult to his sister. This results in a terrible battle in which everyone except five pregnant Irish women and seven Britons are killed. Branwen, who is a figure of dignity and restraint against the fiery tempers of the menfolk, sees the devastation which has been wreaked in her name and wants nothing to do with it. She dies of a broken heart.

As a point of interest, Branwen's mother, Penardun, the daughter of Dôn, and wife of Llyr, is the mother of Efnisien, who has caused the trouble. She had taken a second husband in the person of Eurosswyd and had two sons, Nisien and Efnisien, one a gentle youth and lover of peace, the second given to strife and conflict, thus demonstrating the two eternal sides in the male.

Enid, the daughter of Ynwyl, a chieftain fallen on evil days, is presented as a rather patient young lady. When Geraint marries her, he is constantly demanding that she prove her love and loyalty to him. She, like Guinevere, has become known to the wider English-speaking world through the works of the poet Tennyson. Enid is one of the 'Three Splendid Maidens' of Arthur's court. The others are Dyfr and Tegau Eurfon. Dyfr was popular among the medieval *cywyddwyr*, writers of one of the strict forms of metrical poetry. She is regarded as a standard of beauty on account of her golden hair and it seems that Glewlwyd Gafaelfawr was her lover. Tegau Eurfon is regarded as a standard of chastity. She is, however, the wife of Caradog Freichfras, and rescues him from a poisonous snake. In so doing she is bitten in the breast; it has to be removed because her life is threatened, and is replaced by one of gold. She has a cloak, listed as one of the *Tri Thlws ar Ddeg Ynys Prydain* (The Thirteen Treasures of the Isle of Britain), which will not fit any woman who has committed adultery. Here we see a later Christian motif entering the myths. At Arthur's court, not only was Gwenhwyfar having adulterous intrigues, but Arthur himself was indulging his sexual appetites with three mistresses, according to the Welsh sources. The first was Indeg, daughter of Garwy Hir (The Tall), hailed for her beauty. The second was Garwen, daughter of Henin (The Old). The third was Gwyl, daughter of Gendawd. Yet, in the Anglo-Norman Christian retellings, it is poor Gwenhwyfar who gets the short end of the stick in being sentenced to be burnt for her adultery with Lancelot while Arthur emerges as the virtuous king.

Certainly, Welsh myth is not short on tales of determined women; women such as Goleuddydd, the mother of Culhwch, who, pregnant and knowing she is about to die, goes into the forest to give birth. She makes her husband Cilydd promise that he will only remarry when a briar with two heads grows from her grave. It is in the seventh year that such a briar grows. Or Luned, without whose intelligence, love and help, Owain, son of Urien, would not have succeeded in his quest. This girl rescues Owain from imprisonment at the castle of the Fountain, gives him a ring to make him invisible and also helps him win the hand of the woman whom he wants to marry. After some years he finds Luned again; she is imprisoned and about to face death by burning, and he rescues her.

There are many parallel heroines in Breton tales although, in general, the Breton traditions have been entirely submerged in medieval Christianity and dogma. Some heroines stand out, however, such as Nimue or Niniane, whose name appears in later texts as Viviane or Vivienne. The original name, Nimue, could well be cognate with Niamh. In this story we find Myrddin travelling in the forest of Brocéliande in Brittany. He finds a young woman guarding a fountain, a fountain of wisdom at Barenton − a typical Celtic motif. Myrddin falls in love with her but she refuses his love unless he tells her all his magical secrets. He is aware that in giving up his secrets he will become Nimue's prisoner but he is happy to do so. This story was written down in the later medieval period and seems to be parallel to an earlier Welsh tale of Gwendydd (Gandieda in the Geoffrey of Monmouth version). Myrddin, like Suibhne and also Mis, has become deranged after a battle and is living wild in the woods. Only Gwendydd, his sister, and wife of King Rhydderch, can go near him and she brings him back to health by going to live with him in the woods. It is to Gwendydd that Myrddin passes on his gift of prophecy.

Of all the heroines of the Celtic myths it is Esyllt or Iseult who seems most conjured in the non-Celtic world. It is significant that we can also identify three different Iseults. This story has evolved from Celtic history/mythology to become one of the world's greatest love stories. The core motif is the traditional Celtic elopement tale known, in Irish, as *aithedha*.

Mark of Cornwall is actually a real personage, existing in Cornwall in the sixth century. The name Mark, as previously mentioned, comes not from the Roman *praenomen* Marcus but from the Celtic word for 'horse', and in Celtic form is given as Marc'h. Significantly, in Beroul's twelfth-century rendering of the tale we are told that Mark has ears like a horse. In the *Life of St Pol de Léon*, written in about AD880 by Urmonek, a monk of Landévennec in Cornouaille in Brittany, we are told that Mark has another name – '*quem alio nomine Quonomorium vocant*' (whose other name was Quonomorius), giving the Celtic name of Cunomor or Cunomorus, 'Hound of the Sea'. Urmonek says he was a powerful monarch who spoke four different languages and who ruled in both Dumnonia in Britain and Damnonia in Brittany. His traditions certainly are found in both areas.

In Cornwall, Castle Dore near Fowey is given, in the texts, as his fortress. It was originally constructed in the second century BC, and excavations have shown that it was still in use in the sixth century AD. Most importantly, however, is the fact that a mile or so from the site of Castle Dore, near the disused entrance to Menabilly House, stands an engraved stone dated to the mid-sixth century AD. The accepted reading is '*Drustaus* [or Drustanus] *hic iacit Cunomori Filius*' – 'Here lies Drustanus son of Cunomorus'. Philologically the name Drustanus equates with Tristan and we know that Cunomorus was Mark's other name. So the final reading is 'Tristan son of Mark lies here'. The story of Tristan and Iseult is much more poignant if we see Tristan as the stepson of the tragic Iseult. But in medieval versions Tristan was made nephew, not son of, Mark. The story of Iseult, a corruption of British Celtic Adsiltia – 'she who must be gazed upon', doubtless a compliment to her beauty – is very much like the stories of Deirdre and Naoise or of Diarmuid and Gráinne.

Tristan sets off for Ireland to escort the young woman to Cornwall as the new bride for the ageing King Mark. She is Iseult, daughter of Iseult and Anguish, a royal couple who rule in Munster. Iseult falls in love with Tristan. At first, she denies her love and then the inevitable happens, but the love is fated and can only end in tragedy.

In some versions a third Iseult, a daughter of Hywel of Brittany, comes to compensate Tristan when Mark takes his wife, Iseult of Ireland, back to Cornwall.

In the final scene, Tristan lies dying. He has been badly wounded in trying to help his friend Caherdin pursue a love affair with the wife of another man. The enraged husband's friends kill Caherdin and mortally wound Tristan. Here we have another example of the circle of fate for Tristan is mortally wounded in helping his friend pursue a similar affair to his own.

Iseult of Brittany summons physicians but they cannot cure him. Tristan knows his only hope lies in Iseult of Ireland. He sends a message to Cornwall, begging her to come to him. If his messenger proves successful in his mission, then his ship is to bear white sails; if not, black sails. Iseult of Brittany overhears these instructions and she is jealous.

When the ship appears in the bay, bearing the white sails which indicate that Iseult of Ireland is on the way, she tells Tristan, who cannot leave his bed, that the sails are black. Tristan falls back on his bed and dies. When Iseult of Ireland arrives and finds Tristan already dead she is grief-stricken. Iseult laments:

> My friend, Tristan, when I see you are dead,
> I can live no more.
> You are dead to my love
> And so I die, my friend, of compassion
> For I could not come to you in time
> To cure you of your illness.
>
> Had I arrived in time
> Your life would have been restored
> And I would have spoken gently
> Of the love we had between us.
> As I cannot cure you
> We can die together.
>
> As I could not arrive in time,
> Changing destiny's course,
> Death has arrived before me.
> Now I will drink from the same cup.
> You have given your life for me

And a true friend I shall remain
For I will give my life for you.

According to Professor Jean Markle, the lamentation is a credo of absolute love. The bodies are taken back to Cornwall where King Mark decides to give them an honourable burial, one on each side of the nave of the church at Tintagel. Echoing the usual Celtic motif, a tree grows from each grave and they intertwine over the apse. Three times Mark orders them to be cut down and three times they grow again, symbolising the eternal union of the lovers.

But how much of the story can we trace to a Celtic original? The oldest extant version in a Celtic language (Welsh) dates only to the sixteenth century. However, Joseph Bédlier, in *Le Roman de Tristan par Thomas* (Paris, 1902), discovered that all the known manuscript versions of the story, medieval and modern, could be traced back to one extant manuscript written by Beroul in the middle of the twelfth century. Beroul, writing in French, was obviously translating from a Breton language source which has since been destroyed.

The name Esyllt also appears in the Welsh tale of Culhwch and Olwen in which two women at Arthur's court are mentioned in the persons of Esyllt Fynwen (White Neck) and Esyllt Fyngul (Slender Neck). Esyllt Fynwen is the daughter of Culfanawyd Prydain and said to be one of the 'Three Defiled Women of the Isle of Britain'. This story is one of the few Arthurian texts in Welsh which predate Geoffrey of Monmouth's *Historia Regum Britanniae*.

In Breton tradition we have several determined women who choose their own lovers. A Breton king has fallen in love with a mystic princess and despatches his best warrior, Efflam, to find her. Efflam encounters many adventures and has to overcome many obstacles. He then arrives at the girl's fortress and states the king's case. The girl, in order to determine whether he is worthy, demands three tasks of him. He must spend one night in a lion's cage, the next night in an ogre's den and the third night sorting a pile of wheat. When Efflam succeeds in the tasks, the girl agrees to go with him to see the king. The king is old and the girl has already fallen in love with Efflam. The girl suggests to the king that she possesses magic and that if he will allow her to kill him she could then restore him to life as a twenty-year-old. The king is vain and eager with desire. He agrees. She kills him and then her intention becomes clear. 'Since he is dead, let him remain so, and the warrior who took all the risks and won my heart may receive the reward.' She marries Efflam who then becomes king. The moral of the story is obvious.

The tale is reminiscent of another Breton story, featuring a lady named Marcassa. A Breton king is lying ill and dying and only a certain magical bird called Dredaine, kept in a golden cage in an inaccessible castle, can cure him. Not only is the castle inaccessible, but to enter the room where Dredaine is kept one has to cross three courtyards, one of venomous snakes, another of ravenous tigers and a third of ferocious giant warriors. No warrior will attempt the task on behalf of their king. Finally, a puny youthful servant named Luduenn, 'Drudge', is persuaded to set out. The youth might be puny but he is clever. He reaches the castle, succeeds in crossing the three courtyards, but then finds he has to pass through three rooms to get to the bird. In the first room, he manages to seize a loaf which remains the same size no matter how much is eaten; in the second room he takes a jug of wine that remains filled no matter how much is drunk; while in the third room he finds a beautiful woman sleeping deeply. He kisses the girl without rousing her and enters the fourth room. Here he finds Dredaine and takes the bird back to his king. While the bird improves the king's health, it does not heal him. To be cured the king has to have intercourse with the sleeping girl. Meanwhile, the girl has given birth to Luduenn's child; the 'kiss' has been rather potent! She and the child come to the king's court. She cures the king and is offered marriage by him but she chooses to marry the puny Luduenn.

As Rome asserted its hold on Celtic Christianity, many of the stories featuring women were changed to a new morality. According to Professor Markle: 'This process of debasing women and banishing them, with a great show of morality, into prohibited areas is particularly apparent in the successive changes made to old legends that retain no more of the original myth than its outline dressed up with circumstantial detail.' In this respect, one is put in mind of the story of Ker-Ys, the city of the depths. Gradlon, a king of Cornouaille, in Brittany, built a town for his daughter Dahud. Dahud appears to be an interesting young lady: by the time the Christian scribes set down her story, they could accuse her of being a rebel against Christianity and a nymphomaniac who led a life of debauchery. Along came St Guénole, the sixth-century abbot, known also in Cornwall as

Winwaloe (Gunwalloe), who founded the great monastery at Landévennec in Cornouaille in Brittany. He cursed the town of Ker-Ys for its impropriety and debauchery. God, in the tradition of Sodom and Gomorrah, caused the sea to rise up and engulf it. King Gradlon, previously warned by Guénole, escaped on horseback. Dahud tried to join him on the same horse but it became engulfed in the waves and started to sink until Gradlon, with a burst of self-preservation overcoming his parental concerns, knocked his daughter off and she sank into the sea. Guénole, obligingly, allowed her to become a mermaid.

This sort of story became popular throughout the Celtic world. A similar tale appears in the Irish story of Lí Bán, not the sister of Fand and wife to Labraid Luathlam ar Cledeb, but the daughter of Ecca who wound up as a mermaid in Lough Neagh where, according to the *Annals of the Four Masters*, she was captured in AD558. The Welsh tale of Maes Gwyddneu preserves a similar original theme which seems to have missed the Christian censor. Seithynin Veddw (the Drunkard) rapes a young girl who guards a mystic well. The water then rises up and envelops the land of Cantre'r Gwaelod where Seithynin Veddw comes from.

There is another group of powerful women who appear in Celtic myth and pre-history stories. These are Druidesses: here we use the word not in its original sense which signified the intelligentsia caste of ancient Celtic society, but in the sense intended by Christian scribes who depicted them as enchantresses, prophetesses and witches. We will discuss historical Druidesses in our chapter on 'Women in Early History' but here we confine ourselves to some references to female Druids in mythology. The Celtic tradition for their existence is quite explicit. They feature in many Irish epics and there is even reference to the office of Chief Druidess of Ireland, held by a lady called Gáine, mentioned in the *Metrical Dinnsenchus*. Before the second battle of Magh Tuireadh, two Druidesses promise to enchant 'the trees and stones and sods of earth'. Aoife, the wicked stepmother of the children of Lir, not to be confused with the warrior sister of Scáthach, is clearly a Druidess, turning the children into swans by means of a Druidical wand. Biróg was another Druidess who helped Cian gain access to the crystal tower of the evil Fomorii ruler, Balor. He had imprisoned his daughter Ethlinn in it for it had been prophesied that his own grandson would kill him and he sought to prevent the birth of such a grandson. Biróg was also instrumental in saving the life of the child, the son of Cian and Ethlinn, when Balor cast the boy into the sea.

At Cluain Feart (Clonfert) there was said to dwell a whole community of Druidesses who could raise storms, cure diseases and kill their enemies by cursing them. Fionn Mac Cumhail was raised by Bodmall the Druidess. Smirgat, a Druidess, prophesied that if Fionn drank from a horn he would die, so he was always careful to drink from a goblet or bowl. The Druidess Milucrah was able to transform Fionn into an old man at Loch Slieve Gallion, while in Donegal there lived a beautiful Druidess, Geal Ghossach (White Legs).

Perhaps the two most compelling Druidesses in the Irish sagas are Fidelma and Sín.

Fedelm (Fidelma) Fholtebar (of the Smooth Hair) must not be confused with Fedelm Fholtcháin (of the Beautiful Hair). The latter, while a daughter of a legendary king of Connacht, Brían Mac Eochaidh Mugmedón, became the female progenitor of the kings of Dàl Riada in Scotland through her son Gabhán. But Fedelm Fholtebar is given in some texts as a daughter of Medb and Ailill of Connacht.

In the epic the *Táin Bó Cuailgne*, Medb consults Fidelma, who is sometimes described as being an Otherworld spirit from the *sidh* of Cruachan. Her more usual role is as a Druidess and daughter of Medb. Asked by Medb if she possesses the *imbas forasnai*, the light of foresight, Fidelma says she does and has just returned from studying Druidic lore in Britain. This seems an interesting endorsement of the usually inaccurate Julius Caesar in his statement that the Gauls went to study Druidic lore in Britain and that it was in Britain that the main colleges of Druidism were to be found. Medb asks Fidelma if her army will be victorious over Ulster. Fidelma prophesies its defeat at the hands of Cúchulainn. Fidelma is described as an attractive young girl. Thomas Kinsella's translation of the *Táin* carries this passage:

She had yellow hair. She wore a speckled cloak fastened around her with a gold pin, a red embroidered, hooded tunic and sandals with gold clasps. Her brow was broad, her jaw narrow, her two eyebrows pitch black, with delicate dark lashes casting shadows halfway down her cheeks. You would think her lips were inset with Parthian scarlet. Her teeth were like an array of jewels between the lips. She had hair in three tresses; two wound upwards on her head and the third hanging down her back, brushing her calves. She held a light gold weaving rod in her hands, with gold inlay. Her eyes had triple irises. Two black horses drew her chariot, and she was armed.

Sín is perhaps one of the most 'human' of the Druidesses in the sagas. Her story is recounted in the *Leabhar Buidhe Lecain* (Yellow Book of Lecan). It starts when the High King Muirchertach Mac Erca, an historical king c.AD512–33, is out hunting. He meets a beautiful girl and becomes infatuated with her. He is already married, of course, with children. But he asks her to become his mistress and live at his royal palace of Cletach (Cletty on the Boyne near Rosnaree). Sín is no push-over for the romantic advances of the king. She knows exactly what she wants. She will agree to become Muirchertach's mistress on certain conditions: that the king will submit to her will in all things and that no Christian cleric will ever set foot in the palace while she resides there.

Desire is the overriding factor and the king agrees but not before asking her name. She replies, giving a clear symbolic warning of what is to come, for she presents a list of synonyms for her name: sigh, rustling, storm, rough wind, winter night, cry, tear and groan. In fact, in Old Irish, the word *sín* signifies 'bad weather' or 'storm'. The girl is therefore warning the wretched man of 'the storm' to come. Later, realising that the girl is possessed of supernatural powers, the king hesitantly asks whether she believes in the god of the Christians. She replies emphatically:

> Never believe the clerics
> For they chant nothing save unreason.
> Follow not their unmelodious stave.
> Cleave not to the clerics of churches,
> If you desire life without treachery.
> Better am I as a friend here.
> Let not repentance come to you.

Once installed in Cletach, Sín demands that Muirchertach eject his wife, Dualtech, and his children. They rush off to Cairnech, the local Christian bishop, and demand that he do something about the High King's infatuation. Cairnech orders Muirchertach to send the girl away. The king refuses and Cairnech curses him in a ritual that seems more Druidic than Christian. The High King's entourage are now worried about the extent to which Muirchertach will go to pursue his passion. The girl performs some feats of magic to impress Muirchertach and presumably 'keep him in line'. Curiously, it has an opposite effect. Muirchertach now begins to worry about his soul and rushes off to Cairnech the bishop to confess his sins. He promises to throw Sín out but when he returns, she evokes a vision which mesmerises him.

We now arrive at the moment of truth in the story. Muirchertach awakes, after once more satiating his lust, and finds his fortress ablaze. Seeking to escape, he climbs into a vat of wine and drowns. At this point we learn that Sín's entire family, her mother, her father, her sister and cousins, have all been slaughtered by Muirchertach during the battle of Atha Síghe (Assey) on the Boyne. Sín has planned her vengeance on the king using her Druidical powers to ensnare and destroy him.

Yet there is another punch-line to the tale. Sín realises that, in spite of everything, she has genuinely come to love Muirchertach and after his death she is overcome with grief and dies.

> I myself will die of grief for him . . .
> For the burden of all misfortunes

In spite of the story being written by a Christian scribe, we come away from it with feelings of sympathy for Sín in her predicament. Love or vengeance – which has won?

Finally we can turn to women in a rather unusual role. Where Celtic myth departs from Greek and Latin myths is in the tales of great female warriors and warrior queens. Women warriors even appear on early Celtic coins as a common iconographic theme. The place of female warriors in the myths is a prominent one.

In the landing of the Milesians, the progenitors of the Gaels, in Ireland, there appears a lady named Scota, the widow of the warrior Golamh. Golamh's *nom de guerre* is Míl (Milesius). Míl of Spain had sought refuge in Egypt and there married the daughter of the Pharaoh Nectanebus, Scota. Scota bore Míl's children, among whom were Eber and Amairgen, Ir and Colptha. Míl, hearing of the death of his nephew Ith at the hands of the Tuatha Dé Danaan in Ireland, set out to take revenge by conquering the island. Míl died before reaching Ireland but his widow Scota and their children and followers arrived safely. Scota fought alongside her sons in true warrior fashion but was slain in the ensuing battle at Caherconree (Cú Roí's fort) on the Dingle peninsula. She was buried in Scota's Glen, three miles from Tralee. There are also associations with Slemish (Sliabh Mis) close by where the Tuatha Dé Danaan met the children of Míl and negotiated the end of their power in Ireland. Thus we could argue that Scota, also the mother of Goidel, the eponymous progenitor of the Gael, and herself the eponymous progenitor of the Scots, was the first warrior heroine in Ireland as opposed to the goddess-warriors that went before her.

What is interesting in Irish myth, however, is the appearance of female warriors who are not queens but professional warriors. The best known among them is Scáthach (Shadowy One) whose school of martial arts was situated on the Isle of Skye, Sgiathanach in modern Scots Gaelic. All the famous warriors of Ireland, at the time of the Red Branch epics, were said to have been trained by her. Her most famous pupil was Cúchulainn who was sent to complete his warrior training at her school. She gave him his fearsome spear, the Gae Bolga, and taught him the *Torannchles* or 'thunder feat' as well as his famous battle leap. He even wrested from Scáthach 'the friendship of her thighs'. The symbolism is seen as that of the union of an apprentice with his vocation.

When Cúchulainn arrived at Scáthach's school of martial arts, he was served food by Uathach (Spectre), the daughter of Scáthach. In taking a dish from her hand he forgot his strength and managed to break her finger. Her scream brought the champion Cochar Crufe to her. He challenged Cúchulainn and Cúchulainn slew him. In reparation, Cúchulainn had to become guardian and doorkeeper of Dún Scáthach. Uathach later became his mistress.

In return for her instruction, Cúchulainn helped Scáthach in her own battles, particularly with her war against her equally fierce sister, Aoife. Scáthach's reputation notwithstanding, it was Aoife who was reputed to be the strongest of all female warriors. In fact, Scáthach had tried to leave Cúchulainn behind during her attack on Aoife's fortress, fearing that Aoife might kill him. But the young warrior arrived and challenged Aoife to single combat. As strong and warlike as Cúchulainn was, the champion of all male warriors, he was unable to overcome his fierce female opponent without resorting to a trick and distracting her attention. She surrendered to him. Later they fell in love and she became Cúchulainn's mistress. She was pregnant at the time he had to return to his native Ulster. He left her a gold ring. Years later a young warrior arrived in Ulaidh named Connlaí. By mistake, Cúchulainn challenged him to single combat and slew him, only realising that the boy was his son by Aoife when Connlaí lay dying and he saw the ring he had given Aoife on the boy's finger.

While Scáthach is sometimes given as Scáthach Búanann (Victorious), *Cormac's Glossary* identifies a Búanann, 'Mother of Heroes', as a separate personage who also ran a martial arts academy. She is certainly not to be confused with another female warrior, Búadnat, 'Victorious Lady', who makes an appearance in the Fionn Mac Cumhail cycle of tales.

Cúchulainn's encounters with female warrior enemies were not many but they are significant. One woman he was quite happy to defeat was Scenmed, sister of Forgall Manach who was also the sister of Cúchulainn's greatest love, Emer. When Cúchulainn eloped with Emer, it was this fierce female warrior, Scenmed, who raised an army and set off in pursuit to exact vengeance. Cúchulainn defeated and slew her.

A similar motif runs through the love story of Art, son of Conn of the Hundred Battles, the High King of Ireland, and Delbchaem. Art had to destroy Delbchaem's evil parents – and none was more evil than her mother Coinchend, a monstrous female warrior.

Many other female warriors appear in Irish sagas: Creidne, who had been sexually abused by her father, learnt the martial arts and became one of the relentless warriors of the Fianna; Fionn Mac Cumhail's own daughter Credha; Erni, Medb's personal female warrior who guarded her treasures; and Mugháin Mór, the warrior queen of Munster. In fact, in the *Rennes Dinnsenchus* several female warriors are listed including one called Etsine, who appears in the story of 'The Frenzy of Suibhne', and another named Breifne from whom, it was recorded by the *Dinnsenchus*, the ancient kingdom of Breifne took its name.

Nessa, the daughter of Eochaidh Sálbuidhe of Ulaidh, is described as a female warrior in several texts. She seems to have settled down to a more courtly role after her marriage to Fachtna, the king of Ulaidh. But she continues as a powerful and ambitious woman who sets out to ensure that the kingdom of Ulaidh passes to her son

Conchobhar. We have already discussed how Conchobhar was called Mac Nessa, son of Nessa, and did not take a patronymic.

Nessa's husband Fachtna died and his half-brother Fergus Mac Roth was elected to the throne. Fergus was in love with Nessa but Nessa would only agree to become his wife if he would let her son Conchobhar rule as king for a year first. Nessa than instructed Conchobhar how to be an exceptional monarch and when the time came for Fergus to reclaim the throne, Conchobhar was able to refuse the claim with the support of the people. This laid the groundwork for the eventual war in the *Táin Bó Cuailgne* saga, for Fergus hastened to offer his services to Medb. Nessa, however, had become the most powerful woman in the land.

Nessa's granddaughter also became a famous warrior. Fedelm Noíchrothach (the Nine Times Beautiful) was Conchobhar's daughter and noted for her great beauty. She first married Laoghaire Buadach, son of Ugaine, a Red Branch warrior. They had a son Fiachna, also a warrior. She then married Cairbre, another warrior who was son of a king of Leinster and who took part in the destruction of Da Derga's hostel. Tiring in turn of Cairbre, Fedelm eloped with Conall Cearnach, the Red Branch warrior and foster brother to Cúchulainn who, after Cúchulainn, was probably the greatest of the Ulster champions. But, the epic says, 'none could match her at sword, nor javelin when the battle fever came upon her'.

We will return to female warriors in history later but certainly the myths and sagas demonstrate that women went to war in the ancient Celtic world and took command of men. Specific titles were given to these classes of female warriors such as *ban-gaisgedaig* and *ban-feinnidh*. The first word combines *ban* (woman) and a derivation of *gas* which means a young warrior. The second combines *ban* with *feinnidh*, 'band of warriors', so it seems that women warriors were classed according to age and experience.

From this brief sketch of some of the women who appear in the Celtic myths, it will be seen that they are varied and rich in character. There are no shallow stereotypes. Each character is delicately and carefully drawn and their motivations are as complex and tangled as any that we encounter in reality. They are not there in supporting roles for the handsome, male heroes. Indeed, the men in the myths also provide a rich profusion of characters. Women take their place in the myths in their own right, as thinking people with their own minds and incentives. Nor are they second-class citizens. To repeat what I said at the start of this chapter, I believe that the women of the Celtic myths are a reflection of the historical women of early Celtic society with all their problems, loves, heartaches and triumphs.

[3]

Women in Early History

ONE of the earliest powerful Celtic female rulers of whom we have clear evidence is a woman whose name, alas, we do not know. We know only that she lived in the late sixth century BC and died around 500BC, aged thirty to thirty-five. How we know this is from her spectacular burial chamber at Vix, near Mount Lasois in France. Discovered in 1953, the tomb consists of a three-metre-square chamber. The body of the 'princess', as she is now popularly referred to, lies on a dismantled four-wheeled Celtic chariot. The wheels are detached and rest at one side of the chamber.

She wears a typical Celtic hero's torc, a beautiful hollow, 24-carat golden neck-ring. It is made from 480 grams (a pound) of gold and embellished by fine filigree work. The ends of the torc are fashioned as a lion's paws resting on spheres with a pair of winged ponies on the back of the paws.

It is a very rich grave, demonstrating her power and influence. There are numerous dazzling items but one stands out above the others, a bronze *krater*, or wine-mixing jar, imported from Greece, standing 1.5 metres high with a capacity of 1250 litres. Made in Sparta, it is decorated with Greek warriors, chariots and gorgons, and surmounted by the statuette of a woman on the lid. It is, says Lloyd Laing, 'without doubt one of the most distinguished treasures of archaic Greek art ever to survive'. It is dated to about 550BC and would indicate trade between the Celtic and Greek worlds at this early period. Two hundred years after this date, incidentally, 2000 Celtic warriors were serving in the Spartan army during Sparta's war with Thebes. Rich textiles once adorned the 'princess's' burial chamber, and other items show further contacts with ancient Greece.

Who was this 'princess' of the Celts? Presumably she was a ruler of the ancestors of the Aedui whom Caesar encountered in this area five centuries later. Perhaps she was even an ancestor of the great Gaulish leader Dumnorix, whose name means 'King of the World'.

Another chariot burial of a powerful female ruler, also dating from the sixth century BC, was found at Hömichele Barrow in Germany. In a single wooden chamber lie the remains of a woman on her chariot. In an adjacent chamber are a man and a woman on another chariot, each with a bow and with fifty iron head arrows between them. They lie on a bull's hide. These rich graves are replete with vessels, jewellery and textiles including Chinese silks, indicating a very early trading link.

Another single female chariot burial was discovered at Reinheim where a fourth-century BC Celtic 'princess' was found in a burial chamber overlooking the River Blies. The chamber was oak-lined and the rich grave goods with which she was buried included the contents of her jewel box, comprising some 200 items. Gold, bronze, amber, coral, glass and a mirror were present. As with most other Celtic burials she had vessels for food and drink in the Otherworld including a beautiful gilt-bronze wine flagon engraved with intricate pattern work.

These and other finds confirm what we know from Greek and Roman sources, and also from later native Celtic sources: that Celtic women achieved high positions in society and could lead their people in battle. The symbolism of the chariot burial was not accorded to women in any other position. Prominent female burials have also been discovered among the 700 Arras Culture graves of the Parisii of eastern Yorkshire, dating from the third to the first centuries BC. A total of 95 female bodies and 107 male bodies have so far been identified from these burials. From the remains we can tell that the average height for Parisii females was 5 feet 2 inches (1.58 metres) while the males were 5 feet 7½ inches (1.71 metres). We know that in this area, at this time, Parisii women were quite likely to die in their twenties, largely because of the hazards of childbirth. By comparison, the men from these graves seem to have survived to an average age of thirty, a few living into their forties. Osteo-arthritis of the spine was common among the women, who had quite good teeth although they showed signs of calcium deficiency caused by motherhood. Once again, as an indication of their status, individual females, such as the one at Wetwang Slack, are buried with a dismantled chariot and grave goods.

Professor Fergus Kelly has a problem in coming to grips with the idea of female leaders, especially war leaders. 'The annals provide no instances of a female political or military leader,' he writes in *A Guide to Early Irish Law*. He is, of course, speaking of the literature outside the sagas, which admit to figures such as Medb of Connacht, Aoife and Scáthach. 'Indeed,' he continues, ignoring the female leaders of history, 'the male imagery which surrounds the office of kingship would seem to preclude even the possibility of a female ruler. In non-literary sources I know of only one dubious reference to a female ruler or military leader. This is in a difficult passage in the law-text *Bretha Cróilge* which lists some categories of women who are particularly important in the *tuath*, or clan, including "the woman who turns back the streams of war" (*ben sues srutha coctha for cula*) and "the hostage ruler"(?) (*rechtaid géill*).' He admits that the former could refer to a female military leader, while an ancient glossator clearly notes that *rechtaid géill* refers to a woman ruler who takes hostages (prisoners of war), citing Queen Medb as an example. The Irish chronicler, Tighernach (*c.*1020–88), abbot of Clonmacnoise, records Medb as an historical queen of Connacht, even putting the date of her death at AD70. Some Irish chroniclers record Medb as succeeding Tinne as ruler of her people and marrying Ailill, who is stated to be merely the commander of the Gamhanrhide, or royal bodyguard of Connacht. Yet in most of the Irish sagas, Ailill is said to be king of Connacht. There is clearly a confusion of traditions here. It might well be that there was a Medb who was an historical person and who really did attempt to invade the kingdom of Ulaidh (Ulster). But she has become so swamped in myth and religious symbolism that it is impossible to truly identify her.

In Welsh law there is an office which is described as *arglwyddes*, 'a female lord' or 'the chieftain of a district in her own right'. This reference was so translated by Aneurin Owen in *Ancient Laws and Institutes of Wales*. However, it has to be pointed out that Dafydd Jenkins and Morfydd E. Owen were inclined to argue that the word *arglwyddess* (the feminine equivalent of *arglwydd*, lord) might have been a late medieval change 'due to a realisation that political changes might lead to a woman's exercising the rights of a lord'. I tend to believe that the historical evidence relating to women like Boudicca and Cartimandua proves that the concept of the *arglwyddes* was a far older one than a medieval formation. The Welsh law states that every female chieftain or lord (*arglwyddes*) is entitled to the *amobr* (the fee payable in respect of 'loss of virginity' on marriage to the territorial lord) of her realm or territory. We will be considering these fees in the chapter 'A Woman's Place In Law'. In addition, the wife of the *dung-maer*, who was responsible for organising labour on the chieftains' or royal estates, was entitled, under the law, to the *amobr* of the women of the *maerdref*, those women working under her control.

In an Irish context, there is one person astonishingly overlooked by Professor Kelly when he claims, 'The annals provide no instance of a female political or military leader.' He ignores the annals which record that in 377BC Macha Mong Ruadh (Macha of the Red Hair) became queen of all Ireland. She is said to have reigned for seven years. Granted that many historians do not like to put their trust in the early chronicles relating to Irish prehistory, regarding such people as purely mythical, the fact remains that there are strong traditions of Macha which are, unfortunately, often mixed with traditions of the goddess Macha. Nevertheless, the historical figure, once disentangled from these traditions, seems a fairly tangible one. She is as historical as many of the personages who emerge from Greek or Roman tradition and are accepted without question simply because that is the tradition they appear in.

The interesting thing about Macha is that she had to seize the kingship by force. Her father was Aedh Ruadh, drowned in the cataract at Ballyshannon (Béal Atha Seannaidh, mouth of the ford of the slope) in Co. Donegal. Aedh Ruadh had ruled Ireland alternately with his cousins Dithorba and Cimbaeth. In some texts they are claimed as his brothers. On her father's death Macha was elected in his place. However, Dithorba and Cimbaeth disagreed with the decision and wanted to keep the kingship between them. Macha promptly raised an army and defeated Dithorba, killing him and taking his five sons as hostages. She made them build the ramparts of a new fortress – Emain Macha (Navan). She then came to terms with Cimbaeth and married him, a prohibited marriage if he had been her uncle, but thus perhaps giving her claim to rule a greater authority.

The annals say that Macha established the first hospital in Ireland, which was called Bron-Bherg (The House of Sorrow) and remained in use in Emain Macha until its destruction in AD22. The Brehon laws called for hospitals in all tribal areas. It was, of course, not until AD400 that St Fabiola of Rome established the first Christian hospital there. Ard Macha (Macha's Height) is now better known by its Anglicised form of Armagh, seat of the primacy of the Christian Church in Ireland.

One of the first female Celtic rulers to come to the attention of the Greeks and Romans was a lady called Onomaris, arguably meaning the mountain-ash or rowan tree, which is sacred to the Druids. Dr H. Rankin points out: 'Onomaris was the woman leader of the Celts in their wanderings into south-eastern Europe.' According to J. Weisweiler, Onomaris led her people, the Scordisci, in battle against the Illyrians, who inhabited the Balkans; they eventually settled in what is now Serbia and founded their capital by the banks of the Danube which they called Singidun(um). This is now Belgrade.

From this area there later emerged a powerful queen with a Celtic name who is still the subject of some argument. Some scholars do not accept that she may have been a Celt. Celtic tribes, like the Scordisci, were moving into Illyria as early as the fifth century BC but their main movement came in the mid-fourth century BC. Archaeological finds in Bosnia-Herzegovina show how extensive the Celtic settlement was, causing the Celtic scholar Henri Hubert to speak of 'Celto-Illyrians'. Certainly ancient geographers like the unnamed fourth-century BC scribe who revised the fifth-century *Periplus* (Voyage) of Scylax of Caryanda, also Scymnos of Chios, and the authors of the *Etymologicum Magnum*, mention the Celtic settlements in the area. However, it was not until 310BC that a chieftain named Molistomos and his Celts caused large displacements of the original Illyrian population. It may well be that there was much intermarriage in which the Celtic element was predominant, an idea favoured by Hubert. This is necessary background to make sense of the emergence in 231BC of a ruler known as 'Queen Teuta'.

It was in 231BC that the Romans took some interest in the area of the Illyrian coast. Here they found a group of tribes with their capital at what is now Kotor ruled by a king named Agron. Agron, too, bears a Celtic name for it is the masculine form of the war goddess Agrona whose traditions survive in Wales as 'the Washer of the Ford'. In the autumn of 231BC Agron died from pleurisy. He was succeeded by a woman called Teuta. The Romans recorded her as Agron's widow and said that she ruled with an advisory council of chieftains, which is exactly how the Celts governed. The construction of the government of the Celtic state of Galatia supports this. The woman's name Teuta is fascinating. Was this a proper name or simply a Celtic title meaning 'the people's queen' from *teutates*, 'people', cognate to the Irish *tuath*, 'tribe', and similar to the Gaulish title Toutiorix, 'king of the people'? My interpretation is that Teuta was either a Celto-Illyrian or one of the Celtic ruling class which had established itself among the Illyrians.

Polybius has little good to say about Teuta. 'She suffered from a typically feminine weakness, that of taking the short view of everything.' Teuta decided to extend her empire by attacking the state of Epiros, and her 'shock troops' were clearly identified as Celts. She had initial successes. Polybius, in describing her campaign against the Greeks, and we must remember that he was a Greek, devotes himself to a lengthy passage about the treachery of the Celts. Apparently the Epirots had employed some Celtic mercenaries to guard their city. These Celts then made common cause with their fellow Celts in Teuta's army. 'These were the men, whom the Epirots made the protectors of the republic,' sneers Polybius, 'whom they made guardians of their laws and to whom they entrusted their most prosperous city.'

Significantly we find that, after this success, Teuta had to put down an uprising among the Illyrians. This would make sense if she was, as I have suggested, a member of the Celtic ruling class who was resented by the Illyrians. In the course of this, some Roman citizens appear to have suffered. Rome sent an embassy to Teuta to rebuke her and threaten her with dire consequences unless she behaved in future. Polybius says that 'the queen gave way to a fit of womanish petulance'. It was clear that the Roman ambassador had been both arrogant and offensive to the queen. After the Roman party had left her, she ordered them to be assassinated while they were embarking on their ship back to Rome.

The result was that Rome despatched a fleet of 200 ships under Gnaeus Fulvius containing land forces under Lucius Postumius which systematically reduced Teuta's cities. Teuta herself withdrew into Kotor, which was strongly fortified. From there she finally managed to conclude a treaty with Rome, agreeing to pay reparation and giving assurances of future good behaviour in that she promised not to continue her attacks against Epiros or any other Greek state. Rome duly celebrated their victory in 228BC. After that, no more was heard of this fascinating lady.

Polybius records how Celtic women followed their menfolk into battle. Diodorus Siculus observed, 'The women of the Celts are nearly

as tall as the men and they rival them also in courage.' Ammianus
Marcellinus goes further:

> A whole troop of foreigners would not be able to withstand a
> single Celt if he called his wife to his assistance. The wife is even
> more formidable. She is usually very strong, and with blue eyes;
> in rage her neck veins swell, she gnashes her teeth, and brandishes
> her snow-white robust arms. She begins to strike blows mingled
> with kicks, as if they were so many missiles sent from the string
> of a catapult.
>
> The voices of these women are formidable and threatening, even
> when they are not angry but being friendly. But all Celtic women,
> with equal care, keep neat and clean and in some areas, such as
> among the Aquitanii, no woman can be seen, be she never so poor,
> in soiled or ragged clothing.

One is reminded from Ammianus' description, albeit accepting it as
a caricature, of the story of 'The Feast of Bricriu' during which the
wives of three of Ulster's champions quarrel over their husbands'
relative merits and start to fight among each other, kicking and
punching and shouting almost as Ammianus describes.

Plutarch relates that the historian Polybius met and talked with
another famous Celtic queen, Chiomara, wife of Ortagion, of the
Tolistoboii, who united the Galatian Celts into a powerful state
against Rome at the time of the invasion led by Gnaeus Manlius
Volso in 189BC. Chiomara was captured by the Romans and a centurion raped her. He then discovered that she was of high rank and
demanded a ransom which Ortagion immediately sent. The exchange
took place on the banks of a river. While the centurion was collecting
his gold, Chiomara had him decapitated and took his head, in Celtic
fashion, to her husband. The Greek report of their conversation,
according to Dr Rankin, 'preserved genuine, gnomic, Celtic idiom':

> 'Woman a fine thing [is] good faith.'
> '[A] better thing, only one man be alive who had intercourse
> with me.'

It is, indeed, an echo of an Irish triad implying that the marital fidelity
of a chieftain's spouse was highly regarded. '*Cid as dech do mnáib?
Ní hannsa: ben maith ad fitir fer romat ríam.*' 'What is the best sort

of wife? Not hard: a good woman whom a man has never known before you.'

From Plutarch comes another story of a Celtic heroine of Galatia – Camma, priestess of the goddess Brigid (if we accept that Brigid, or Brigantu, was the Celtic equivalent of Artemis). Camma was married to a chieftain called Sinatos. Sinatos was murdered by a man called Sinorix (the name, appropriately enough, seems to mean 'King of Storms') who then forced Camma to marry him. But, as the ceremony involved drinking from a common cup, Camma contrived to put poison into it. She allayed Sinorix's suspicions by drinking first and so accepted death herself. Sinorix drank and died.

The tradition of a Celtic female being able to become a war leader and ruler is nowhere more clearly confirmed than in British Celtic history.

When the Romans began to drive their conquest northward in Britain they came across a confederation of tribes collectively called the Brigantes, arguably named after the goddess Brigid, though the meaning of the 'High Ones' has been suggested or even the 'Hill Dwellers'. From the time of their first encounter with the Brigantes, the Romans noted that they were ruled by a remarkable and powerful female queen named Cartimandua, 'Sleek Pony'. Tacitus describes her as *pollens nobilitate* (powerful in lineage). She was, he adds, 'flourishing in all the splendour of wealth and power'.

It appears that Cartimandua, for reasons we may speculate about, decided to become a client ruler of Rome. It should be pointed out that Rome's policy, at this time, was to form friendly 'buffer states' on its frontiers, so their initial approaches to Cartimandua may have been along these lines. Certainly, it would appear that by AD47, four years after the Roman invasion of Britain, Cartimandua had formed such an alliance. But in AD48 a south-western section of her kingdom, a tribe called the Setantii, had rebelled and threatened the safety of Ostorius Scapula's expedition into what is now Wales for the purpose of overcoming the Catuvellauni king, Caractacus. He was high king of the southern tribes in Britain, still valiantly holding out against the conquest.

Ostorius finally defeated Caractacus' army. Caractacus then made the mistake of attempting to seek political asylum at Cartimandua's court. Cartimandua obviously saw Caractacus as a threat to the peace of her kingdom so she broke the laws of hospitality: she had Caractacus and his family bound and handed over to the Romans.

Caractacus and his family were then taken in chains to Rome and only his eloquence caused Claudius to spare his life from the ritual executions planned. Caractacus and his family lived out their days in exile within the confines of Rome.

Cartimandua had married a British chieftain, Venutius of the Jugantes. Venutius was, says Tacitus, 'since the loss of Caractacus, the first in fame for valour and military experience'. Within a few years Cartimandua had fallen out with Venutius. According to Tacitus' Roman viewpoint, 'The Britons by that event were fired with indignation. They scorned to submit to a female government . . .' But it was obvious that Venutius was no more than Cartimandua's consort and was in no way seen as her equal in kingship. When Venutius tried to raise an insurrection, Cartimandua had no compunction in requesting the governor, Didius Gallus, to send a Roman legion to help her assert her will. The legion, under Cesius Nasica, was duly sent. Her quarrel with Venutius was patched up, and she remained in firm control of the Brigantes. This fact, and her continued alliance with Rome, probably explains why the Brigantes did not join in the Boudiccan insurrection in AD61.

In AD69, however, Cartimandua and Venutius were quarrelling again. Cartimandua divorced Venutius in favour of Vellocatus, his armour-bearer and charioteer. Venutius stirred up another insurrection and sent for warriors from tribes outside the Brigantian confederation to join him. This gave Cartimandua an excuse to request more Roman troops. Tacitus says that the Romans suffered several reverses and finally settled for rescuing Cartimandua and Vellocatus, taking them out of Brigantia, and leaving Venutius as undisputed ruler of the Brigantes.

It was a few years later, in AD72, that the Roman general Quintus Petilius Cerialis, whose IX Hispania Legion had been virtually destroyed in the Boudiccan uprising, finally caught up with Venutius near Stanwick. But even before this defeat, the powerful figure of Queen Cartimandua disappears from history. The defeat of Venutius and the Brigantes allowed Julius Agricola, during his governorship in AD79–81, to garrison the whole of Brigantia. It ceased to be a client kingdom, becoming simply part of Roman-occupied Britain. One interesting fact is that Claudius Ptolemaeus, the Greek geographer (c.AD100–178) placed the Brigantes in Ireland. This might not have simply been a mistake but a record that elements of the Brigantes had fled, like many other Britons, to seek political refuge among the Irish. In 1927 some excavations were carried out at Lambay Island, off the coast of Co. Dublin, which showed a cemetery of the period. The artefacts – swords, shields and five Roman *fibulae* – were all untypical of the Irish weapons of the time but closer to the artefacts from cemeteries of the 'Iron Age' in Brigantia. Professor Barry Raftery, in *Pagan Celtic Ireland*, suggests that the settlers on Lambay could well have been the refugees of the Brigantian defeat by Rome. The Roman garrison of Brigantia was, however, not enough to contain the people and in about AD118 they rose in a serious revolt which took two years to quell. Further insurrections took place in AD155 and 193–7.

It is, as I have mentioned earlier, the figure of Boudicca, or Boadicea, that people conjure to mind when talking of Celtic women and warrior queens. Most people are familiar with the statue of Boudicca, standing in her fanciful scythe-wheeled chariot with her two daughters, opposite the Palace of Westminster. It is a curious place for such a thing: Boudicca's Celtic descendants were conquered, reviled and driven from their lands by the ancestors of the English, the people who now seem to venerate her as 'an *English* warrior queen'.

Boudicca's name means 'Victorious'; we can still see the form in modern Welsh (*buddugol*) and Irish (*buach*). Her husband was Prasutagus, king of the Iceni in what is now Norfolk. The Iceni were a rich and cultivated people, issuing their own coinage since about 10BC. Boudicca had two teenage daughters. According to Cassius Dio, quoting from earlier sources, Boudicca 'in stature was very tall, in appearance most terrifying, in the glance of her eye most fierce, and her voice was harsh; a great mass of the tawniest hair fell to her hips; around her neck was a large golden neck-ring [*torc*]; and she wore a tunic of divers colours over which a thick mantle was fastened with a brooch. This was her invariable attire.'

In AD60 Boudicca was about thirty-five years old. She had probably married Prasutagus of the Iceni on the eve of the Roman invasion of AD43. It would appear that Prasutagus, watching the defeat of the southern tribal confederation under Caractacus, or, indeed, having been part of it like his neighbours the Trinovantes, then accepted the emperor Claudius's offer to make an alliance and become a client king. But Claudius died in AD54 and his adopted son Nero became emperor. Under him, Roman policy changed and client kingship was not encouraged. Nero preferred 'direct rule'. Professor Peter Salway, however, is more of the opinion that the direct causes of the insurrection 'reflect ill on the Roman administrations of the day and cannot be blamed on Nero himself, since in 60 his government was still largely in the hands of those "good men", Seneca and Burrus.'

The Roman view of events was that Prasutagus had reigned a long time and had considerable wealth. 'By his will he left the whole to his two daughters and the emperor in equal shares, conceiving, by that stroke of policy, that he should provide at once for the tranquillity of his kingdom and his family.' If we look at things from a Celtic perspective, we have some problems in accepting this statement. Firstly, Celtic kingships were electoral and secondly absolute private property was not a Celtic perception. Thirdly, there was no way under Celtic law that Prasutagus could have named Nero as co-heir to the kingship. It may well be, however, that Prasutagus had been instructed in Roman law and knew that when he died, Nero's administration would step in and impose direct rule on the Iceni. To avoid this he went through a Roman form of will-making. Perhaps Roman advisers had dropped hints to the king that this was the only way of avoiding conflict. Tacitus does not mention whether Prasutagus left anything to his wife, Boudicca. Does this mean that his two daughters had already been elected as 'heirs apparent' to the kingship? If the traditions we glean from other sources apply, then this would put their age at the 'age of consent', that is fourteen years old, the minimum age for them to aspire to office.

The fact is that Prasutagus died in AD60. In spite of the stratagem adopted by Prasutagus, if such it was, Rome quickly responded with its new policy. The procurator, or civil administrator of the province, Catus Decianus, was under orders to extend direct rule on the death of client kings. As Tacitus' father-in-law, Julius Agricola, was serving on the staff of the military governor of Britain at this time, he can be regarded as more trustworthy than most Romans in knowing the causes of the insurrection. The military governor of Britain, Paulinus Suetonius, had taken half of his military strength to attack 'the isle of Mona; a place inhabited by a warlike people, and a common refuge for all the discontented Britons'. But Catus Decianus was not particularly concerned at the absence from southern Britain of Suetonius and his legions. If any trouble arose there was the II Augusta Legion in the south and the IX Hispania Legion at Lindon (identical with *lleyn*, a lake), a Celtic settlement where the Witham widened, which is now Lincoln.

Retired veteran soldiers had already started to seize the land of the Trinovantes, driving them out or making slaves of them, with the blessing of the local administration. The Iceni were not the first nor the last people to realise that appeasement to an aggressor invites only more aggression.

Catus Decianus and his soldiers marched into the Iceni kingdom to assert the new order. Tacitus admits that the fault lay entirely on the Roman side, which must have been Agricola's view at the time. The Iceni kingdom was ravaged and looted. When she protested, Boudicca was stripped and whipped in public while her young teenage daughters were raped in front of her. Other 'relations of the deceased king were taken into slavery' while Iceni chieftains were robbed and beaten. Catus Decianus was doubtless proud of his work in bringing the barbaric Britons to heel! The Iceni had witnessed at first hand the unbridled power of Rome.

The crimes committed by the Romans were grave in the eyes of the Iceni, both legally as well as politically. From Celtic perceptions, and under law, the Iceni had the right to *dial* or vengeance.

The fascinating point behind these actions is that Boudicca emerges as absolute ruler of the Iceni and their war leader. We should now be able to accept without question that women would take such positions in Celtic society as a matter of course. Boudicca herself emphasised the point, according to Tacitus: 'This is not the first time that Britons have been led to battle by a woman.' Unfortunately he does not record the other times nor the names of the other women war leaders. But the interesting thing is that Boudicca was accepted not only as queen and war leader of the Iceni but as supreme commander of the many tribes who now joined the Iceni in a general rising against Rome.

We are left with several questions to be answered. If Prasutagus was king of the Iceni, under Celtic law Boudicca had no legal right of succession unless she, in her own right, was a candidate for office. Boudicca, therefore, must have had the right to stand and have been duly elected by the assembly of the Iceni. This means that she and her dead husband might have been cousins since rulers were usually elected from the same family, a simple marriage-link not being a qualification.

After the Roman atrocities among the Iceni, Boudicca must have sent out emissaries to neighbouring tribes. The Trinovantes immediately pledged their support. 'The neighbouring states, not as yet taught to crouch in bondage, pledged themselves, in secret councils, to stand forth in the case of liberty,' observes Tacitus. Doubtless the tribal confederation against Rome also included the Coritani and Catuvellauni, although both these tribes had been defeated and garrisoned by Roman troops. Is it possible that Tacitus might be indicating that the insurrection spread to an even wider area than those south-eastern tribes? We certainly have no reference to tribes other than the south-eastern ones taking part in the uprising.

Boudicca's first major target was the town once sacred to the Celtic war god Camulos, which the Romans now called Camulodunum. This was the former Trinovante capital which the emperor Claudius had used a battalion of elephants to reduce, and where he, personally, had taken the surrender of many southern British rulers. Eleven British rulers are said to have formed an alliance with him as 'client kings'. He had then ordered a great temple to be erected in his honour. Camulodunum was the administrative capital of the new Roman imperial province of Britain. 'In the eyes of the Britons,' confirms Tacitus, 'it seemed the citadel of eternal slavery.'

Tacitus goes deeply into the portents which the Romans are said to have foreseen and which told of its annihilation. Catus Decianus, in Londinium, sent 200 legionaries to reinforce the small garrison of retired veterans and auxiliaries. Messages were sent to Quintus Petilius Cerialis, commander of the IX Hispania Legion, at Lindon in the land of the Coritani, asking him to hasten southward to protect the Roman capital.

Here, Boudicca showed her prowess as a military strategist. General Quintus Petilius Cerialis was commanding 6000 legionaries, divided into sixty centuries, with a detachment of 500 cavalry. The IX Hispania were no novices at war. The legion had been raised about 200 years previously and had seen ruthless fighting against the Celts of Spain before being transferred to Pannonia in about AD6. It was considered an élite legion and had been personal escort to Aulus Plautius, commander-in-chief of the Roman invasion forces in AD43. Neither was Cerialis a dilatory commander. The fact that in AD71 he returned to Britain as military governor and finally defeated Venutius and the Brigantes is an indication of his record as a general. His had been no political appointment.

But, when facing Boudicca, in the opening weeks of her campaign, this crack Roman legion was all but annihilated. Cerialis, marching confidently south to protect Camulodunum, was ambushed by Boudicca and his infantry slaughtered. Doubtless, he had the same arrogant attitude towards his opponents as many another general has displayed. He managed to fight a retreat with only 500 cavalry, saving the legionary standard by which the legion could be reconstituted. Having saved only 500 cavalry out of his 6000-man command, he reached the safety of his fortress headquarters at Lindon and barricaded himself inside. Not even Caractacus had managed to defeat a Roman legion in battle before.

The successful Boudicca now unleashed her main assault on Camulodunum. The Roman defenders were forced to withdraw from the perimeters of the city, back to the Temple of Claudius which, according to Tacitus, was strongly fortified. 'The temple [initially] held out but, after a siege of two days, was taken by storm.'

Boudicca and her army turned triumphantly towards Londinium (London).

It was only now that the Roman commander-in-chief Suetonius learnt of the disaster. The procurator Catus Decianus had, wisely, fled Britain and crossed to Gaul. General Suetonius, with an advance guard of cavalry from his army, managed to reach London before Boudicca. This was originally a small Celtic settlement named Londo, 'the wild place', a trading port of the Trinovantes; following the conquest, Roman traders had established a larger township there. A new bridge spanning the Tamesis, the 'sluggish river', had been started in AD43, and the streets were laid out with substantial timber buildings. During the invasion, the settlement had been converted into a principal supply-base for the armies and it was obvious that it was the financial headquarters for the Romans in spite of Camulodunum having been designated administrative capital of the new province. Tacitus, who gives us the first literary reference to the town, pictures it as a hive of commerce and packed with traders from all parts of the Roman world. Some estimates place the population at this time in the region of 20,000.

Reaching the town, Suetonius decided to sacrifice it to the oncoming Britons. Firstly, he was shocked by the news of the annihilation of the crack IX Hispania. Secondly, he had only an advance guard from the cavalry units of the XIV Gemina and XX Valeria Legions, not enough to face Boudicca's army with. Thirdly, his orders to the acting commander of the II Augusta, Poenius Postumus, the camp marshal, encamped within a day's march from London, had not been obeyed. The II Augusta's acting commander simply refused to march his legion to London's defence, fearing annihilation like that which had befallen the IX Hispania. When the campaign was over Poenius Postumus fell on his sword, in Roman tradition, rather than face a court martial. Suetonius therefore ordered any in the town who could follow him to do so and headed north.

Boudicca and her army came upon the undefended trading township. Tacitus paints a picture of a merciless enemy. Curiously he observes that the Britons 'sold no captives as slaves and went in for none of the usual trading of war'. This was certainly the Celtic custom for they, unlike the Romans, did not believe in slavery, although they usually did hold hostages for ransom. However, it is clear from the accounts that the Britons slaughtered the Roman inhabitants as well as traders from other parts of the empire, who were still in the settlement and had not fled with Suetonius. The settlement was razed to the ground.

Boudicca now turned north after Suetonius, towards Verulamium. The former capital of the Catevellauni, Caractacus' tribe, 'lovers of the god Bel', had been taken over as the third major Roman settlement of Britain. Caractacus' fort, which had once spread over 1250 acres, was replaced by a Roman township of 116 acres. As in Londinium, the Romans had erected mainly timber dwellings, although at least two masonry buildings had been constructed by this time. After years of Roman military conquest, the administration, following Caractacus' final defeat, felt that the tribe had been pacified. In AD50 Verulamium was created a *municipium*. Many writers on Roman Britain seem to think this indicated that within a few short years the Catevellauni had become Romanised. Hardly so. Like Londinium, Verulamium was populated by Romans, retired veterans, settlers, traders and merchants from many parts of the empire. There was also a small garrison. Any Celtic population which remained dwelt, not in the Roman city, but in the surrounding hills.

Boudicca's warriors treated Verulamium as they had treated Londinium. The archaeological evidence for the Boudiccan destruction is clear and unequivocal. Traces of burnt buildings and debris have been found not only in the town but among neighbouring farmsteads.

Boudicca continued to head north, after the Roman military governor who now possessed the only sizeable army the Romans had left in Britain. She realised that if she could destroy it, then she would have freed Britain from Roman occupation. Cassius Dio says that Suetonius was forced into battle by a shortage of supplies. The site is dubious. Dr Webster suggests that it was in the vicinity of Mancetter in Warwickshire. The name still retains its basic Celtic form, Manduessdo, to which the Anglo-Saxon *ceaster* was added. An inland site, like Manchester, it is curiously named after the Celtic ocean god, Manawydan (Mannánan). The site was certainly well north-west of Verulamium and in the Midlands. The figures given by Tacitus and Dio are widely exaggerated in Rome's favour. Dio claims Boudicca's force was 230,000 strong. Suetonius is claimed to have only 10,000 troops. Tacitus claims 80,000 British dead as against 400 Roman dead. A more reasonable estimation of those actually engaged in battle is perhaps 20,000 Britons as against 12,000 Romans, bearing in mind Suetonius had now been joined by the bulk of his troops from the XIV Gemina and XX Valeria plus some isolated garrisons of the II Augusta, and auxiliary cohorts.

Suetonius took the high ground with a dense forest behind him. Infantry was placed in the centre and cavalry on either wing. Boudicca had her army drawn up in loose array with, we are told, war chariots. This seems curious; war chariots would have been forbidden by Rome during the occupation and not so easy to conceal. Chariots would surely have been a major consideration when Rome started to disarm the southern tribes. But Tacitus, who is in a position to know, as his father-in-law Agricola was at the battle, and Dio both mention the war chariots. Can the Britons have built new chariots during the campaign or had they managed to keep large numbers hidden during the Roman disarming attempts? It is an interesting point.

Boudicca gave her speech, according to Tacitus, from her chariot, with her two daughters standing either side of her.

Tacitus has her start out by saying, 'This is not the first time that the Britons have been led to battle by a woman.' He goes on to report that she said she took the field, like the meanest among them, to assert the cause of freedom and seek vengeance for her body seamed with the stripes of Roman whips, and for her two daughters who had been raped. She pointed out that none were safe from the pride and arrogance of the conquerors but on that spot they must either win victory or die. There was no alternative. 'You must either win on this battlefield or die. This is my resolve, and I am a woman; men may live and be slaves!'

Suetonius lured Boudicca into attacking uphill towards his positions and then launched his wedge of infantry at them. The British line crumbled and retreat turned into a rout. The war chariots became entangled with the baggage wagons and with the women and children and old people who were camp followers. The Romans slaughtered anyone who fell into their hands. Suetonius followed up his victory with a systematic persecution of anyone suspected of disloyalty to Rome. Reinforcements were called for to help him in his campaign of suppression; 2000 legionaries, eight cohorts of auxiliaries (4000 men) and 1000 German cavalry arrived in Britain. But so harshly did Suetonius treat the vanquished Britons that the new procurator who had succeeded Catus Decianus, Julius Classicianus, urged Rome to recall Suetonius and appoint 'a man, who would bring with him neither ill will to the natives, nor the pride of victory. The vanquished would, by consequence, meet with moderation and humanity.' It was some time, however, before that happened and then only after an official inquiry conducted by Polycletus, the emperor's envoy. Suetonius was replaced. It was agreed that Suetonius' ravages might spark off a new uprising.

What had happened to Boudicca and her daughters?

According to Tacitus, after the defeat, she escaped capture by the Romans and took poison rather than fall into their hands. One presumes that her daughters also followed suit. Dio Cassius, however, says she simply fell sick and died. Tacitus, whose source is the first-hand account of Agricola, is more to be trusted in this. But Dio also says that the Britons gave her a rich burial. That we cannot doubt for if Boudicca's retinue survived with her there is little question that they would have followed the Celtic custom of burial. What an archaeological treasure that grave would be if it has, somewhere, withstood the ravages of time and grave robbers.

There is little doubt that had Boudicca been captured her fate would have followed that of many another Celtic leader, such as Vercingetorix. She would have been transported to Rome and there would have been a ritual execution. Indeed, about ten years later Eponina, a Gaulish Celtic woman, was executed along with her husband in just such a ritual to appease the Roman blood lust. In AD69 there was a Gaulish uprising against the occupying Romans. Eponina's husband, 'Julius Sabinus', a Celt named Sabrann who is now known by a 'Romanisation' of his name, took part in it. It is fascinating, in view of the evidence of many early Irish names applying equally to males and females, that Sabrann was the name of a goddess whom I have already mentioned in connection with the Severn. Sabrann was chieftain of the Lingones. When the rising failed, Sabrann, in order to elude the Romans, faked his own suicide. Eponina hid him, smuggling food and clothing to him for nine years. At the same time she sought through diplomatic means to obtain a Roman pardon for him, even going to Rome to plead his cause. When Sabrann was finally caught, the emperor Vespasian had both Sabrann and Eponina ceremonially executed. The story emerges in the records of Tacitus and Plutarch.

Dio Cassius claims that among her other offices Boudicca was a priestess of the goddess Andrasta, a goddess of battle and victory. This seems to be the same goddess as is worshipped by the Vocontii of Gaul under the form Andarte. The implication is that Boudicca was a Druidess. This is quite possible for the Greeks and Romans often speak of *dryades* or Druidesses. As the Druids were merely the intelligentsia of ancient Celtic society, equivalent to the Brahmins of Indian society, there is no reason to argue with the idea. Of course, a Druid could become a king or a queen but a king or queen did not necessarily become a Druid.

The fourth-century AD Gaulish Celtic writer, Ausonius Decimus Magnus, who wrote his works in Latin and some epigrams in Greek, had an aunt called Dryadia, whom he mentions in his work *Parentalia*. Why would his aunt be called 'Druidess' so many centuries after the Romans claimed to have stamped out such a class in Gaul? The answer, simply, is that she was of the Druid caste.

Tacitus, like most Romans, had difficulty sorting out Celtic and Germanic peoples. He mentions a 'prophetess' of the Bructeri, which he wrongly calls a 'Teutonic' tribe. This was in the time of Vespasian (AD69–79). Tacitus gives the name Veleda to the prophetess. Veleda clearly is a Celtic name which derives from the root *gwel*, 'to see', cognate with the Irish *filí*. Therefore the name Veleda simply means 'seeress' and perhaps is a title rather than a name. She is described as a virgin ruling over a wide territory. 'Her name was held in veneration . . .'

Thankfully, Dio Cassius does not mix up his Celts and Germans and refers to the successor of Veleda as 'a virgin prophetess among the Celts', thereby confirming that Veleda not only bears a Celtic name but is a female seer of the Celts not the Germans.

Veleda was also a force in politics and chosen to arbitrate between the Tencterians and the Grippinians on the opposite banks of the Rhine, together with Claudius Civilis. According to Tacitus, no ambassadors were allowed to see Veleda in person. 'The deputies, however, were not admitted to the presence of Veleda. To increase the veneration paid to her character, all access to her person was denied. She resided in the summit of a lofty tower. A near relation, chosen for the purpose, conveyed to her several questions, and from that sanctuary brought back oracular responses, like a messenger who held commerce with the gods.'

Tacitus, still muddling the Celts and Germans in his *Germania* – identifying, for example, Ambiorix of the Eburones as a German chieftain – has much to say about the female prophets or 'wise women'.

> There is, in their opinion, something sacred in the female sex, and even the power of foreseeing future events. Their advice, therefore, is always heard; they are deemed oracular. We have seen, in the reign of Vespasian, the famous Veleda revered as a divinity by her countrymen. Before her time, Aurinia and others were held in equal veneration; but a veneration founded on sentiment and superstition, free from that servile adulation which pretends to people heaven with human deities.

The consultations with Veleda remind one of the female prophet in the story of Fíngín Mac Luchta of Munster, who, on every feastday of Samhain, would visit her and obtain a prophecy for the next twelve months.

Dio Cassius says that Veleda's successor in office was Ganna, whose name seems to derive from a Celtic word meaning 'intermediary'. The word appears to survive in the modern Welsh *canol* while a Cornish language magazine was named *Gannas* (The Ambassador). Dio relates how Ganna, 'a virgin among the Celts', accompanies Masyos, king of the Semnones, on an embassy to the emperor Domitian, the younger son of Vespasian (AD81–96). Flavius Vopiscus identifies Gannas as being of the Gaulish tribe of the Tungri, modern Tonges, near Liège, Belgium.

Women in priestly form also appear in the ancient Celtic world. Tacitus refers to the women on the island of Mona (Anglesey) running among the Celtic warriors, dressed in funeral garments, hair streaming, carrying torches. Pomponius Mela, in *De Chorographia*, mentions nine priestesses who dwelt on the island of Sena, off Pointe du Raz, on the western coast of Armorica (Brittany), who knew the future and gave oracles to sailors. He calls them Gallicenae (Celts). In Breton tradition they are called Groac'h or Grac'h, implying 'fiery-headed'. J.F. Campbell sought to make the word cognate with the Scottish Gaelic *gruagach*, a word for a female brownie, used adjectivally, meaning having a beautiful head of hair. The nine Gallicenae have a parallel in the legend of the nine female magicians who guard the thermal waters of Gloucester in the Welsh tale of Peredur. Fascinating is the Larzac inscription, a lead tablet found in a necropolis near Millau. It is dated to AD90–110 and mentions nine Gaulish women (Druidesses), each by name.

Strabo also mentions an island similar to Sena, which he places at the mouth of the Loire, where women called Namnites served a deity resembling Bacchus, the god of wine and ecstasy. Strabo goes so far as to confirm marriage among the pagan Celtic priesthood and points out that Gaulish priestesses were very independent of their husbands. It is of interest that the tradition of isolated Celtic female communities also survives in the Norse sagas. Gaulish priestesses are recorded as inhabiting what are now called the Channel Islands. In the former territory of Gaul, there have survived several inscriptions which speak of priestesses, such as those at Arles and Le Prugnon where a goddess called Thucoliss was venerated. And at Metz an inscription refers to '*Arete Druis Antistita, somno monita*' or Druidic priestesses.

Aelius Lampridius, one of the authors of *Historia Augusta*, written around the fourth century AD, has a Druidess foretelling the defeat of Alexander Severus before he set out on his expedition in AD235. Lampridius puts these words, which he says were delivered in the Gaulish Celtic tongue, in the mouth of the Druidess: 'Go forth but hope not for victory nor put your trust in your warriors.' Lavius Vopiscus has Gaius Aurelius Diocletian (AD284–305) residing in an inn in the land of the Tungri of Gaul. He was then a soldier of humble birth. When he came to settle with his hostess she upbraided him on his apparent meanness in haggling over his account. He retorted that he would be more liberal with his money if he was emperor. To this jocundity, the hostess, who was a prophetess, replied: 'Laugh not, Diocletian, for when you have slain the Boar, you will indeed be emperor.' Diocletian rose in rank and slew the Prefect Arrius, nicknamed The Boar, and became emperor. Vopiscus gives yet another example of a Celtic Druidess, stating that the emperor Aurelian (Lucius Domitius Aurelianus, *c.*AD215–75) consulted 'Gaulish Druidesses' (*Gallicanas Dryades*) as to whether his children would retain the imperial crown. The Druidesses gave a negative answer. These references seem to confirm the insular Celtic traditions of female Druids who emerge as prophetesses and witches in the sagas written down by Christian scribes. We find that Patrick and his biographers often refer to Druidesses and, according to the *Rennes Dinnsenchus*, Brigid was a *ban-druí* before she was converted to Christianity.

Arriving at the start of an age when many Celtic women were to take prominent positions in the rise of the new Christian religion, we find a most extraordinary lady named Elen Luyddog, or 'Elen of the Hosts'. It is right, I think, to end our examination of 'Women in Early History' with this remarkable woman who stands at the crossroads between the end of prominent pagan Celtic women and the rise of women in the phenomenon known as Celtic Christianity.

Elen Luyddog was the daughter of a British chieftain named Eudaf who ruled from his capital at Segontium (near Caernarfon), and from whom the kings of Cornwall later claimed descent. She lived during the last decades of the fourth century AD. In fact, she became such a powerful figure that many later traditions place her as the wife of Myrddin (Merlin), intermixing her traditions into mythology. Other traditions recorded in the twelfth and thirteenth centuries confused her with St Helen, mother of the Roman emperor Constantine. In fact, Elen Luyddog married a soldier from Iberia who had been posted to Britain as a general in the Roman army.

Magnus Maximus, who, some traditions have it, was a Celto-Iberian and who was known in Welsh tradition as Macsen Wledig (*gwledig*, a ruler) had, in AD382, defeated a combined army of Irish and Caledonians and thus been acclaimed by his legions. He was declared emperor by the army in Britain, who were fed up with the way Rome was out of touch with them. In the ensuing conflict, Magnus took his army across to Gaul and defied the emperor Gratian who was captured and slain by one of Magnus's officers. Magnus was now *de facto* emperor of the west, controlling Britain, Gaul and Iberia. Theodosius, the eastern emperor, acknowledged him as co-emperor. He was approved of by the Church, and Martin of Tours became a frequent visitor to Magnus's court.

Sulpicius Severus in his *Dialogues* mentions that Martin of Tours also became a close friend of the emperor's wife, Elen. He converted her and their talk was often about religious philosophy. Elen and

Magnus had many children but Elen was not content to confine herself to a domestic life. Severus says she was a leading figure in the intellectual life of Magnus's court.

Meanwhile Magnus crossed the Alps in 387 to occupy the imperial city of Milan, with Valentinian II, a rival for the western government, and his court fleeing just ahead of him. Theodosius realised that Magnus Maximus was now constituting a threat to his eastern empire and took the field against him. Several battles took place in which Maximus is recorded by Ammianus Marcellinus as bearing a standard depicting a red dragon on a purple background. Some Welsh scholars see this as the origin of the national flag of Wales. However, at Aquileia, Maximus was betrayed, captured and put to death on 28 July 388.

Elen decided to leave Gaul, where Magnus had established his court, and take her family back to Britain. In Britain she began to work assiduously on behalf of the Christian Church. Many place-names attest to her influence, from Llanelen in Monmouth to Llanelen in the Gower to Capel Elen in Penrhosllugwy in Anglesey. She is even claimed as initiating the building of roads across Britain; in parts of Wales sections of roadway were called Sarn Elen.

Her son Plebig became a disciple of Ninian; another son, Leo, became king of the Cantii; Cystennin has his tomb at Segontium in Gwynedd; Owain is claimed as the ancestor of the kings of Glywsing (South Wales); while Demetus was a founder of the dynasty who ruled Dyfed. Yet another son, Antonius, is claimed as the ancestor of the Celtic kings of the Isle of Man. Elen's daughter, Sevira, married Vortigern – the name means 'Overlord' – the High King of Britain who invited the first ancestors of the English into Britain to serve him as mercenaries. Sevira's son Brydw was blessed by St Germanus of Auxerre during one of his visits to Britain.

The traditions place Elen's home at Dinas Emrys, the fortress at Bedgelert. This one-hectare fortress, with a pool and artificial cistern, was first constructed in pre-Roman times. But it was rebuilt in the years after the Roman withdrawal and reinforced in the fifth and sixth centuries. A fascinating point in placing Elen's home here is that, according to Nennius, it played a central part in the overthrow of Vortigern, regarded as betraying Britain to the Anglo-Saxons, and its name, Fort of Emrys (Ambrosius), commemorates the very person who record has it toppled Vortigern.

Elen's position is also a special one in that all the Celtic rulers in

Britain, and even beyond to the Isle of Man, acknowledged her as their source of sovranty. From her and her several children, they claimed their authority to be legitimate kings of their peoples. In this aspect Elen seems to be given the role, by later chroniclers, of the mystic Celtic goddesses of sovranty. She appears as the heroine in 'The Dream of Macsen Wledig', one of the two historical tales in the *Mabinogion*, in which Elen enters the sleeping brain of her husband.

In this story Elen has two brothers, Cynan and Gadeon, who conquer Rome with Macsen. Significantly, bearing in mind that Elen's father ruled from Segontium, there is a reference in the *Notitia Dignitatum* (AD429) to a legion of Britons called the Segontientes serving in the Balkans. Could this be one of Macsen Wledig's lost legions? According to most traditions Elen did have a brother named Cynan Meiriadog who went to the Continent; we find him as one of the leaders of the British colonisation in Armorica (Brittany), leading his people in a settlement of the Nantes area. Some traditions have him being made ruler of Armorica (*Brytaen Fychan*) by Macsen. There is a rather anti-female legend which says that Cynan, in order to preserve the purity of the language of the British exiles, had the tongues of all the women cut out. The idea was that women were the teachers, passing on the '*mother*-tongue'. The story was meant to explain an old Welsh name for Brittany – Llydaw (*lled-taw*, open silence).

Elen Luyddog was probably dead by AD410 when Celtic Britain had re-emerged from the long centuries of Roman occupation as an independent country again – a period which was to last scarcely a generation or so before the invasion of the Jutes, Angles and Saxons. Her life marks the end of the old Celtic society in Britain and the start of a new order of things in which the role of women was beginning to undergo fundamental changes.

[4]

Celtic Law: the background

To truly judge the role of women in Celtic society, we, of course, have to know something about the role of women in other contemporary societies in order to make a comparison. This is not the place to discuss the theory of the changing role of women in all Indo-European societies. But we should be aware that it has been proposed that all Indo-European societies were continually changing and altering their perceptions and codes of behaviour to the detriment of women. The hypothesis of this argument is that at the dawn of time women had a coequal role in society but that gradually men sequestered this role and became dominant. One could therefore argue that women were found in a coequal role in Celtic society because that society was clinging to ancient cultural paradigms rather than undergoing change as Greece and Rome were doing; that it was, in fact, other societies which were out of tune with the original paradigms of the female role, not the Celts.

This could be supported by conclusions drawn from an examination of our first comparative society – Greece. Early Greek literature depicts female characters as enjoying quite a free social life. It was clear that in the seventh century BC, in Lesbos, the poetess Sappho enjoyed considerable social freedom. But when the Greek city states like Athens emerged as dominant political entities, women were severely limited in their rights. Indeed, they had no political rights at all and could not take part in the decision making for the government of the city. Under the law a woman had no independent existence. Her marriage was arranged by her father or a male relative. She could not inherit or own property nor enter into any transaction involving more than the value of a bushel of grain. Any business that needed to be done had to be dealt with by a male guardian, whether husband, father or brother.

If a man died and had only a daughter but no direct male heirs, then a male next-of-kin, however distant, could inherit by marrying the daughter, incidentally divorcing his wife if he had one. The daughter, if she had a husband, had to divorce him to comply with the inheritance laws.

Women were kept in seclusion and had their own separate quarters in the house where no man was allowed to enter apart from the husband or male guardian. 'It is better for a woman to stay inside the house instead of showing herself at the door,' warns Xenophon (c.428–354BC). Menander (c.342–292BC) says 'a decent woman must stay at home; the streets are for low women.' Young girls would live in the female quarters under their elders' supervision until they became of marriageable age. Fifteen was about the age for marriage. Women were more or less prisoners of the house and seldom left it, being responsible for running the household affairs, raising children, weaving, spinning and making clothes. If dire necessity forced them to leave the house then they had to go covered and always in the company of a slave, who was their chaperon.

In Rome there was little difference. The *paterfamilias* had absolute control over his wife. There was a period, at the end of the republic, when women had, in law, secured a few more rights and could marry without passing wholly into the legal possession of the husband. It was still necessary to have a male guardian to conduct business. After Augustus's reign things tightened up again. But women did not live in the total seclusion their Greek sisters were forced into. Roman women could even take their meals with their husbands!

Ironically, it fell to a Celt to make a comparison between Roman and Greek attitudes to women and point out that Rome seemed more progressive. It was Cornelius Nepos (c.100–25BC), a Vocontii from Cisalpine Gaul, who wrote in *De viris illustribus*:

Many things which we consider proper are thought shocking in Greece. What Roman, for instance, has any scruples about taking his wife to a dinner-party? What Roman woman does not appear in the reception rooms of her own house and take part in its social life? But it is quite different in Greece, for there a wife may not be present at dinner, unless it is a family party, and spends her time in a remote part of the house called 'the *gynaeceum*' which is never entered by a man unless he is a close relative.

Roman women were free to leave the house, provided they wore a *stola matronalis*; they could visit shops and public places such as theatres and law courts. In the seclusion of their own homes they could take part in business discussions with their husbands and their husbands' friends. Some women, such as Fulvia, the first wife of Mark Antony, were said to overstep the boundaries of their role by overtly showing their control and power in public, but they were exceptions.

Cicero summed up the Roman attitude when he wrote: 'Because of the weakness of women's judgement, our ancestors wanted them to be subject to guardians . . .'

Gaius Suetonius Tranquillus (*c.*AD70) reports that the emperor Augustus recommended Romans to read a speech by Quintilius Caecilius Metellus Macedonicus, urging Romans to compulsory marriage to increase the then declining birth-rate in Rome: 'If we could get on without a wife, Romans, we would all avoid the annoyance, but since nature has ordained that we can neither live very comfortably with them nor at all without them we must take thought for our lasting well-being rather than for the pleasure of the moment.'

This typical male chauvinistic viewpoint permeated Roman life and perceptions. Professor Jean Markle sums up the general attitude thus: 'The Romans looked upon women as bearers of children and objects of pleasure . . .'

Bearing in mind Greek and Roman attitudes towards women, it is valid to ask how Celtic women appeared in their eyes. Certainly the Romans found the idea of Celtic women being rulers and war leaders distinctly disturbing. Romans not only comment on this but record that women were also to be prominently found in many professions; Plutarch particularly mentions that women were often used as ambassadors. Celtic women ambassadors negotiated the treaty between the Celtic Volcae and the Carthaginian general Hannibal.

It is interesting that the word 'ambassador' itself is actually a Celtic one. The Romans adopted the word into Latin as *ambactus* which they observed meant a 'messenger'. This then made its way into German as *amt* meaning public office and also from Low Latin into French, Italian and English.

But what do we actually know of an ordinary woman's place in ancient Celtic society as viewed from Greek and Roman sources? There are a few intriguing glimpses given in the surviving texts.

For laws relating to Gaulish and British women in early times we have to fall back on our untrustworthy authority Julius Caesar. Speaking of the Gauls he says:

> When a Gaul marries he adds to the dowry that his wife brings with her a portion of his own property estimated to be of equal value. A joint account is kept of the whole amount, and the profits which it earns are put aside; and when either dies, the survivor receives both shares together with accumulated profits.

Here the comments are a reasonable reflection of how a Roman might interpret the system. But, inevitably, Caesar goes overboard when he then says:

> Husbands have power of life and death over their wives as well as their children. When a high-born head of a family dies, his relatives assemble, and if the circumstances of his death are suspicious, they examine his widow under torture, as we examine slaves; if her guilt is established, she is consigned to the flames and put to death with the most cruel torments.

His ideas about the customs of the British Celts are equally bizarre. 'Wives are shared between groups of ten or twelve men, especially between brothers and between fathers and sons; but the offspring of these unions are counted as the children of the man with whom a particular woman cohabited first.' This is a total misrepresentation of the polygamous society of the early Celts. The Romans seemed preoccupied with the 'liberated' attitude of Celtic women to men. Dio Cassius (c.AD150–235) comments on the fact that the empress Julia Augusta went so far as to criticise what she saw as a lack of morals because Celtic women were free to choose their husbands and lovers and did so openly without subterfuge. The object of her criticism was the wife of a North Briton chieftain named Argentocoxos (the name has 'silver' as its root). The encounter took place early in the third century AD. According to Dio, the wife of Argentocoxos turned to the empress and replied with dignity: 'We Celtic women obey the demands of Nature in a more moral way than the women of Rome. We consort openly with the best men but you, of Rome, allow yourselves to be debauched in secret by the vilest.' How the empress reacted, alas, we do not know.

The Roman attitude to women was not really very different from that of the Anglo-Saxons, although there have been attempts to rehabilitate the Anglo-Saxons. Christine Fell, in her study *Women in Anglo-Saxon England*, argued that 'the statements that are made about the subordination of Saxon women, and the relative freedom of "British" (i.e. Celtic) ones, are blatant misrepresentations of such evidence as we have. Early Celtic law shows women in a far less favourable position than Anglo-Saxon law.' This hardly squares with the statement in the gnomic verses of the *Exeter Book* which succinctly sum up the Anglo-Saxon idea that 'a woman's place is at her embroidery'. Also, it does not concur with archaeological evidence of women in pagan Anglo-Saxon times being thrown alive into graves on top of carefully placed corpses and buried. Dr Ray I. Page, in *Life in Anglo-Saxon England* (1970), has referred to the Sewerby, Yorkshire, burial as an example. In this burial a woman was placed on top of the body of an obviously wealthy woman. The second body, found 'lying face downwards, was contorted as though she had died violently. Across her pelvis rested part of a quern stone, hurled in to keep her down before the grave was closed. Was this, too, a slave sacrificed so that she could serve her mistress in death as in life?' Similar burials have been found in which the unfortunate woman was thrown in the grave on top of the dead body of a male.

Peter R. Cherici, in *Celtic Sexuality*, observes:

In the strict patriarchy of the Saxons, women held low status. They were little better than chattels, destined to serve men and suffer hardship in silence. Regardless of social rank, they could be bought and sold at the whim of their husband or father. And they imperilled their life if they rejected the sexual advances of the man who controlled their destiny. When their male master died, they were sometimes killed and interred in the same grave to serve him even in death. So rigid were the gender roles in Saxon society that the very notion of women bearing arms was monstrous, a story-teller's device to evoke terror in the audience.

By the time Alfred, at the end of the ninth century, gathered the Anglo-Saxon laws and codified them, making amendments, the women of the Anglo-Saxon upper and middle classes were certainly more liberated than before. In law and in practice they had more freedom than under pagan law, and this allowed for the emergence of several prominent female church leaders and queens who played political roles, although usually in support of their husbands. Alfred's laws were a progressive development in Anglo-Saxon society. Indeed, Sir Frank Stenton has pointed out that the new laws of Alfred display a concern for the weakest in society that does not occur in previous Anglo-Saxon thinking. Yet this was a basic tenet of Celtic law. Could this 'new approach', the more liberal attitude to women's rights, have arisen because the man whom Alfred of Wessex asked to supervise the codification of the Anglo-Saxon laws was none other but a Celt named Asser from St David's in Dyfed?

Christine Fell does not seem to be swayed but holds firmly to Anglo-Saxon superiority over the lot of their Celtic sisters. In spite of this, the little we know of the codes of Ine of Wessex, Offa of Mercia and Aethelberht of Kent, the Anglo-Saxon law systems prior to Alfred's great codification, shows that the place of women was not nearly as liberated as Miss Fell would have us believe. And whether Celtic women suffered a worse fate under their own law system can be easily assessed.

It is argued that it is Irish law that has survived in a form closest to the original Celtic social system of the 'Iron Age'. Before we examine the native Celtic law systems, we should remind ourselves that from the First Synod of Patrick, Christian canon law began to be introduced into Ireland. Gaul and Britain had already been influenced not only by the Romans but by Rome's version of Christianity before this time. Therefore, while Ireland's ancient law system is certainly less corrupted from its original source than are the laws of Wales, it still shows the influence of Roman Christianity. For example, the concept of 'sexual crime' was introduced by Patrick, in which divorce and casual lovers, and sexual relationships between male and female *religieux*, were forbidden under penalty of excommunication. This was followed by documents known as Penitentials. At the end of the sixth century the *Poenitentiale Vinnia* (Finnian's Penitential) was being widely used in religious communities; it stressed physical punishment, such as flogging and fasting, for any transgressions of its tough sexual codes. It contained a lengthy list of prohibited sexual relationships. Columbanus quoted it and used it as the basis for his own set of Penitentials, as did the seventh-century *Poenitentiale Cummeani* which we will discuss later.

So, in fact, in Ireland, we have the position of the native law system existing side by side from the fifth century with an ecclesiastical law system which diverged utterly from it in matters of codes of sexual behaviour; a law system which criminalised many things relating to the position of women, and the relationship of men and women, which the Celts considered normal behaviour. The earliest surviving texts of these ecclesiastical laws are the *Collectio Canonum Hibernesis*, compiled in the eighth century, which were set down with their application to Celtic society. If Christine Fell was making her judgement between ecclesiastical law and Anglo-Saxon law, then she might have a point. But to judge properly, the comparison should be between Irish criminal and civil law and the equivalent Anglo-Saxon law, for the canon law of both countries was virtually a vehicle for the concepts, with local variations, of Roman Christianity. Perhaps I should emphasise that when I talk of 'Roman Christianity' I refer to the western Christian movement which Paul of Tarsus founded in Rome and from which eastern and African Christian movements eventually dissociated themselves.

The Celtic peoples had developed a sophisticated law system by which their lives were governed at an early point in their history. The Greeks and Romans often commented on the role of Celtic judges. Caesar mentions a judicial gathering in the land of the Carnutes (Chartres) and says that in 52BC one Vergobret was elected chief magistrate and judge of the Aedui. Once more Caesar misinterprets things for Vergobret is actually a title, a job description, from *vergo* (effective) *breto* (judgement), cognate with the Old Irish term *brethach* from which derives *breitheamh* or Brehon, the word for a judge.

At one period a common Celtic law system must have existed: this can be seen from similarities in those law systems we know. We are lucky in that two complete Celtic law systems survive.

The oldest surviving Celtic law system is the Irish one, that which we call the Brehon law, the word deriving from *breitheamh*, a judge. The correct name was the Law of the *Fénechas* or land tiller. The first known codification of these laws occurred during the reign of the High King Laoghaire (AD428–36). He appointed a commission of nine eminent persons, including Patrick the patron saint of Ireland, to study, revise and commit the laws to written form. Tradition has it, however, that it was in 714BC that the High King of Ireland, Ollamh Fódhla, founded rule by legislature and drew up a code of laws. He founded the great Féis Temhrach, or Festival of Tara, at which laws were discussed and revised every three years. However we view the tradition, certainly the Féis was an assembly held into historical times at which legislation was enacted.

The law system was therefore not static, but constantly developing. Laws were modified or changed as circumstances warranted. We have a record of the famous gathering at Druim Ceatt (Co. Derry) in AD576, when Colmcille's law relating to women was enacted. Thus we can point to changing laws on women, from pagan traditions through to Christianity and the influence particularly of canon law, the legislation of Church councils which usually dealt with the governance of the clergy and the Church, including the administration of the sacraments, but which often also tried to interfere with the civil and criminal procedures of society.

The regular meetings, usually annual or triennial, in which laws were discussed and changed were called *airechts* or councils. According to Dr P.W. Joyce, in *A Social History of Ancient Ireland*:

The women had *airechts* or councils of their own to discuss those subjects specially pertaining to women; and at these assemblies no man was permitted to be present; while, on the other hand, no woman was allowed to enter the special council meeting of men. In those formal sittings that were open to both sexes, the women were seated with their own people, in the special places set apart for the representatives of these respective tribes.

So in the mixed councils, men and women from the same tribe, or clan, were seated together. The sexes were not seated separately but as clans. These meetings were usually held during the great Aonach or 'fair'. We are told that the fair at Carmán (Wexford) was held every three years from 1 August until 6 August – the feast of Lúnasa. The eleventh-century 'Poem of Carmán' says: 'There they discussed and debated the rights and taxes of the province: every legal enactment right piously, every third year it was settled.' As well as the provincial king, no fewer than forty-seven chieftains, or sub-kings, attended. The *Book of Leinster* shows that women played a conspicuous part in this fair and one of the days was especially set aside for entertainment for the women who attended. One group of people was especially entrusted with the duty of guarding the jewellery worn by the Leinster women who had to lay it aside during the entertainment and games. Indeed, a law says that any creditor who held a woman's brooch, necklace, ear-rings or other jewellery as a pledge against a loan had to return it to the owner so that she could wear it at the great assembly. The pledge had to be returned to the creditor afterwards. If the creditor refused, then they could be fined for 'humiliation'.

Our second complete law system is that of Hywel Dda, or the Welsh law system. This was codified at a much later date than the Irish system, during the reign of Hywel Dda (910–50) of Wales. He is said to have called upon his chief legal adviser, Blegywyrd ab Einon, archdeacon of Llandaf, a man learned in law, to summon an assembly to consider and codify the laws. Bishops and scholars and six representatives of each of the local sub-divisions of the country, presumably elected civic leaders, met to discuss the Welsh laws for forty days. Their recommendations were then set down in a single code. The majority of the Welsh law texts survive from copies made between 1200 and 1500.

Both Irish and Welsh systems point to the common root and we can use them as a yardstick to analyse and confirm the role of Celtic women as seen by the Greeks and Romans and, indeed, as demonstrated in the stories enshrined in the Irish and Welsh epics and sagas.

There are references and fragments of law systems from other parts of the Celtic world. Unfortunately, there are no extant Breton texts on the subject, although some ideas survive in texts relating to the ninth century and, indeed, some basic structures are amalgamated into the treaties which incorporated Brittany as an autonomous province of the French state in the sixteenth century. One particular reference shows that in ninth-century Brittany women could still be appointed to public political office. Each area in Brittany had an officer called a *mac'htiern* (horse lord) at this time, whose role was to regulate business transactions and ensure their legality. The *Cartulary of Redon* mentions that in one case this position was occupied by a lady named Aourkan of Pleucadeuc. Her husband was *mac'htiern* of an adjacent area. According to Dr Wendy Davies, who is not convinced about the extent of Celtic women's political freedoms, and who views Aourkan's position as 'unusual':

Although their number was small a few women presumably played a direct part in politics when they had control of large properties and when the course of politics was directly related to property interests. This may well be the underlying reason for Aourken's unusual position, for her husband's family had property in Pleuca-deuc and her father-in-law had previously been *mac'htiern* there. However, political women are more likely to have operated in Ireland than elsewhere, for the leaders of some powerful religious communities were women.

Geoffrey of Monmouth mentions the legendary Molmutine law of Cornwall which, he says, was concerned with the protection of the weak against oppression. Domnuil I of Alba (Scotland) had the ancient laws of Dàl Riada, obviously a version of the Brehon system, promulgated at Forteviot and Fortriu between AD858 and 862, when the kingdom of Alba incorporated that of the Strathclyde Britons and Cumbrian Celts. It was felt that a legal document needed to be drawn up to resolve any differences between the Goidelic Celts and the British Celtic system. In the *Leges inter Bretonnes et Scotos* of the eleventh century there are found terms which are similar to both the Irish and Welsh systems. Professor Kenneth H. Jackson has stated: 'This may imply the existence of a common Brittonic legal tradition of considerable antiquity.'

When the Manx laws came to be written, the original Celtic system, which would have been similar to the Brehon system, had been intermixed with Norse concepts and later with English feudal concepts. Magnus III, the last independent king of the Isle of Man (Ellan Vannin), had died without issue in 1265. He had left his kingdom to Alexander III of Scotland. But for the next century England and Scotland fought over the Island until in 1405 the Stanley family were established as its suzerain lords. During this time the Manx parliament, Tynwald (*thing-völlr*, parliament field), and its elected body, the House of Keys (*kiares-es-feed*, the twenty-four, named after the number of its members), continued to meet. Tynwald is the oldest continuous parliament in the world. We hear of one law passed in 1098 by the Tynwald which made it necessary for wife as well as husband to sign a deed of property. In the same law it states that the women of the northern half of the Island were entitled to half their husband's property while women from the southern half were entitled to only one-third of their husband's property. There is a reason behind this piece of discrimination.

When Godred Crovan died in 1095 his son Lagman repented that he had mutilated his brother Harald so that he would not become king of Man and the Isles. He went off on a pilgrimage to Jerusalem and died there. The chieftains of Man then sent to the Irish High King, Muirchertach Ua Bríain (d. 1119), and asked him to send an Irish prince to rule until Olaf, the third son of Godred, had become old enough to rule. The High King of Ireland sent one Domhnall Mac Thadhg to fulfil the role of regent but Domhnall seems to have abused his position of power and was driven out. In the wake of this there was an internecine war in the Isle of Man with the north pitted against the south. The northerners were commanded by Ottar, a *thegn* of Magnus who now claimed the throne of Man, and the southerners were commanded by MacMaras or MacManus. According to A.W. Moore, in *A History of the Isle of Man*: 'A battle took place at Santwat near Peel in which the north gained the victory, according to tradition, by the assistance of their women.' The law was then passed 'because of their bravery in joining the fight'.

Although ecclesiastical laws were enacted on the Island between 1266 and 1405 the main law was the 'breast laws', an oral tradition of laws, equivalent to common law, remembered by the Island's Deemsters, or judges, from oldest times. In 1429 the Tynwald met under the presidency of the governor of the island, Henry Bryon, who then caused the laws and constitution to be reduced to writing.

According to this customary law, the wife was entitled, on the death of her husband, to one-half of his possessions; if she left her husband, which she could do 'for any crime, either adultery, or for any other cause', she could still claim half of his possessions. If her husband was found guilty of a crime, a woman did not forfeit her share of his property. However, during the seven-month 'reign' of Ferdinando Stanley, fifth earl of Derby and Lord of Man (1593–94), the earl declared that such a practice was 'against the laws of God and good government'.

If a woman was guilty of a felony, a husband could divorce her. If he stood by her and concealed her crime, he was deemed as guilty before the law as she was. Conversely, the husband became responsible for all his wife's debts. If a woman was raped, the punishment, brought in by the English lords of Man, was death. However, the Deemsters, remembering the old Celtic form of compensation, would usually offer an unmarried woman a symbolic rope, sword or ring so that she might 'have her choice to hang with the rope, cut off his head with the sword, or marry him with the ring'.

The age of majority was fourteen and parents were obliged by Manx law to maintain the child until then, as elsewhere in the Celtic world. With children born out of wedlock, if the parents married within one or two years, and the mother 'was never slandered nor defamed with any other man before', then the child was deemed as legitimate. But an illegitimate child had no right of automatic inheritance unless by will or at the discretion of a judge.

It is difficult to reach back to the hypothetic common Celtic law. We have so few references, and those are from outside observers.

'In Britain,' observed Tacitus, 'there is no rule of distinction to exclude the female line from the throne, or the command of armies.' Indeed, it has been argued that some Celts developed a matrilineal form of kingship by which the succession was governed through the maternal line. Bede (d. 731) is often quoted as believing that the Pictish kings came to the throne by matrilineal succession. In fact, Bede's source appears to be an Irish claim that the Pictish kings and chieftains took Irish wives on condition that the kingship passed through the female line. Lloyd and Jenny Laing in *The Picts and the Scots* (1993), believed this reference to be simply Irish propaganda. 'As things stand, the case for Pictish matriliny is not proven, and would not appear to be supported in any way by the evidence that survives except in the very curious succession pattern.' This 'very curious succession pattern' is nothing more than the usual electoral method of Celtic kingship, the election by the *derbfhine* of the family, ignoring the primogeniture system of inheritance by the eldest son.

However, the Scottish king lists do have their monarchical claim based on a female progenitor, i.e. Scota. In one tradition she is the daughter of the Egyptian Pharaoh Cingris, wife of Niul, a Druid, whose son was Goidel. The other Scota is the daughter of the Pharaoh Nectanebus, who became the wife of Míl and mother of his children, the Milesians or Gaels.

In fact, as already pointed out in several stories, many heroes in Irish and Welsh literature are named after their mother and not their father. The most famous example, already discussed, was Conchobhar, known as the 'son of Nessa'. Gwyddyon of Wales was the son of his mother Dôn while Cúchulainn, whose original name was

Setanta, was the son of his mother Dechtire. Could this be a vestige of an early system of matrilineal descent? Such a system certainly continued for a time in some other societies, for example, that of the American Natchez. Interestingly, in the Natchez creation legend men were created first but they were not interested in life, even when the creator, the god Thoume Kene Kimte Cacounche, gave them tobacco. They were useless and didn't fend for themselves. So the creator made women to organise and rule them.

Certainly, as we have seen, women could and did rule in their own right. And one interesting example of the struggle over female succession between Celtic law and Salic law, the law of the French monarchy excluding females from dynastic succession, occurred in Brittany. Brittany was still independent at this stage but constantly bickered over by France and England. Yann III (1312–41) of Brittany had been thrice married but had no legitimate children. His brother Guy (d. 1331) had married and his daughter, Jeanne Penthièvre, became the heir when her father died. Breton law, in accordance with the Celtic system, allowed for female succession. Needless to say, her hand in marriage was eagerly sought by the English royal family. Edward III was marriage broker for his brother John. The French royal family offered a suitor in the person of Charles, count of Blois, a nephew of Philip VI.

Charles de Blois was the successful marriage candidate. The war between France and England made Brittany a strategic country. When Yann III died, Jeanne de Penthièvre was the natural successor under Celtic law. However, Jeanne's half-uncle Jean de Montfort, son of Arthur II (1305–12), claimed he should be recognised as legitimate ruler of Brittany. He had spent little time in Brittany and had few supporters. He managed to attract one powerful supporter in Edward III of England, who was making another attempt to control Brittany since his brother John had been unsuccessful in the marriage game. With a little persuasion, a civil war broke out in Brittany over the succession. The war continued on and off until 1364 when the English general Sir John Chandos, companion and friend of the Prince of Wales, led his army to Auray and defeated de Blois and his Bretons. Charles de Blois was killed.

Jeanne de Penthièvre was forced to concede Jean de Montfort's right by military conquest to become ruler of Brittany, although she was allowed to keep her title until her death. De Montfort's claim was based on the foreign Salic law of France. Curiously, de

Montfort, it turned out, believe in an independent Brittany and once in power, by political marriages, he produced a strong line of independent rulers. The last of these was also to be a woman – Anne.

In 1488 the Breton armies under her father Francis II (1458–88) were defeated by the French at St Aubin du Cromier. The Bretons were forced, by the treaty of Le Verger, to recognise the French king's suzerain right over Brittany. When Francis II died three weeks after this calamity, his daughter Anne (1488–1514) became ruler of Brittany. But she was only eleven years old. Anne's advisers reinstituted resistance to French interference. In 1490 she was married to Maximilian, king of the Romans, in a proxy ceremony. Maximilian was not willing to come to Brittany and Anne and her advisers were not willing to leave. There appeared to be a palace coup: a new set of pro-French advisers had Anne's marriage annulled and forced the young girl-monarch into a marriage with Charles VIII of France on 6 December 1491. As Patrick Galliou and Michael Jones remark in *The Bretons*: 'with the French marriage Brittany ceased to exist as an independent and essentially sovereign state'.

In 1408 Charles died and Anne managed to achieve some measure of independence again but only by marrying his successor Louis XII (1498–1515). She used her influence with Louis to get his approval for the continuance of the Breton royal council and parliament. Anne tried to have her eldest daughter Claude, heiress to the ducal throne of Brittany, betrothed to the heir of the house of the Austrian Habsburg dynasty, traditional enemies to France. This was an attempt by Anne to achieve Breton independence again. But Anne died in 1514 and Charles then married Claude off to François, the heir presumptive to the French throne, which simply tightened French royal control of Brittany. The 'union of crowns' was complete. And in 1532 the Breton parliament was forced to agree a new treaty with France which secured the succession of the French monarchs as dukes, and thereby rulers, of Brittany. On the other hand the French monarchy pledged to respect the political and administrative rights of Brittany, agreed not to levy taxes there without the consent of the Breton parliament, and also agreed that only Bretons were to be appointed to public office in Brittany nor were Bretons to serve as soldiers outside Brittany. Brittany had become an autonomous state within the French kingdom and remained so until 1790 when it was annexed completely.

Anne was, therefore, the last ruler of an independent Breton state and, ironically, the French monarchy's claim over Brittany was made contrary to their own Salic law, for they accepted Anne's right as a woman to inherit the throne under Celtic law.

[5]

A Woman's Place in Law

USING the two complete surviving law systems, Irish and Welsh, we are able to examine the role of women in those Celtic societies not only during the period when the laws were in force but, to a certain degree, during the earlier pre-Christian period by assessing what must have been common Celtic law. Picking one's way through any legal system can be a tortuous task. This chapter is, therefore, divided into sections dealing with specific areas for easier comprehension.

CHILDHOOD

In Irish law, a child, male or female, under the age of fourteen had no legal responsibility nor any right to independent legal action. According to the *Bretha Crólige*, the *eneclann* or honour price of a girl of any social class until the age of seven was the same as for a cleric. Eight *cumals*, a variable unit of currency generally fixed at three milch cows, would be the penalty for killing a child before the age of seven. After the age of seven, when children were sent to fosterage or to acquire an education, the child's honour price became half that of his or her father or foster father and stayed at that level for as long as they were dependent on him.

Irish law takes heed that children were most likely to be killed or injured in accidents, even while playing games with others. If a child commits an offence while under age then their parents are responsible. If a child is injured then the culprit is normally required to provide the sick-maintenance. If the child is under seven years old then they must be maintained at the financial level accorded to a cleric and must be accompanied during their stay in hospital by the mother, who also has to be provided for. The child, if aged between seven years and ten years, must be fed the normal diet to which they would be entitled during their fosterage, provided the physician does not think that it is injurious to their health. After the age of ten the boy or girl is entitled to adult sick-maintenance according to the rank of their legal guardian.

The rearing of children, male or female, is the responsibility of both parents in normal circumstances. If the child was conceived through wrong-doing on the part of the man, such as rape, adultery etc., then the man alone is responsible. In cases where the mother is sick or has a disability, she may require her husband to assume total responsibility. This can also apply if, under law, the mother is shown to be unsuited to rearing a child. If his wife dies, then the father is responsible for the rearing of his children.

Welsh law demonstrates many similarities in this area, although it has become considerably less generous to the female. Females are indistinguishable from men only until baptism and their *sarhaed*, compensation for insult, or *galanas*, compensation for unlawful death, is calculated as half that of any male sibling. Welsh law, therefore, does not recognise that special *grád maice* or 'status of childhood' found in Irish law.

The Welsh girl remains *wrth noe y thad*, beside her father's plate, until she marries – usually after the age of twelve to fourteen years.

EDUCATION OR FOSTERAGE

In all Celtic societies, children underwent an education which was termed 'fosterage', by which they were sent for a period to foster parents who undertook their instruction in various fields.

There were two types of fosterage in ancient Ireland: fosterage for affection (*altramm serce*) for which no fee was paid, and fosterage for which a fee was required. This fosterage was where the child acquired its full education. Interestingly, the fee for the fosterage of a girl was higher than that for a boy. Each child had to be educated according to their rank. Fosterage was a legal contract between parents and foster parents. While the child was in the foster parents' care, the foster parents became responsible for all legal fines incurred by the child. The *Cáin Iarraith* gives fourteen as the age for a girl

to complete her education, seventeen for a boy. An addition, however, in the *Bretha Crólige* allows a girl to continue until the age of
seventeen 'if required'.

There is plenty of evidence that young women also attended 'higher
education' – the bardic and ecclesiastical schools in Ireland. In both
schools, secular or lay, pupils could study for up to twelve years and
obtain one or more of seven degrees, the highest, after the twelfth
year, being that of *ollamh*, which is still the modern Irish word for
a professor. We find that old records mention the abilities of female
scholars. Women's writing styles (*delg graiph*) are favourably
referred to in one text. When Mugint of Ireland founded his university in Scotland it was open to girls as well as boys. The daughter
of Cualann was sent to Finnén of Clonard, 'doctor of wisdom and
teacher of the saints of Ireland', for her education. Brendan, when
setting off to get his education, was enjoined by his mother to avoid
studying in the same school with any young, attractive women in
case he might be distracted by them.

There seemed few professions that women could not join, nor was
there any barrier to their rising to prominence in such professions
as they chose. We have references to women in all the professions,
even as judges in the courts. The *Bretha Crólige* refers to female war
leaders, physicians, artisans or wrights (*bansáer*), judges and local
magistrates, and poets. I have already briefly mentioned Bríg Briugaid, a female judge, who was qualified to correct a wrong judgement
in law given by a male judge, Sencha. She was no isolated example.
Aine ingine (daughter of) Iugairu was noted for the 'purity' of her
judgements and referred to in Donal O'Davoren's *Glossary* of 1569.
The *Tripartite Life of Patrick* mentions a *religieuse* named Darí who
was the authoress of a set of laws known as the *Cáin Darí*, but what
these referred to we do not know as the texts have been lost.

One very successful lady, who achieved the pinnacle of her profession, was Ulluach. In the tenth century, she was actually elected
to the highest office any poet, male or female, could achieve and
became the chief bard of Ireland. Alas, we cannot say when the
lady named Gáine, noted in the *Metrical Dinnsenchus*, became Chief
Druidess of Ireland, but it was obviously before the early fifth century. Gáine's office would imply that she had legal authority as a
judge.

A WOMAN'S LEGAL RESPONSIBILITY

Professor Kelly may argue that the Irish laws 'reveal a society in which a woman is generally without independent legal capacity', but a study of the law shows how loosely he uses the term 'generally'. Under the law, a woman can inherit land from her father and like any landowner she has a right to distrain goods and make a formal legal claim on her inheritance. If she marries a man without wealth or property, or a stranger from another country, then she makes the decisions of her household, and she is responsible for paying his fines and debts. If she has inherited her father's property, then, on her death, it does not necessarily pass to her widower. Under both Irish and Welsh law, women of property in their own right (Irish *bé cuitchernsa* and Welsh *gwraig briod*) can dispose of their property as they think fit. However, joint property cannot be so disposed of.

Where the woman brings property into a marriage, she remains the owner of it. She is subject to the same inheritance laws as the male and if she does not have sons then her daughter can inherit the property. Like male landowners, when warriors are needed for war service she is bound to send them but, if she gives up half her property, as a fine, she is freed from such an obligation – a withdrawal clause not given to men. This might be seen by some as a legal way of depleting a woman's property holdings on the basis that she might prefer to pay the fine rather than send her workers off to war.

Later law texts, such as the *Bretha Nemed déidenach*, give nuns a special position and legal rights not possessed by women in secular society. The evidence of a nun may be accepted against that of a cleric although the evidence of an ordinary woman may not unless it is supported by other witnesses.

An Irish queen usually has no more rights than an ordinary woman in society but if she is the mother of a king, bishop or sage (*suí*) she has the same honour price as her son and more legal rights. In Wales the queen, in medieval times, had special rights and her own household of eight officers, consisting of her principal steward, priest, chief groom, chamberlain (who served the queen with food and drink and kept the keys of her coffers), handmaid, doorkeeper (whose job was to carry the drink but not to serve it), cook and candleman. The queen shared ten other officers of the court with her king, who also had sixteen of his own officers. The Welsh queen has one right above other wives. She can dispose as she pleases of one-third of the *dofod* or casual acquisitions accrued with her husband during her marriage.

It is clear from historical evidence that Irish women could take part in the military muster of the clan and command the armies in battle. In Ireland, this role seems to have finally ended when Adomnán succeeded in having his *Lex Innocentium* or 'law of the innocents' adopted at the Synod of Birr in AD697. It was designed to protect non-combatants in war, such as elderly women and children as well as clergy. The law was approved of by an attendance of no fewer than fifty-one kings and provincial rulers and forty leading churchmen from all the Celtic lands and was made binding throughout the Celtic realms, becoming a sort of 'Geneva Convention' among the Celtic peoples. Compared to what was happening elsewhere in the European world, it was an amazingly progressive piece of legislation. This same law went on to forbid women to become warriors or military commanders. According to a *Life of Adomnán*, the abbot of Iona was moved to propose the law on the appeal of his mother Rónait. She and Adomnán were crossing a battlefield together after the slaughter and saw the terrible sight of a beheaded woman with her child still suckling at her breasts, 'a stream of milk on one of its cheeks and a stream of blood on the other'. As a justification for the new law, Adomnán painted a picture of men flogging their unwilling wives into the forefront of the battle, indifferent to their wounds or sufferings. Then, after the battle, the same unwilling naked women were forced to provide sexual service to coarse male warriors.

However, another interpretation of the *Lex Innocentium* might be that this was yet another move by Christianity to remove some of the rights of women and their authority to command, although superficially the law seemed commendable. According to Peter Cherici:

Women did indeed fight alongside men in battle and it would not have been unusual for warriors of both genders to engage in sexual relations before and after combat. But literature and historical chronicles provide little evidence that women were forced into battle or sexual encounters. In traditional Celtic society, women enjoyed a relatively high status. Their right to bear arms was a duty and a source of pride, despite the physical risks of combat. And any man who sexually assaulted a woman warrior would have to contend with her sword as well as the Brehon law prohibiting rape.

Peter Cherici believes that by granting women a religious immunity from military service and command, Adomnán was modifying the expectations of women in society and lowering their status. Banning them from the profession of warrior would not only diminish them, but would ultimately pave the way for banning them from making political decisions and from the professions of judge, healer, poet and scholar. Colmcille had presented a similar law at Druim Ceatt in AD575, but it seems that this was not popular enough to be obeyed and Adomnán's law had to be passed before notice was taken of it: perhaps because the punch-line of Adomnán's law was that women were incapable of determining their own destiny and needed the protection of male society or social institutions. Indeed, in the *Cáin Adomnáin* women, under the 'protection' of Iona, had to pay a quarterly tax assessed on their means to the abbot of Iona – in this case Adomnán himself. If they failed to pay, the saintly and charitable Adomnán would curse them and prophesy the decay of their children.

FEMALE SLAVES

At the bottom of early Irish society was a class of people who have been described, wrongly in my opinion, as 'slaves'. I have applied the collective term 'non-free' to this group for it is my contention, supported by many other scholars, that they cannot be compared with the popular concept of slavery which we find epitomised in ancient Greece or Rome, where slaves were subjected to conditions of servitude and bondage without rights, as the property of an owner. Laurence Ginnell in his pioneering examination of the Brehon law system, comments:

> There being no prisons or convict settlements in Ireland, except where the natural prison afforded by a small island was available, reduction to a species of slavery, permanent or temporary, was considered a reasonable punishment of criminals guilty of capital offences . . . and of prisoners who could not or would not satisfy fines imposed on them. Therefore, in many ways, the better comparison was to the recent French law where a penalty of civil degradation was passed by the Chambre Civique which meant a loss of civil rights, cessation of pensions, prohibition to practise in professions or be employed by the civil services.

This class was sub-divided into three. The *fuidhir* consisted of cowards who deserted their clan when needed, of prisoners-of-war and hostages. No *fuidhir* could bear arms, nor had they any political rights within the clan that held them. The *saer-fuidhir* could, however, work his or her own land, paying taxes for its use, while the *daer-fuidhir*, those who were untrustworthy, could not. The *fuidhir* remained in this state until he or she had paid compensation or a tribute had been paid on their behalf. The third-generation *fuidhir* was automatically granted full citizenship in the clan. St Patrick was a *fuidhir*, having been taken as a hostage in Britain. With slightly more rights than the *fuidhir*, but still of the non-free class, was the *bothach* (*bothan*, a cabin), who was allowed to be a crofter or cow-herd, and the *sen-cleithe*, who was a house servant. Neither the *bothach* nor the *sen-cleithe* was restricted as to who they could work for in the territory, but they were not allowed to leave the territory without special permission. They did not have political rights but they were capable of acquiring their own plots of land by contract and through this means returning to their former status as full citizens.

It is Professor Kelly's belief that 'the advent of Christianity seems to have contributed to some small improvement in the position of the slave in Irish society.' However, it is clear that the position of the *fuidhir* continued well into the Christian period, and the law text *Di Astud Chirt agus Dligid* disapproves of any attempt to change it. It is true that the *Penitential of Finnian* in the sixth century legislated against the use of a 'slave' woman for sexual purposes. But previous native laws had already made it clear that if a man made a 'slave' woman pregnant then he must pay compensation and arrange for the rearing of the child, while if a woman allowed herself to become pregnant by a male 'slave' then she alone was responsible for rearing the child, unless she could prove rape.

Mug is usually interpreted as a male 'slave' while a female 'slave' is called a *cumal*. Again, I have to argue that the use of the word 'slave' is not accurate. The meaning of the word *cumal*, within the texts themselves, is actually given as servant, maid, or woman-in-waiting to a chieftainess or queen. What has worried many feminist observers is that the same word appears as one of the ancient units of currency, generally fixed at the value of three milch cows. The average *eneclann* or honour price was eight *cumals*, equal to twenty-four milch cows. The word also means 'fine' or 'compensation'. This usage has led some to the claim that early Irish society was therefore based on slave economics: the final insult to womanhood was that the unit of currency was fixed on the value of a female 'slave'. This could be an over-reaction, for *cumal* has yet another meaning: 'champion'. Fionn Mac Cumhail's father is, as we can see, named Cumal. Cumal was the son of Trenmor, chief of the Clan Bascna, and a leader of the Fianna, whose son Demna grew up to be Fionn (Fair) and become the greatest leader of the Fianna. Etymologists see *cumal* as an ancient word signifying 'sky' and perhaps a 'sky god'. They see the word as cognate with the Brythonic Celtic form Camulos, who was a war god known among both Britons and Gauls. Colchester, once capital of the Roman province of Britain, was known as Camulodunum, the fortress of Camulos. The same name was given to Almondbury, in Yorkshire, while Camulosessa, the seat of Camulos, appears in southern Scotland. At Bar Hill on the Antonine Wall is an inscription 'to the god Mars Camulos'. Camulos was also known among the Remi in the region of Reims and in Dalmatia where there are inscriptions to him.

The assertion, therefore, that the Irish coin *cumal* signifies the value of a female servant is open to argument although Irish society would not be unique if such a coin were named after a female slave. Claude Lévi-Strauss, in *L'Attraction Passionnée* (Paris, 1967), pointed out that many societies applied the name of currency to the value of women. But apart from the similarity of the names, there is nothing to suggest a link in this case.

In Welsh law there is a comparative group called *caeth*, now also interpreted as 'slaves'. The word is borrowed from the Latin *captus*, perhaps showing a lack of a suitable native word. These were prisoners taken in war who, under law, were not allowed to be killed. The value of a male *caeth* was given at 240 pence. Should a female *caeth* be married, then her *amobr* was fixed at 12 pence compared with the daughter of a free chieftain at 120 pence. A free male who makes a female servant pregnant has to provide a replacement while she is unable to work, and after the child is born he has to accept responsibility for raising the child. If the woman dies in childbirth then the man is responsible for the payment of compensation and, if the child has survived, he remains responsible for raising it.

MARRIAGE

A girl reached her maturity at the age of choice (*aimsir togu*), which in Ireland, according to the *Gúbrétha Caratniad*, was at the age of fourteen years. In some cases, as the *Bretha Crólige* says, this was raised to seventeen years. She was then free, if she wished, to marry.

The *Cáin Lánamna* is the Irish law text dealing with the subject of marriage. There are nine specific types of union described in the text. In the first and primary type of marriage (*lánamnas comthinchuir*) the woman is called a 'wife of joint input' (*bé cuitchernsa*) with the man. In this marriage, man and woman have come into the partnership on grounds of financial equality. The second type of marriage (*lánamnas mná for ferthinchur*) is one in which the woman contributes little or nothing to the property. The third category (*lánamnas fir for bantichur*) is where the man contributes little or nothing.

The other forms of marriage are: fourthly (*lánamnas fir thathigthe*), through a man cohabiting with a woman at her home (with her kin's consent); fifthly (*lánamnas airite for uráil*), when a woman goes away openly with a man without the consent of her kin; sixthly and seventhly (*lánamnas foxail agus lánamnas táide*), when she either allows herself to be abducted without her kin's consent or when she is visited by a man in secret without her kin's consent; eighthly (*lánamnas éicne no sláithe*), marriage by rape, which we will discuss in our section on rape, and lastly (*lánamnas genaige*), the marriage of two insane persons.

In pre-Christian Celtic society, and indeed for a while after Ireland converted to Christianity, marriage was a polygamous institution. Men and women could engage in various sexual unions. While the Church opposed polygamy the *Bretha Crólige* finds justification in the Old Testament, pointing out that 'the chosen people of God lived in plurality of unions, so that it is not easier to condemn it than to praise it'.

The *Bretha Crólige* distinguishes three ranks of wife for the purposes of sick-maintenance: a chief wife, entitled to half her husband's honour price; a second wife, entitled to one-third; and any other wife, entitled to one-quarter. A concubine (*adaltrach* or *dormun*) could decide her worth from either kin, partner or son.

Significantly, there is no Old Irish word for a dowry. But the husband gives a *coibche* or 'bride-price' to the bride's father or head of her kin. The law is clear that the bride is entitled to a portion of this *coibche*. Incidentally, if the marriage results in divorce through the fault of the bride, then the *coibche* must be returned.

The nine marriages of the Irish law correspond to the nine types of marriage found in the Laws of Hywel Dda, and, significantly, to the eight types of marriage in Hindu law. The Welsh types of marriage are as follows (the number in brackets refers to the corresponding Irish marriage):

1. *priodas* (1).
2. *agwedi* (2).
3. *caradas* (4).
4. *deu lysuab*. There is no Irish counterpart to this law, which is encapsulated by Culhwch's stepmother's proposal that he marry her daughter, i.e. his father's stepdaughter.
5. *llathlut goleu* (5).
6. *llathlut twyll* (6).
7. *beichogi twyll gwreic lwyn a pherth* (7).
8. *kynnywedi ar liw ac ar oleu*. This law, which specifically deals with a union by abduction of a woman without her consent, may be covered in the eighth Irish marriage.
9. *twyll morwyn* (8).

The ninth Irish marriage, *lánamnas genaige*, the marriage of insane people, has no equivalent in Welsh law.

Both lists of the types of marriages are based on the same principles as those found in the *Dharmasutras* of Hindu law. Marriage, as in the Irish system, is basically an economic union and an exchange of wealth. Indeed, in every civilisation, marriage, as an institution, is a legal contract about finances.

The Welsh system has become more developed towards feudalism than the Irish system, and the Irish women certainly had more rights in marriage than their Welsh sisters. The feudal aspect of the Welsh law is seen in the general forms of marriage. When the Welsh girl married, a sum called *amobr* became payable to the local lord. This payment was apparently a sum for the symbolic loss of virginity. However, when the wife went to the marriage bed, the husband then paid the wife a sum called the *cowyll*. This was not paid until the morning after the wedding night. During that first night of marriage the *neithiorwyr* or wedding guests remained in the house or its vicinity to witness the event. The wife remained within the seclusion of the marriage bed for the next nine days before returning to the world. At the end of the seventh year of marriage she became entitled to a payment known as *agweddi* from her husband if he or she legitimately decided to divorce. The *agweddi*, therefore, was the property which a wife was entitled to on separation from her husband whichever partner was the instigator.

The word *gwraig* seems to mean a woman as opposed to *morwyn*, a girl. Only when the girl reached maturity did she become *gwraig*, having achieved *teithi oedran gwraig*, the characteristics of womanhood. *Morwyn* occurs as the word for a virgin. If a man took a wife on the understanding that she had *ar fraint hithau yn wraig*, or the status of a virgin, and found this was not so, then he was able to divorce her – a matter we shall discuss shortly.

As with Irish law, we find the native Welsh law system existing side by side with canon law; the Church often took a different view of what was correct in law. The *gwraig briod* seems to be the only wife recognised by Church law as opposed to the native law. Primogeniture was entering the equation and *Llyfr Iorwerth* states, 'Church law states that no son is entitled to his father's holding except the father's eldest son from the *gwraig briod*.' The literal translation of *briod* (*priodas*) is property.

The *Cartulary of Redon*, an eleventh-century work which gives references from as early as the ninth century, also gives examples of Welsh women, as well as Breton women, who owned property in their own right and so could dispose of it without male interference.

We will return to the subject of the changing structure of marriage in Ireland in our survey of 'Women in Medieval History'.

DIVORCE

Divorce in Irish law (*imscarad*) was permitted for many reasons. And a woman in ancient Ireland had the right to initiate such proceedings. A woman could divorce her husband and retain her *coibche* if, for example, he was physically violent to her and caused bruises; if, without her consent, he left her for another woman (in that case she had an automatic right to the ownership of the house); if he told lies about her or circulated a satire; or if he had tricked her into marriage and she later discovered he had lied.

There were various sexual failings which were also grounds for divorce such as impotency, or if the husband became so obese as to be incapable of intercourse, or if he became a practising homosexual, either with other men or with boys. If a man was incapable of having children he could be divorced or separated, as he could be if he decided to take holy orders and follow a life which was incompatible with his obligations (*cuinliged*) to his wife.

Professor Jean Markle comments: 'Like all other peoples, the Celts knew homosexuality.' Aristotle (384–322BC), writing in *Politica* (Politics), comments on 'the Celts, who respect manly love quite openly'. Athenaeus of Naucratis (*fl.* AD200), the author of *Deipnosophistai* (Men Learned in the Arts of the Banquet) writes: 'And among the barbarians, the Celts also, though they have very beautiful women, enjoy boys more; so that some of them often have two lovers to sleep with on their beds of animal skins.' These rather breath-taking generalisations may reflect the prevailing attitudes of ancient Greece, but we cannot level the charge of general or institutional encouragement of homosexuality at Irish or Welsh law.

The reference giving homosexuality as grounds for divorce makes it clear that it was not socially acceptable. As a reason for divorce it is mentioned in a legal heptad, No. 52 (Binchley, *Corpus Iuris Hibernici* i 48.5-6 and *Ancient Laws of Ireland*), which lists the causes for divorce. The heptad says: '*bean doguidtar caemda combi ferr leis feis la gilliu manabe deithbir do*' which Professor Kelly translates as 'a wife whose bed is spurned so that he (her husband) prefers to lie with boys, unless it is blameless for him' (is entitled to divorce). Professor Kelly explains this clause 'unless it is blameless for him' as a conscientious attempt to cover any situation where a husband found himself having to spend a night with a boy but for no sexual motive. A later glossator adds an explanation: '*cona ferr lais beith a neunlebaid maraon risna gilliu*', 'so that he *prefers* to be in one bed together with boys'.

The heptad does not, unfortunately, give the native term for homosexuals but uses *gilla* (plural *gilliu*), 'lad', for the homosexual partner.

It is certainly true that in some of the epics, such as the Red Branch Cycle, there are discreet references to homosexual relationships. And there are similar references to lesbian relationships, such as that between Brigid of Kildare and Darlughdacha which we will come to when we study 'Women in the Celtic Church'. In a Penitential (edited by E.J. Gwynn, *Ériu* 7 (1914) 144 § 25), the text refers to lesbian practices: '*Is amlaid dano cid mna no ingena dognet immenetur*', 'it is the same [penance as for males] if women or girls do it [the sexual act] among themselves'. A later glossator adds, perhaps with distaste: '*daingin sin a pennadoir*', 'that is hard, o penitential!'

There is a reference in the *Táin Bó Cuailgne* (the version in the twelfth-century *Leabhar na Nuachonghbhala* or *Book of Leinster*) to someone who is a *fergráda*. This was translated by nineteenth-century scholars as 'confidential servant'. I believe, in spite of the acceptance of this definition in the Royal Irish Academy's *Dictionary of Old and Middle Irish*, that the word is obviously from *fer*, 'man/male', and *gráda*, 'lover'. I believe that the implication of the name is clear. Professor Fergus Kelly would disagree with this, pointing to other examples in the RIA dictionary which give *fiallach gráda* as 'band of retainers' and *oes gráda* as 'men of trust'. In a letter of 5 September 1994, Professor Kelly tells me: 'So far as I can make out from these examples, the idea is the bond of loyalty between a lord or champion and a group of trusted followers. There is not, I think, necessarily a homosexual bond.' But I find it hard to accept that such a powerful word for 'love' and 'affection' can be interpreted as 'confidence' or 'trust', and it is not so translated elsewhere in the texts. The Old and Middle Irish word for trust and confidence is clearly *muinigin* from which the modern Irish *muinín* derives.

Homosexuality is mentioned in canon law which, after the First Synod of Patrick, had begun to run concurrently with Brehon law. In these texts homosexuality is called *ferchol*, literally 'man-sin', expressive of the Christian morality. When Cummian Fota (also recorded as Cummean Longus), the abbot of Magh Bíle (Moville), d. AD662, wrote his *Poenitentiale Cummeani* he paid particular attention to homosexual practices within the male religious orders. His *Poenitentiale* records almost every sexual variation with its penalties. For anal intercourse, the punishment was seven years of atonement. Mutual masturbation incurred several years of reduced rations. A simple kiss between men involved six fasts while passionate kissing incurred eight fasts. These Penitentials, in sexual matters, diverged from traditional Celtic attitudes, criminalising solitary and consensual acts such as masturbation, cunnilingus and fellatio. In another Irish Penitential (edited by E.J. Gwynn, mentioned above) a passage reads: '*fir dogniat ferchol itir sliastaib no toin .ii. anni pendite*', 'men who have intercourse between the thighs or anal intercourse [must do] two years' penance'.

The Irish law texts show that divorce was not a thing easily entered into and a woman could not leave the marriage without just cause. Neither could a man. Even where a man or woman had adequate grounds for divorce, the woman, for example, would forfeit her *coibche* if she left her husband without the formality of law. There were seven grounds for a man to divorce his wife, including unfaithfulness, persistent thieving, bringing shame on his honour, having an abortion without telling him, and smothering her child.

A divorce meant that a woman could take out of her marriage all the property that she had brought into it. But furthermore, she was automatically entitled, at separation, to one-ninth of the increase of her husband's wealth even if she had no property at the time of marriage.

For women who did not want to go so far as divorce, there were eleven circumstances in which a married couple might separate without penalties exacted from either partner. These separations tended to be of a temporary nature. One particularly interesting one was that if either partner was infertile, the wife or husband might go away 'to seek a child'. The wife of an infertile husband, if she did not wish to divorce him on these grounds, might leave him temporarily so that she could become pregnant by another man. The resultant child was then treated as the child of the husband.

But a woman who absconded illegally from her marriage, no matter what her rank, was deemed an *élúdach*, an outlaw; she lost her rights and had to pay compensation. Similar judgement applied to a man who likewise absconded, and also to anyone who absconded and so failed to look after an elderly parent or parents.

In Welsh law also, separation and divorce could be enacted for a variety of reasons. After seven years the wife was entitled to half of the man's goods. The Welsh law says that 'it is right for them to share everything in two halves . . . it belongs to the woman to divide and to the man to choose.' Even the debts are to be halved. A divorce by the woman before the seven-year period on legitimate grounds allows her to take with her the *agweddi*, her personal property (*argyfrau*) and her *cowyll*. But if she left her husband for another man, she was only entitled to her *cowyll* and her *wynebwerth* (honour price). Presumably she was also entitled to her own property as well, although this is not mentioned. If her husband was found with another woman, and this was a cause of the divorce, then she was entitled to *gowyn*, a compensation payment. If the husband was of

'stinking breath', had some other malady or could not have intercourse, the woman was entitled to divorce and her fair share of the
property. If the couple had separated and the husband died, and the
widow was still living in a house owned by him to which she was
not entitled, she was given nine days and nine nights to vacate the
premises with those goods to which she was entitled.

A feudal aspect of the law is that if the marriage was contracted
on the grounds that the girl was a virgin and this proved not to be
the case – the girl and her relatives could appeal in law about such
accusations – the *twyllforwyn* (false virgin) could be divorced after
nine nights, and her share of marriage wealth (*agweddi*) due on such
a separation was not paid. She was simply given a one-year-old steer
with a greased tail and if she could keep hold of it then it became
her own property.

In thirteenth-century Wales, when the idea of one wife had been
generally accepted, one of the provisions for divorce was that if
a man left his wife and went off with another woman, she was
automatically free 'since no man is entitled to have two wives'. The
divorced woman was then free to do what she wished. 'Every woman
is entitled to go the way she will, for it is not right for her to be
car-returning, and there is no right to anything from her save her
amobr, and one *amobr* at that, for a woman has no *ebediw* [death
duty] save her *amobr*; therefore it is right that a man should pay
only one *ebediw*, in the same way it is right that a woman should
pay only one *amobr*, since she has no *ebediw* save her *amobr*.' The
concept of car-return (*karrdychwel*) means that a woman does not
have to return to her family, taking the car (in the thirteenth century,
usually a sledge drawn by an ox or ass) in which she had taken the
goods she possessed when she went to her husband's house. It also
means that her *amobr* was payable only once, no matter if she married again.

An interesting point is that if a Welsh wife found her husband
committing adultery, she was exempt from any legal penalty if jealousy caused her to attack him, his mistress, or even members of their
families, but the exemption was only for a period of three days from
the time of learning of her husband's affair. By that time, Welsh law
reasoned, the woman would have recovered from any shock which
would cause such 'irrational acts'. Anything that happened after that
was considered calculated vengeance.

RAPE

It is only in this century that many western societies have come to accept sexual harassment as something which should be regulated by law. Among the Celts it was already recognised. In Ireland the laws are clear, stating that compensation must be paid if a woman is kissed against her will, or if a man attempts to interfere with her clothing. The *Cáin Adomnáin* places the fine at ten ounces of silver if a man is found guilty of familiarly touching a woman or attempting to put his hand inside her clothing. If he, in fact, put his hand under her dress, the fine rose to seven *cumals* plus three ounces of silver.

And sexual harassment was not just confined to physical familiarity but also to verbal assaults. There are a wide range of verbal assaults listed, from mocking a woman's appearance, coining a nickname, being derisory about any physical defect, taunting, or repeating an untrue story about them. In all cases the person's honour price constituted the fine.

Rape, intercourse without consent, was also a punishable offence and early Irish law recognised two distinct types, although both carried the same penalties. In this recognition there is a parallel to early Hindu law. Firstly, there was forcible rape (*forcor*), a crime of a violent nature with possible physical injury to the victim. The second form was all other eventualities in which rape could occur, such as a seduction by stealth of a girl or woman who is intoxicated, asleep or has a disordered mind. This is called *sleth*, and often one finds *sleth* associated with intercourse with a drunken woman, which is regarded as just as serious as forcible rape.

There are listed in the law eight categories of women who get no redress, under law, if they claim to have been raped. Most of these are regarded as promiscuous or adulterous women. For example, a woman who makes an assignation to go to bed with a man and afterwards complains she did not consent, or a married woman who agrees to meet another man in secret. A married woman who went unaccompanied to an ale house sometimes received no compensation if it became clear that she went there for male companionship. There was also no redress for a woman who tried to conceal the fact that she had been raped. One law triad states 'three darknesses into which women should not go; the darkness of mist, the darkness of a forest, the darkness of night'. However, this is clearly not a statement of law but simply advice for there is no evidence that a woman raped under these circumstances was denied compensation.

One point of law is emphasised, that if a woman is assaulted in a town or near habitation, she is obliged to call for help, but does not have to do so if the assault occurs in an isolated spot.

In the *Cáin Lánamna*, listing nine types of sexual union, there is one to which I have briefly referred earlier as *lánamnas éicne no sláithe* or marriage by stealthful rape. This occurs when the family of a girl does not agree to her choice of suitor. Therefore, an elopement without consent was regarded, under law, as marriage by rape. However, in this case the woman consents to the union, although her kin does not. The result is that, unless there is a reconciliation with the woman's kin, the man is responsible for the rearing of any children from that marriage. It is a different concept from the Roman idea of marriage by capture and rape and the Sicilian method of acquiring a wife by rape, which was socially acceptable until recent times.

By the time that the Welsh law system came to be codified and then amended, there were obvious changes to original Celtic concepts. Rape was still regarded as a heinous crime but fell into two different classes, the rape of a virgin and the rape of a married woman. The attacker of a virgin had to pay any one of several specified fines to the girl involved but in addition he had to pay the *amobr* to the guardian of the girl and a fixed penalty (*dirwy*), usually twelve *kine* (cows) or £3, to the king's coffers. This last penalty was a recognition of the concept that the king was ultimately responsible for peace in the kingdom and infringement of it was an action against the king himself.

In the case of the rape of a married woman, the fine (*sarhaed*, or honour price) was payable only to the woman and her husband. The king did not receive any payment for the law was that a married woman was under the protection of her husband and not that of the king. However, this *sarhaed* was a particularly high one, with three augments since such a crime could give rise to kin enmity. Unless the *sarhaed* was agreed and paid, according to law, it was a blemish not only on the woman and her husband but upon her kin and they might take vengeance (*dial*).

In all cases the violence of rape was regarded, like any other assault, as an insult to the victim and the main fine or honour price was payable to her. One interesting point in the Welsh law relating to rape and related crimes is that no other section of the law texts preserves the old Celtic concepts of honour and shame so succinctly. At this time – the thirteenth century – sexual offences in western Christendom were generally under the jurisdiction of the Church but the Welsh texts seem singularly free from ecclesiastical influence. The Welsh legal terms clearly go back to a pre-Christian period.

In the text known as the *Cyfnerth Redaction* it is noted that if a man is found guilty of rape and cannot pay the necessary compensations 'let his testicles be taken'. This is the only reference to castration as a punishment. If a woman is raped and the man denies it and the woman says she was a virgin until the rape, the Welsh law says that it is proper to test whether she is telling the truth. The officer organising this test was the *edling*, a word obviously borrowed into Welsh at a later period from the Anglo-Saxon *aethling* or heir apparent. The older Welsh word for this office was *gwrthrychiad* and equivalent to *tanaiste*, now the word in modern Irish for Deputy Prime Minister. As in Irish law, women physicians had to carry out the examination to confirm whether the victim was a virgin and report to the officer in charge.

If a woman is raped and becomes pregnant, and does not know who the father is, she does not have to pay *amobr* to the lord, the reason being that her *amobr* is extinguished because the lord has not protected her from rape. A boy born through rape is adjudged according to his mother's family status unless it is discovered who the father was. A girl is also so adjudged. If the woman claims that her illegitimate child is the child of a particular man, and if her accusation is proved wrong, the law says she is not subsequently entitled to accuse any other man.

WOMEN AND CRIME

If an unmarried woman commits a crime or incurs debts then it is the responsibility of her kinfolk, her father, if alive. In the case of a married woman, the status of the marriage determines the person responsible. If, for example, she has been abducted then her abductor pays all fines and compensations.

Before the law courts, according to later ecclesiastical Irish law, 'the testimony of a woman is not accepted, just as the apostles did not accept the testimony of a woman about the resurrection of Christ'. The fact that the woman in that particular Bible story was correct in her testament was not considered in this text. However, this ecclesiastical law seems to contradict the older native law, where the evidence of women *is* accepted, as for example in the *Din Techtugad*. Indeed, a woman could take action at law on her own account and the *Senchus Mór* gives a list of many actions in which she could be involved. It also clearly states that 'though the law cedes headship to the man for his manhood and nobility, he has not the greater power of proof upon the woman on account of it . . .'

It is clear that a female witness giving evidence about ill-treatment or abuse carried greater weight before the courts. Female evidence is also regarded as conclusive in sexual matters. During cases where a man claims that he has been unable to consummate his marriage owing to a physical defect in his wife, she is examined by female physicians whose evidence is fully accepted. Similarly, if a woman claims her husband has not consummated the marriage when he claims he has, an examination by female physicians is again regarded as conclusive.

The *Din Techtugad* is an archaic text which includes an account of the Brehon named Sencha who made a wrong judgement about the methods by which a woman might claim her inheritance against opposition from other claimants. As previously mentioned, a female judge named Bríg Bruigaid, in some texts given as his wife, corrected his judgement. Women were not only accepted as plaintiffs and witnesses before the court, but could act as both judges (*breitheamh*) and advocates (*dálaigh*). It is interesting that Brígh's name means power, strength, authority and virtue. As another example, we hear of Darí of Connacht, a female Brehon who was the authoress of the *Cáin Darí*, a law, according to the *Annals of Ulster*, written in about 300AD. No text seems to have survived. Also, the text of the *Gúbretha Caratniat* (False Judgements of Caratniad) shows a female judge arguing points of law with a king.

WOMEN AS HOMICIDES

The Welsh law states, 'If it happens that a woman kills a person, let her be a homicide like a man.' That is, a woman is to be treated equally before the law. But further, 'If she has not goods which she can pay [the compensation and fines incurred] she is entitled to a *ceiniog paladr*.' This translates as a 'shaft penny', usually rendered as a 'spear penny', i.e. shaft of the spear. Thus the law recognised that the destitute woman had no protection (or spear) except her distaff (or femininity) and was entitled to a grant towards her fine.

In Irish law women also stood equal with men. Homicide was clearly divided into what would today be termed manslaughter and murder. The guilty woman, like her male counterpart, had to pay the *eneclann*, or honour price, and the body fine, *eric*-fine or *coirp dire*, usually of seven *cumals* for a freeman or woman (this varied downwards depending on the social status of the victim). The fines and compensation payments for murder were exactly double those for manslaughter. These are detailed in the *Book of Acaill*. Nevertheless, if no compensation was forthcoming, the victim's family could wreak physical vengeance on the perpetrator. But as Dr Joyce says: 'The idea of awarding death as a judicial punishment for homicide, even when it amounted to murder, does not seem to have ever taken hold of the public mind in Ireland.' Dubhthach Maccu Lugir (*fl.* AD430–50), Chief Brehon of Laoghaire the High King and one of the nine-man commission who compiled the *Senchus Mór*, says: 'At this day no one is put to death for their intentional crimes as long as *eric*-fine is obtained.'

We find it is Patrick who, according to the *Tripartite Life*, attempted to introduce capital punishment into Ireland. It seems that Patrick won over Dubhthach to Christianity and the Brehon later enthused: 'Let every one die who kills a human being.' And again: 'Every living person who inflicts death shall suffer death.' Dubhthach is doubtless echoing the views of Patrick, echoing the 'eye for an eye, tooth for a tooth' philosophy of Hebraic-Christianity. Yet one wonders when this conversion came about. Was it inserted by later Christian commentators to 'tidy' the texts? Certainly, execution did not become the norm until much later into the Christian period in Ireland.

Significantly, we find that the ecclesiastical law of Ireland laid more stress on the death penalty than did the native law system. Admittedly, *outside the native law courts*, arbitrary execution began to take place among the people and we find glosses talking about *crochad* and *riadgadh*, hanging by the neck. There is a chilling tale from the late eleventh century, *Aislinge Meic Conglinne*, in which Ainiér Mac Conglinne is sentenced to death by the abbot of Cork for complaining about poor hospitality in the guest house of the monastery. The sentence is not carried out but from the tale one deduces that an abbot seems to have absolute power of life and death. The *Annals of Ulster* record that in AD745/6 six men were hanged for attempting to rob the monastery of Downpatrick.

Can it be that we have, with the two law systems in operation – the native and ecclesiastical – two sets of punishment taking place in Ireland? If the transgressor fell into the hands of the ecclesiastics then he or she could expect physical punishment. If the delinquent came under the native Irish law system then the punishments were the fines and compensation that had to be secured.

There is an interesting aside on the death penalty when we find that in Waterford in 1537 complaints were being made about an Anglo-Irish widow, Lady Katherine Power (the name is usually given as de Paor). She had appointed to the local court an Irish judge named Shane McClaunaghe (Seán Mac Flannchadha). This Seán Mac Flannchadha is referred to in a tract of 1578 as a 'professor of the Brehon law to the Earl of Desmond' (*ollamh Iarla Desmumhan le breithemhnus d'écc*). The family name of the Desmonds was, of course, Butler. Lady Katherine, until her marriage to Lord Power of Waterford, had been a Butler. The complaint was that, under this judge and contrary to the Statutes of Kilkenny, Irish law was being used, by which a thief could expiate his crime by paying a fine. The complaint says that 'the lady Katherine suborneth the King's laws ... pardoning thieves by taking canes [*cáin*, fine] and letting felons at liberty.'

Another early mode of punishment, which occurs in many extreme cases where the *eric*-fine was not obtainable for homicide, is where the guilty woman was put in a boat without oars, sail or rudder and set adrift. The offence became *fuidir cinad o muir*, an offence of the sea. According to Professor Fergus Kelly: 'It seems likely to be a form of punishment introduced with Christianity and was evidently regarded as particularly suitable for dealing with serious crimes by women, no doubt from a general reluctance to put a woman to death by the direct methods of hanging or slaying.'

The *Cáin Adomnáin* undoubtedly proposes this method of punishment, particularly if a woman commits murder or arson, or breaks into a church: she is put into a boat with one paddle and a vessel of gruel, and set adrift on an offshore wind. If she is swept back to shore she becomes a *fuidhir*, or non-free person. The judgement is then left to God. The same punishment is listed elsewhere for those women who encompass death by *indeithbirw* (carelessness), *anfot* (negligence) and *fingal* (kin-slaying). Therefore, in spite of the intro-duction of the death penalty, there seems a distinct reluctance to carry it out, especially in respect of women.

The native laws, based as they were on compensation, did not mete out capital punishment. Punishments such as death, mutilation and flogging were introduced by Christianity. Professor Kelly's view is that all things progressive in Irish law were brought in by Christian-ity and so he states that it was 'the influence of the church which must have helped raise the status of women in early Irish society'. I would argue the reverse, that it was Christianity which accelerated the decline of the status of women in Celtic society under law. It was certainly the Church, in the text of the *Cáin Adomnáin*, which laid down heavy physical penalties for murder. Under these new Christian ideas, payment of compensation was rejected in favour of vengeance. A man who killed would be liable to have a hand and foot cut off and then be put to death while his kin paid a fine of seven *cumals*. Alternatively, depending on circumstances, if the perpetrator could pay fourteen *cumals* and spend fourteen years without civil rights, he escaped death and mutilation. The principle now was that the more you were able to pay, the less punishment you received, unlike the native fixed sum of reparation.

Indeed, it is also when we come to the *Cáin Adomnáin* that the law starts to talk of mutilation as a punishment. Again, while there is no sign of flogging as a punishment under the native Irish law texts, it does appear in canon law. Fines for injuries to women and by women were equally severe under the new ecclesiastical laws. But there is no evidence that these new laws, enacted mostly in the seventh century, were ever put into general practice. The old tried and trusted concepts of fixed sums of compensation to the injured continued to be the basis of Irish law rather than mere physical retribution.

The main punishment under native Irish law for a wide variety of criminal or anti-social crimes for both men and women was a loss of civil rights or outlawry. This loss of rights or outlawry was not permanent and it is quite clear that the man or woman could regain their rights after due time and payment of compensation or other restitution. Compensation for the victim and rehabilitation for the perpetrator rather than Old Testament vengeance seemed a better basis of justice.

PROSTITUTION

It is curious how few, if any, historians have come to terms with the practice of prostitution in early Celtic society. The granting of sexual access for payment is an institution whose origins are lost in the mists of prehistory. Prostitution usually flourishes in societies where the role of women is constricted, specifically restricted economically. A society which demands chastity and segregated confinement for one section of its female population usually demands the opposite from another section. This was especially true of ancient Greece where Athens was renowned for its prostitutes and brothels. According to Athenaeus of Naucratis, Nicander of Colophon, the famous didactic poet of the seventh century BC and author of such works as the *Georgica*, built a temple to Aphrodite on the earnings he made from keeping brothels. Even the great Greek reformer, politician and writer Solon (*c.*640 to after 561BC) is reported by Philomenon to have erected public brothels in Athens. Strabo (64BC–AD24) in his *Geography*, speaking of prostitution in Corinth, says: 'The city drew crowds of visitors and grew rich; sailors were especially prone to ruin themselves there.'

In Rome, prostitution was a legalised institution but marriages between freemen and former prostitutes were strictly forbidden.

Some writers have claimed that there was no institution of prostitution among the early Celts because the Irish word for a prostitute is *meirdrech*, a loan word from the Latin *meretrix*, by which Cicero describes public prostitutes; while the medieval Welsh word *putain* is clearly borrowed from the Norman French.

It does seem likely that in the pre-Christian society of the Celts, because of the more liberal sexual attitudes displayed in that society, there would have been little need to purchase sexual favours from women: polygamy was practised, together with concubinage, and there was freedom of divorce on both sides. This is, of course, a subject open to argument. But Peter R. Cherici suggests:

The Celts, however, had no need of the prostitute. If a man or woman desired more sex than their present partner could offer, they could easily take another lover. Although the Celts exchanged sex for power, the notion of men paying women to experience sex for its own sake was alien to them.

The trend of the native law systems was certainly to sanction a wide array of human sexual behaviour. The canon law introduced by Christianity denied this freedom of behaviour and attempted to introduce 'ideal patterns' which the new dogma decreed. These patterns were borrowed from Greek and Roman concepts; they were more rooted in an 'idealised' society than in reality, and initially found little currency among the Celts, specifically the Irish. The ecclesiastical system initially confined itself to the religious communities. Then its dogmas began to spread outside the religious establishments and influence the general public. The people found themselves living under parallel legal systems that were opposed in their respective views of sexuality.

Canon law was quick to seize on the fact that Irish women could own property. The text known as the *Cáin Díre* had this interesting sentence: '*Cach ben nad-faccaib cin na ciniud na soethar i tóaith, is meise torad a da llám do chor fri eclaise*', 'Every woman who does not leave liability to fines nor offspring to be supported nor any other trouble among her people is entitled to leave the fruit of her two hands to the Church.' In other words, no legal obstruction was placed in the way of women leaving their entire property to the Church.

I would take the view that as Celtic society became more restrictive over the role of women, whether this was due, as seems evident, simply to the incoming of Christianity or, as Mary Condren believes, to a process begun in pagan Celtic society, the market for prostitution increased. It is clear, in Welsh law, that there were prostitutes at the time that the laws were codified and the usual phrase to describe them was *gwraig llwyn a pherth*, 'woman of bush and brake'. Again, it has been pointed out that this term had its equivalent in Anglo-Saxon and Low German – *busk unde brake* – and that the concept is obviously not native.

In Irish law *meirdrech* and *meirdrechas* were, however, not the only terms for a prostitute and prostitution. Incidentally, the ninth-century St Gall *Priscian Grammar* has a gloss by an Irish scribe which gives *meirdrech-loc* as the word for a brothel, *loc* in this sense meaning a dwelling-place. So brothels had been established by the ninth century. But an even earlier word for a prostitute does occur in legal Irish: *echlach*. This word, which seems to derive from the same word as messenger, courier and servant, appears to be used most often. Then there are several euphemisms such as *bé-carna* (woman of flesh), *bé-táide* (woman of secrets) and *baitsech*, a curious word which is glossed in a few places as meaning *bé-táide*. From the context of the laws these last two terms (*bé-táide* and *baitsech*) more often refer to a woman who is engaged in illicit sexual relations than to a prostitute – that is, women who are having affairs with married men or having children by them. The word *táide* has a variety of meanings: secrecy, stealth, hiding or concealment. A *bé-táide* is given in law not only as an adulteress but sometimes as a concubine, a woman who cohabits without being married. The laws refer to *clann táidhe* as 'illegitimate children'.

There are several other words that occur in the Irish law texts applying to prostitution: *striopach*, for example, with its offshoots of *striopachas* and *striopamail*, which is again an obvious Latin loan-word from *stuprum*, 'pollution by lust', debauchery, ravishing. *Cormac's Glossary* has several words such as *giabur*, which O Cléirigh later glosses as *giabhair*; he gives *lót* and *lótrad* in the phrase 'whoredom is destruction for a woman'. There is the word *partchuine*, or *portcheine*, a place of assignation, which then turns up as a euphemism for a prostitute. Finally, Cormac mentions *druth* which also means an unchaste woman or a wanton. It is fascinating that at this time Irish astrologers referred to Venus as '*planed na ndaoine óg ndruith*', 'planet of wanton young people'. O'Davoren's sixteenth-century Glossary also gives the word *traill*, as a drudge, trull or harlot. The word seems to be a Germanic loan-word from *thrall* meaning a slave. As trull, meaning a low prostitute, the word only entered the English language in the early sixteenth century. Therefore, O'Davoren was recording a new word in Irish rather than an old Irish term. To *traill* seems to have also taken the meaning of 'kneading dough'.

It becomes clear, from all these terms and euphemisms, that prostitution, as in all other societies, did exist in the early Christian period. So how did prostitutes fare under the law? Irish law, in fact, seems harsher to the prostitute than Welsh law. Under Irish law, according to the *Corpus Iuris Hibernica*, a prostitute was not entitled to an honour price, and if she had children then she, and she alone, was responsible for their upbringing. She could claim nothing from the father. If she was raped or even abducted, no punishment was inflicted on the perpetrator and no compensation was usually payable. It appears that this might have been modified at a later date for a gloss says: '*bean is meirdreach itir imat na muine i leth enelcann fagbas fris iar fo-eigem*', 'a woman who is a prostitute among the bushes, half-honour price is left to her after she cries out'. In other words, if a prostitute is raped and charges rape and it is proved, she will receive compensation of half her honour price, presumably that which was bestowed on her at maturity.

A prostitute could not acquire property through marriage or cohabitation and, unlike other women, if a profit had come through her work within such a union, she had no claim to a share of it. There was no division of property with the man when the relationship ended. The law states: 'The *echlach* women, an unlawful contract, without a word: they are not given a bride-price [*coibche*] unless they come under the law.' It is obvious that if the prostitute 'comes under the law', presumably renounces her previous way of life, and sets up as a married woman, her *coibche* is a small one. The law states: 'An excessive *coibche* to a prostitute is an unlawful contract, and such has no binding effect.'

The fragmentary text on inheritance, *Maccshléchta*, says that the prostitute's son cannot claim an inheritance of land from the father. 'If his mother is dead, and there is admission [by the father] of connection with her, the father gives seven *cumal* for reception [to the clan] and each *cumal* has the force of an oath [swearing his paternity]. If there be admission of paternity, the father swears by seven graveyards.'

In a legal sense, it appears that a prostitute could not give evidence against anyone, according to the *Derrad Airechta*. The point is further emphasised in the ruling on the inadmissibility of hearsay evidence. 'Everyone's hearing is a prostitute [*bé-carna*] so that a report which is heard is invalid, whether the matter concerning which the report is heard be true or untrue.'

Dr Joyce points out that *Cormac's Glossary* derived one of the words for a prostitute, *druth*, from *dir*, 'right' and *aod*, 'fire' – 'as much as saying to burn her were right'. Dr Joyce believes, contrary to the evidence of the law texts, that it was a very ancient Irish custom to burn women for adultery. He cites the story of Corc Mac Luigdech, the legendary founder of the kingdom of Cashel, in the *Leabhar na Nuachonghbhala* or *Book of Leinster*, compiled in about 1150. Corc Mac Luigdech says that 'it was the custom at first to burn any woman who committed lust (*dognid bais*) in violation of her compact'. I am not sure why Dr Joyce places *dognid bais* after the word 'lust' for *do-gni* means 'I do, make, cause, approach, consider, etc.' while *báis* means 'death'. Even so this statement, on face value, seems totally contrary to the evidence of both law and custom. From the same book comes a quotation, but from a Greek princess: 'My crime of unchastity will now be found out, and I shall be burned immediately.' The only other evidence Dr Joyce can offer is the story of Murna and Cumal. After Murna eloped with Cumal and became pregnant, and Cumal was killed, her father, not recognising the legality of her marriage, urged his people to burn her. As much as I admire Dr Joyce's work, I believe that he is in error and that this was not an ancient Irish custom but an idea which only permeated Irish literature in the medieval period.

However, it is obvious, from the foregoing, that prostitutes did not have any agreeable position under Irish law. In fact, the general attitude to prostitution seems summed up in the phrase of Cormac Mac Cuileannáin: 'Whoredom is the destruction of women.' In Wales they seemed to fare only slightly better. In fact, if a prostitute had a child and could identify the father, the father was responsible for its upbringing. 'If it happens that a person makes pregnant a woman of bush and brake [*gwraig llwyn a pherth*] it is right for him to maintain the child; for the law says that though she may lose the man, it is not right for her to suffer want from him or because of him, though she gets no benefit, and therefore it is right for the man to rear the child.'

Apart from that the law is also very clear. 'A prostitute has no status. Though she be raped, she is not entitled to receive compensation.' There then seems a contrary addition in that compensation becomes payable if the prostitute suffers insult (*sarhaed*), presumably not the insult of rape. The *sarhaed* has to be paid according to the status of her brother and if the prostitute is killed then the compensation for the homicide, or her *galanas*, is also fixed on the status of the brother and not on her 'non-status'.

Prostitution had certainly begun to flourish under the Normans after their conquest of England. Every main centre in England boasted its brothel, usually run under the protection of a noble, an abbot or a bishop, who took a percentage of the earnings. Usually, the brothel was leased to overseers from the laity to avoid charges of impropriety against the clergy. Henry II had to issue a law to regulate these brothels and forbid the employment of nuns or pregnant women in them. Such brothels were also to be found initially in Dublin, Wexford and other centres of Anglo-Norman administration. By the fourteenth century, R. Gillespie writes in *Women and Crime in Seventeenth-Century Ireland*, 'the female operated *meird-rech-loc* was quite common in Ireland at which clients could purchase food, drink and a sexual romp with a woman.'

Peter R. Cherici comments:

> The existence of formal prostitution reflected the diminished status of women in feudal society. Few avenues for financial gain were open to women born without wealth or position. Men regarded women of the lower classes as drudges, camp followers and whores, as lesser beings whose sole purpose of existence was to serve. Prostitution became one of the only viable means for women to earn a living without backbreaking labour.

From these two law systems we can, therefore, obtain a fairly clear picture of a woman's life in Celtic society from the fifth century to the medieval period. We can also use them to help us put more detail on the sketches which the Greeks and Romans have left us about pre-Christian Celtic society. No serious commentator can argue that Celtic women lived in a socially liberated paradise. On the other hand, the society they lived in was a truly remarkable one and women enjoyed considerable freedoms compared to their Greek and Roman sisters, not to mention the women of the restrictive, militaristic Anglo-Saxon culture.

[6]

Women in the Celtic Church

WHEN the Celts began to accept Christianity, Celtic women, as they had been in pagan times, were equal with men in preaching religion. As Brendan Lehane admits in *Early Celtic Christianity*, 'Women could play as great a part as men in the new religion and did.' There is even evidence that they were able to perform Mass and give the sacrament. In fact, three Roman bishops at Tours wrote an outraged letter to two Breton priests, Lovocat and Catihern, *c.*AD515–20, calling on them to refuse to allow women to celebrate Mass. 'You celebrate the divine sacrifice of the Mass with the assistance of women to whom you give the name *conhospitae*. While you distribute the Eucharist, they take the chalice and administer the blood of Christ to the people . . . Renounce these abuses . . . !' We are told, however, that both Brigid of Kildare and Beoferlic (St Beverley of York) of the Celtic Church in Northumbria were ordained not simply as priests but as bishops as well.

The evidence from the early Christian movement in all the Celtic countries is that women played a prominent role in converting the Celtic peoples to the new faith. Certainly, women were foremost in debating the new religion and the social implications of its theology. Professor James Carney, in *Medieval Irish Lyrics and the Irish Bardic Poet*, notices and translates an interesting dialogue between Patrick and a lady called Ethne who wants to know more about the religion. Ethne puts these questions to Patrick.

> Who is God and where is He?
> Of whom is He and where does He dwell?
> Has He sons and daughters?
> Is he rich, this God of yours?

Is He Ever-Living and beautiful,
Was His Son fostered by many?

Are His daughters beautiful
To the men of this world?
Is He in the Otherworld
Or in this one?
Is He in the sea, the rivers
Or in the mountains or valleys?

Speak to me of Him and tell me
How will I know Him?
How can He be approached?
Can He be loved?
Is it in my youth or in old age
That I will find Him?

Ethne was, of course, one of the two daughters of the Irish High King Laoghaire (or Loéguire mac Néill, AD428–c.463). His other daughter was Fidelma. They had both been educated (fostered) by the Druids Caplait and Mael and therefore, with their religious background, were probably more interested than most in what Patrick had to say. The story of their conversion appears in Bishop Tirechán's seventh-century *Life of Patrick*, preserved in the *Book of Armagh*, compiled by Feardomhnach in about AD807. Feardomhnach says that the two sisters had come to Clébac, near Tulsk, Co. Roscommon, 'as is the women's custom, to wash in the morning'. Ethne and Fidelma were converted, after their discourse with Patrick; then Caplait and Mael arrived and after further discussion they, too, were converts to the new faith.

A study of the role of women in the early Celtic Church has yet to be written. Most of the surviving lives of these influential ladies date from a period where the woman's role had been diminished by the influence of Rome and later histories merely show them in the traditional Roman position as subservient to male saints and clerics. Dom Louis Gougard, for example, in his otherwise excellent study, seems to go out of his way to argue that women were not equal with men and that there was strict celibacy among the Celtic *religieux*. When faced with evidence of the *conhospitae* or mixed houses of men and women, who were raising their children in the service of

God, he makes the extraordinary claim that these houses were peopled by male ascetics who lived with women as an experiment to test their sexual strength, rather like self-mortification.

Certainly, there is some evidence to support the idea that a few ascetic monks practised this, although the evidence comes from a later period when Roman ideas were finding more currency. Oengus (*fl.* AD800–50), in his famous *Féilire*, more popularly known as the 'Martyrology', talks of St Scoithíne (the name comes from *scoth*, meaning blossom), who has become known for his austerity and asceticism. He is not to be confused with Scoithíne, a well-known abbot of Durrow, d. AD950. In the text there is also a reference to Brenáinn. There are seventeen saints who bear this name, popularly rendered as Brendan, 'a prince'. The writer does not make clear which one he means, although it has been generally accepted that the popular Brendan the Navigator was the monk in question. Oengus records his story as follows:

Two young, attractive girls used to sleep with Scoithíne every night so that his conflict with the Devil might be that much greater. Hearing the news, Brenáinn came to him in order to accuse him of fornication. Scoithíne decided that night to demonstrate his test.

When the time came for repose and Brenáinn had gone to his *cubiculum*, Scoithíne sent the two young maidens to him. They went to his room, bearing wood for the fire, but then climbed into bed with him. 'What are you doing?' demanded the cleric. 'We do this every night with Scoithíne,' they assured him. But Brenáinn could not settle to sleep for the longing of the flesh. The girls said: 'Scoithíne lies with us and feels nothing at all. Either you must do what you must or get into a tub of cold water.' Brenáinn climbed out of the bed, mortified. 'This is a wrong test for Scoithíne has better control than me.'

Oengus says of Brenáinn and Scoithíne: 'Thereafter they made a union and an understanding and parted in happiness.' Scoithíne, presumably, resumed sleeping with his two young female companions.

Another argument Dom Gougaud makes is that the 'marriages' among early Celtic *religieux* were no more than the practice of *syneisactum* or having 'spiritual marriages' by which *religieux* of different sexes 'married' or became 'soul friends'. It was a practice banned in other areas by the decisions of the Council of Nicaea. But in attempting to find alternative explanations for the mixed houses and married *religieux* one suspects that Dom Gougaud 'protests too much'. In desperation to dismiss the subject, Dom Gougaud says: 'The references to sons or wives of priests or bishops which we meet in subsequent insular texts cannot furnish any argument against the law of ecclesiastical celibacy.' Why? He does not elucidate.

Patrick himself was the son of a British Celtic deacon of the Church, Calpurnius, and the grandson of a priest, Potitus. In his writings, he twice refers to the large number of women working in the early movement. Perhaps Brigid, the 'Mary of the Gael', became the best known, but we also have Darerca, the foundress of Killery near Armagh. She is said to have been the daughter of Mochta, a British Celt and an early disciple of Patrick, or the daughter of an Irish chieftain from the Co. Louth area. She is not to be confused with the Darerca who was said to be one of Patrick's five sisters nor the Darerca who was the mother of Ciarán of Clonmacnoise nor the mother of Mel of Longford. The name 'Dar Erca', meaning daughter of the hero Erc, was popular at this period and so we have a confusion of four 'saints' of the time bearing the name. The term 'saint' as used in the early Celtic Church did not mean that the person was canonised; it was the custom to call all missionaries and teachers 'saints', a distinction to show that they were women and men of eminent virtue.

Darerca of Killeavy was born in Magh Coba in north-western Co. Down among the clan Conaill. She was baptised as a Christian by Patrick himself. Patrick asked her to take charge of teaching women converts and her first group consisted of nine women, one of whom was a widow who had a small boy named Luger. We are told that Darerca fostered the boy and he grew up to be a bishop and founded a church at Rúscaigh (Rooskey, Cooley, Co. Louth).

Darerca and her converts journeyed through Ireland and eventually visited Brigid at her foundation at Kildare. Darerca was obviously impressed with Brigid's organisation. After staying with Brigid 'she went to the bishop Ibhair, who had converted Brigid to the faith, and Darerca lived under his direction in Ard Conais'. Ard Conais is an unidentified site but possibly near Wexford. There were many women, widows, former queens and others, who lived at Ibhair's foundation and Darerca became their abbess. After a while, she returned to Co. Down to be with her family. Then she moved on and went to live on the slopes of Faughart, Co. Louth, for a while, and then to Slieve Gullion, Co. Armagh, before founding a new abbey at Cill Shléibhe (Church of the Mountain), Killeavy, Co. Armagh.

Her hagiography, which survives in the *Salamanca Codex*, is, of course, full of reputed miracles performed by Darerca. But there are some interesting points in her story demonstrating the realities of life at this period and Darerca's exceptional organisational abilities. At one point she decided to send Brígnat, one of her most promising pupils, to Ninian's famous monastery at Rosnat, Candida Casa (White House), now called Whithorn, in Galloway, Scotland, to be instructed in the rules there. This shows that Whithorn, during Ninian's time, was also a mixed community.

Darerca's foundation was instrumental in bringing the new faith to the plains of Muirtheimne, to Cuailgne and Cobha, where the legendary hero Cúchulainn fought with the warriors of Medb. Even the king 'Eugenius', son of Conaille, and doubtless a relative, came to her abbey to seek favours. When she died Bia took over as abbess, then Indiu and then Derlasra, who remained abbess for forty years. Killeavy was one of the most influential religious centres during the first century of Christianity in Ireland. Darerca is without doubt one of the most important influential female advocates for the new religion at the time of Patrick.

However the most famous was undoubtedly Brigid (or Brigit) of Kildare (*c.*AD455–*c.*525). The cultus of Brigid spread far beyond her native land where she was revered as 'Mary of the Gael'. According to the *Rennes Dinnsenchus*, Brigid was a *ban-druí*, a female Druid, before she converted to Christianity. She was born at Faughart, near Newry, Co. Down, where her father was a Druid named Dubhtach and where Darerca lived and taught for a while. Her birth and upbringing, according to later hagiographies, were steeped in Druidical symbolism. Her mother, Broiseach, is given by a ninth-century hagiographer as being a bondservant of Dubhtach. She is said to have been sold by him to a Druid named Maithghean. But Maithghean sent her back to Dubhtach after Broiseach bore her child, named after the Celtic goddess of fertility of whom we have already spoken. This goddess was a daughter of The Dagda, the Father of the Gods, and a divinity of healing, poetry, arts and crafts.

We are told that Brigid studied under Bishop Ibhair. He had prophesied that the Virgin Mary would appear in his church. On the appointed day, as he and his followers anxiously awaited the fulfilment of the prophecy, Brigid walked in. To save his reputation as a prophet, Ibhair hailed her as 'Mary of the Gael'. This humorous tale seems quite believable. Brigid converted to Christianity and started to give away her father's goods to the needy. When she gave away his sword to a beggar, her father decided to place her as a bondservant to the king of Leinster with the idea of eventually marrying her off to the king. The king was not interested but some time later a suitor for her hand in marriage emerged. We are told Brigid, to dissuade the young man's ardour, thrust a finger into her eye, pulling it from the socket until it dangled on her cheek. Appalled, the suitor beat a hasty retreat. 'Celtic women', observes Peter R. Cherici, 'did not shy from extreme measures to avoid a demanding suitor.'

She left the king of Leinster's service and studied under Mel, the bishop of Ardagh, who was in fact the son of Darerca, the sister of Patrick. Mel had already been rebuked by his uncle for living with a *religieuse*. Whether this indicates that Patrick personally disapproved of such relationships or whether it was tacked on to the story for later sensibilities is unclear. As we have already pointed out, such relationships were common enough not to arouse much criticism. Mel's sister, Lallóc, another early 'saint', was also living with a *religieux* named Sétna. According to one intriguing reference, Mel not only ordained Brigid as a priest but conferred on her an episcopal title – that is, she was ordained as a bishop. The reference occurs in the *Hymn to Brigid* written at the beginning of the seventh century by St Broccan Cloen (d. 653) at the request of Ultan of Armagh. The hymn survives in an eleventh-century copy. The reference goes further and says that 'hence Brigid's successor is always entitled to have episcopal orders and the honour due to a bishop.' Brigid was not the only female bishop. Hilda at Whitby, who adhered to Celtic customs in spite of the results of the famous Synod held in her abbey in AD664, was succeeded by Beoferlic (St Beverley of York), who, like Hilda, was also raised in the Celtic traditions. She is also recorded as being ordained as a bishop. It was not until the twelfth century that the abbesses of Kildare had the dignity and honours of a bishop removed from their titles.

Brigid's first recorded community was at Drumcree (Druim Criadh, the ridge of clay) overlooking the plain of the Liffey and, significantly, under the shadow of a high oak, sacred in pre-Christian Celtic religion. Her foundation at Kildare was also based on oak symbolism, 'the church of the oaks'. Only six miles away was the famous pagan fortress of Dún Ailinne. Second only to Emain Macha in the north, Dún Ailinne was named after the daughter of Laoghaire Mac Fergus Fairge, son of the king of Leinster, who fell in love with Baile, son of Buain, heir to the kingdom of Ulster. But Leinster and Ulster were deadly enemies. When Ailinn and Baile arranged to meet, Baile reached the spot first. A stranger told him that the warriors of Leinster had discovered Ailinn's secret and killed her. Baile died from a broken heart. The stranger then went to Ailinn and gave her news of Baile's death. She, too, died of grief. From the graves of the two doomed lovers grew a yew from Baile and an apple tree from Ailinn. The poets of Leinster and Ulster cut the branches of the trees and inscribed this prototype *Romeo and Juliet* on them in Ogham. The wands were then placed in one of the *Tech Screpta* or libraries in the time of Art the Lonely (c.AD220–50). The story goes that when the wands were placed there they sprang together and could not be separated. Doubtless, the community of Kildare knew the tragic tale. Dún Ailinne was once capital of the kingdom of Leinster, enclosing thirteen hectares, and traces of its occupation have been dated from 390BC to AD320, so it had fallen into disuse by the time Brigid founded her community at Kildare.

The evidence of Cogitosus, a monk of Brigid's community, writing his *Life of Brigid* in AD650, scarcely a hundred years after Brigid died, makes it abundantly clear that she ruled a mixed community of men and women. Some might even speculate on the relationship between Brigid and Conlaed, the bishop, whom she had persuaded to join her in running her community. The question whether Conlaed might have been her lover is not as outrageous in the context of what was happening during this period as it seems to be today.

According to Peter R. Cherici, speaking of the character of Brigid which emerged in later clerical writings:

Brigid was largely the creation of Christian male celibates who controlled access to literacy in the Celtic lands. She reflected their values and their views of the feminine ideal. As with Mary, they moulded Brigid into a model for how Christian women should act, not how they did act. And a portrait emerged of a woman who believed that marriage was a horror worse than disfigurement and blindness.

While we might speculate on her relationship with Conlaed, we seem to be left in little doubt that Brigid had a lesbian relationship with another member of her community. She certainly shared her bed at Kildare with Darlughdacha, whose name means 'daughter of the sun god Lugh'. It is recorded that once Darlughdacha had the temerity to look appraisingly at a passing young warrior. As a punishment, Brigid made her walk in shoes filled with hot coals. As Darlughdacha became Brigid's successor as abbess at Kildare, one presumes that, after this penance, she dutifully returned to Brigid's bed. One could also argue that Brigid's sexual inclinations become clear in that she had maimed herself rather than marry a male but was content to share her bed with a female over whom she displayed signs of intense jealousy.

It was her biographer, Cogitosus, who mixed various motifs of the goddess Brigid with those of the saint of Kildare. It was not until later that Brigid was claimed to be the initiator and abbess of the first women's religious community in Ireland. This is, of course, an absolute myth. Kildare was a mixed house and there had been other similar foundations in existence before Kildare. When she died, Brigid was buried in Kildare but, during the Viking raids of the ninth century, her relics were removed for safety to Downpatrick, Co. Down, and reburied. Her cultus spread throughout the Christian world. In Wales, for example, Brigid's name was transformed into St Ffraid.

There were in fact, in these early centuries in Ireland, no fewer than fifteen women named Brigid who became 'saints' of the early Church. One other famous Brigid of the sixth century was the daughter of Cú Cathrach, whose church was on the banks of the Shannon. Her story was that she was in love with Senán of Inis Cathaig (Scattery Island) in the Shannon estuary. He did not return her love and forbade any woman to land on his island. Not daunted by this proscription, Brigid is said to have sent gifts to the man floating on little rafts. The stories about him suggest Senán to be a man of complex character. He is said to have studied in Wales with Dewi Sant.

As we have emphasised, Brigid's foundation in Kildare was clearly a mixed house which was not unusual in the Celtic world. As Celtic Christianity spread into the Anglo-Saxon kingdoms — and be it remembered that it was Irish missionaries who first converted the ancestors of the 'English', bringing them literacy and learning — the idea of mixed houses was accepted. Hilda, the famous abbess of Whitby (Streoneshalh), ran a mixed community. Hilda was the patroness of Caedmon (d. AD680), who was a member of her community, the earliest known 'English' poet.

Another Northumbrian abbess ran a famous mixed community during this time. Aebbe, the sister of King Oswald of Northumbria, had, like her brothers, been taken as a child to Iona after their father Aethelfrith had been killed. Here they were brought up by Irish *religieux* and converted to Christianity. When Aebbe returned to Northumbria, *c.*AD634, she founded a community at Coldingham, which stood on St Abb's headland, a place-name which preserves Aebbe's name. The mixed community stood for fifty years but the ascetic Adomnán criticised its dubious reputation. He wrote that 'the cells that were built for prayer and for reading have become haunts of feasting, drinking, gossip and other delights; even the virgins who are dedicated to God . . . spend their time weaving elaborate garments with which to adorn themselves as if they were brides, thus imperilling their virginity, or else to make friends with strange men'. A mysterious fire caused the monastery to be destroyed in AD686, a few years after Aebbe's death; this was promptly declared by Roman clerics to be a punishment for the debauched lifestyle of the community.

Mixed monasteries were found throughout the Celtic world at this time. In Gaul an Irish woman, Ita, not to be confused with Idé or Ita of Kileedy, married Pepin of Landen and they established a mixed community at Nivelles. St Ita had two daughters, St Gertrude and St Begga. St Begga married St Arnulf of Metz becoming the mother of St Pepin of Herstal, thus demonstrating that it was perfectly in order for the *religieux* of the time to marry. St Gertrude (AD626–59) took over as abbess at Nivelles and particularly encouraged the settlement of Irish *religieux* in her community. In fact, it was Ita who gave Foillan, the brother of Fursa and Ultan, some land near Nivelles, at Fosses, where he established another community and became abbot. Foillan, Fursa and Ultan had already played a leading part in converting the East Angles to Christianity. When Foillan was returning from a visit to Gertrude at Nivelles he was set upon by robbers in the forest of Seneffe and murdered. His body was not found until three months later. His brother Ultan took over as abbot.

The mixed communities founded by St Salaberga and St Burgundofara in Gaul were also influenced by Celtic ideas. Burgundofara was the sister of Faro (d. AD672) and Cagnoald (d. AD635). The brothers and their sister seem to have studied under the Irish missionary Columbanus, the former monk of Bangor, Co.

Down, at his community at Luxeuil. Burgundofara then established her own mixed house called Faremoutiers, 'the place of Fara's family' (from the Celtic word, *muinntir*).

It is of interest that three years after Leinster-born Columbanus died at his final foundation of Bobbio in Italy in AD615, a young monk named Jonas entered the abbey and wrote a life of the Irish monk. Throughout his work he portrayed Columbanus as a man tormented by sexual desires. Jonas was able to get first-hand information from many of the monk's surviving friends and colleagues. He recounts one story of Columbanus as a young man studying under an Irish *religieuse*. This woman convinced him to forsake all women although the desires of his intellect could not control the desires of his body. 'The old enemy aroused against him the lusts of lascivious maidens, especially of those whose fine figures and superficial beauties are wont to enkindle mad desires in the minds of wretched men.' Alas, we do not know who this Irish woman was who persuaded Columbanus, and doubtless others, both male and female, to suppress their natural feelings. We know it left Columbanus in a conflict about women for he wrote in a poem:

> Let everyone who is dutiful in mind avoid the deadly poison
> That the proud tongue of an evil woman has.
> Woman [Eve] destroyed life's gathered crown:
> But woman [Mary] gave long-lasting joys of life.

Undoubtedly, the third most influential female Irish saint of this early period was Idé, more popularly known as Ita, but not to be confused with Ita of Nivelles. This Ita died *c.*AD570. Oengus calls her 'the bright sun of the women of Munster'. She was, according to the chronicles, a daughter of Fáelan, king of the Dési. Her sister was Nessa, the mother of St Mo Cháemmoc. Idé established a community in Limerick at a place which is still called after her – Kileedy, Cill-Idé or the church of Idé or Ita. She opened an ecclesiastical school here and among her more famous pupils was Brendan the Voyager (*c.*AD486–578). Significantly, like the Druids, she taught in triads and the main philosophy of her school was:

> Faith in God with purity of heart,
> Simplicity of Life with religion,
> Generosity with love.

The fact that Brendan studied at her community points to its being a mixed house. As already stated, Dom Louis Gougaud tries to justify the mixed houses by saying that they were tests of religious celibacy. He admits their existence in disapproving terms, stating that 'the association of the sexes in monasticism was contrary to the discipline of Irish saints of the second order (second half of the sixth century)'. During this period, as the Roman ideas began to dominate the Celtic Church, the *conhospitae* or mixed houses began to vanish. But not without a struggle.

There is evidence that mixed houses and a non-celibate clergy lasted in Wales even until the Reformation. The Church there, as in other Celtic lands, was based on the clan system and was monastic. These monasteries were organised on a *clas* or family community basis. Members of the community were often related; wives and husbands brought their children up in the service of the religion. In the thirteenth-century *Brut y Tywysogion* (The Chronicle of the Princes) we find that in AD961 the hierarchy attempted to introduce a rule that the priests under the jurisdiction of Llandaff were not to marry without the specific permission of the Pope. When the rule was introduced in the diocese of Teilo there was such a reaction from the clergy that it was agreed that they could continue to marry without such permission. But the attempts to introduce celibacy were increasing and in the Welsh law system (of the tenth century) we find that the son of a priest born after his father had entered holy orders could be deprived of his paternal inheritance. Willis Bund, in his *The Celtic Church of Wales*, gives evidence to demonstrate that clerical marriages continued and that such marriages were regarded as perfectly lawful. Even Dom Gougaud has to concede: 'We admit that in the eleventh and twelfth centuries there set in a sad lowering of the standard of clerical morality in Brittany, Wales and Scotland . . .' In fact, the standard had never been changed. The Celts of these countries simply continued with their own non-celibate practices.

Giraldus Cambrensis mentions several instances of sexual behaviour among the Welsh and Irish clergy which he thought 'scandalous'.

Wales, too, had its fair share of influential women in the early Church movement. We have mentioned the work of Elen and her family in Britain just before the ancestors of the English began to invade and carve out the land that now bears their name. After Elen in importance came Non, or Nonna, from Dyfed, whose life and work have been almost eclipsed by her son, Dewi Sant, popularly St David, the patron saint of Wales. One wonders if there was a tendency among medieval hagiographers to play up the work of the sons of these early female 'saints'. Efrddyl and Tudful, of Merthyr Tydfil, remain fairly shadowy figures yet it is obvious from references that they were powerful personalities. Tudful lived in the late fifth century and was said to be one of the daughters of Brychan Brycheiniog, a king of Powys. According to folk tradition, recounted by Charles Wilkins in *Tales and Sketches of Wales* (1879), Tudful was killed by Picts while returning from a visit to her sister Tangwystl whose community was five miles from Merthyr Tydfil. But the traditions recording her martyrdom are very late and it has been pointed out that the word *merthyr* has a meaning of 'memorial' nor 'martyr' – this form is found in Merthyr Cynog in Brecon.

Dwynwen, said to be another of Brychan's daughters, is considered as the patron saint of lovers in Wales. She is obviously the same person as Adwen who in Cornish tradition takes this role and is also recorded as one of Brychan's twenty-four children. The stories later attached to her include one in which she was in love with a youth named Maelon but rejected his sexual advances. God appeared to her and offered her a sweet drink which caused her love for Maelon to be dispelled and which, when tasted by Maelon, turned him into ice. However, both Dwynwen and God relented and Maelon was revived while Dwynwen became patron saint of lovers but never married. There are also traditions associated with her in Anglesey as well as Glamorgan.

The work of Gwladus, and her husband Gwynllyw, at Snow Hill, Newport (Monmouth), is overshadowed by that of their son Cadoc, one of the more influential male 'saints' of Wales who founded the monastery at Llancarfan. But another interesting sixth-century female saint seems to be an Irish princess who fled to Wales to escape the unwanted attentions of a chieftain who wanted to marry her. This was a lady called Melangell. She arrived in Powys and taught the new religion. One day she encountered Brochfael Ysgithrog, prince of Powys, out hunting. His quarry was a hare and Melangell is said to have picked up the hare and hidden it in her robes. The prince was so impressed by her serenity, beauty and actions that he gave her lands around what became known as Pennant Melangell (Montgomery) where she formed her community. She became the patron saint of all small creatures and the local name for a hare for centuries was *oen bach Melangell*, 'Melangell's little lamb'.

Perhaps the most famous female Welsh saint of this early seventh-century period is Gwenffrewi, more widely known through an Anglicised form of her name as Winifred. More than one Life was composed about her traditions. Her father was Trefyth and her mother was Gwendi, a daughter of a king of Powys. In late hagiographies she is claimed as a niece of St Beuno of Clynnog, Caernarfon. According to her traditions, Gwenffrewi had to repulse the unwanted sexual attentions of a chieftain's son, Caradoc of Penarlag (Hawarden in what was formerly Flint). Angered by her rejection of his attentions, Caradoc is said to have struck off her head. Where it fell there gushed a holy well. Once again we encounter the common theme from Celtic myth of the mysticism of water. This was at Holywell (Trefunnon, Welltown). Beuno then arrived and performed the obligatory miracle, putting her head back on her shoulders and bringing her to life. She became abbess at Gwyntherin in Denbigh where she is said to have lived with St Eleri.

Her cultus became widespread in this area and then, in 1138, her reputed relics were taken to England and enshrined in the Benedictine abbey at Shrewsbury. Elizabeth of York, mother of Henry (VII) Tudor, was a devotee of Gwenffrewi and the saint's cultus spread throughout England. It became popular to go on pilgrimage to Holywell. Even after the Reformation, pilgrimages here were still popular; Samuel Johnson visited the site in 1774, with the Welsh poet Hester Piozzi (former Salusbury) from Bachegraig near Tremeirchion. Johnson recounts that he saw people washing themselves in the well. Gerard Manley Hopkins (1844–89), the English poet and Jesuit priest, who became professor of Greek at University College, Dublin, wrote two poems devoted to Gwenffrewi.

The story of Gwenffrewi and Beuno has an interesting parallel in the Breton story of Tryphina and Gildas. And in this story we also meet Mark (Marc'h of Cornwall) in his guise as ruler in Brittany. We are told that Marc'h Cunomorus, sometimes given in the Breton text as Kynvawr, reigned in the sixth century in Domnonée (the Breton equivalent of Dumnonia). He had been widowed several times but then married Tryphina, daughter of Waroc'h, another historical king. Marc'h, according to the story, was in the habit of maltreating his wives as soon as he discovered that they were pregnant. Tryphina did become pregnant and Marc'h began to ill-treat her. She fled and Marc'h gave chase. The result was, as with Gwenffrewi, that Tryphina's head was cut off.

Then Gildas, taking the part of Beuno, arrived and replaced the head on her shoulders and brought her back to life. Tryphina gave birth to a boy, Tremur. In turn, Marc'h beheaded the boy and Gildas, in rage, led an assault on Marc'h's fortress, destroying it and all its occupants. This curious story is kept separate from the romance of Tristan and Iseult. Marc'h is referred to in several other texts and tales apart from the Tristan romance and always in the role of a tyrant. Doubtless there were valid reasons for this depiction of Marc'h, an historical sixty-century king of Cornwall, whose rule appeared to extend to Brittany.

Even in a comparatively small area such as Cornwall we can trace the foundations of over twenty influential female missionaries in the early Christian period. This may give an indication of women's input into the spread of the new religion among the Celts. Alas, most of these Cornish female saints are shadowy figures steeped in legend. The most interesting provides us with a story of one of the few martyrdoms for the Christian faith in a Celtic land. Piala (Phillack) and her brother Gwinear are said to have arrived in Cornwall to convert the people. They landed in the Hayle estuary where they were met by the local ruler Tewdrig (Tudor) who had them put to death. The story of the martyrdom of Piala and her brother is told in a fourteenth-century *Life of Gwinear* while Tewdrig appears (as a Muslim!) in the *Life of Meryadoc*. Newlina (Newlyn), appearing in Breton tradition as Noulen, is also said to have been martyred. The period seems to be the fifth century, a time when several Irish missionaries arrived in Cornwall. Among them were Breaca and Crowan, Buryan – said to be daughter of a Munster chieftain – and Ia (St Ives), also a Munster chieftain's daughter, who founded their churches in the West Penwith peninsula of Cornwall. Kew was the sister of Docco of Gwent and they both seem to have arrived in Cornwall in the fifth century. In fact, the town of St Kew was originally called Lan Docco (church of Docco). At the same time Anta set up her foundation at Lan Anta (Lelant), which was where Twedrig had his fortress – but presumably this bellicose Cornish ruler was long dead when she converted the local population.

Moving into the sixth century we have the legends of the children of Brychan, the king of Powys, who is said to have given all twenty-four to the service of the Church. We have already mentioned his daughters Tudful and Tangwystl. In Cornwall, we find foundations and stories associated with no fewer than nine daughters of Brychan: Adwen (Dwynwen in Wales) who became patron saint of Cornish sweethearts, Endelienta, Juliot, Keria, Keyne the beautiful, Mabyn, Minver, Teath and Wenna. Other female missionaries of the sixth century in Cornwall who left legends and foundations behind are Crida (Creed), Ewe, Gulval (Wovela) and Merteniana. Perhaps the most interesting, and one of whom we have some historic knowledge, is Sitofolla, the sister of Paul Aurelian or Pol de Léon, one of the few British Celtic saints of whom a *Life* exists which was written before AD1000. The *Life* was completed in AD884 by a Breton monk named Wrmonec in the monastery of Landévennec in Brittany. Sitofolla was the daughter of a chieftain of Morgannwg. She was older than her brother Paul Aurelian and educated at Illtud's famous monastery at Llanwit Major. Sitofolla then started her missionary work among her fellow Celts. Her foundations are remembered in Sidwell, a suburb of Exeter, and she was the same person as St Sativola of Laneast, Launceston. She finally settled in St Mount's Bay in Cornwall.

Meanwhile, her brother had also received an education at Llanwit Major where his companions were Dewi Sant (St David), Samson and Gildas. Paul and some comrades decided to cross to Brittany to begin their work but the journey was via Cornwall so that he could visit Sitofolla. According to Wrmonec he believed his sister's foundation was in an unsuitable place and he persuaded her to move to a new location on the edge of Gwavas Lake. The ancient church of Paul (Mousehole) is dedicated to him. He then crossed to Brittany where he became the famous bishop and saint of Léon.

The female saints of ancient Cornwall, shadowy and legendary as many of them now are, are certainly an indication of the prominent role taken by women in the Celtic Church of the fifth and sixth centuries.

One of the earliest influential Christian women in what is now Scotland was Teneu, the daughter of Lleudonos, king of the famous Gododdin tribe, immortalised in the sixth-century poem *Y Gododdin*, which tells of how their warriors attempted to recapture Catraeth (Catterick) from the Angles. The Gododdin, whose capital was at modern Edinburgh, were earlier known to the Romans as the Votadini, one of the most powerful Celtic tribes in the area now known as the Lothians, which, significantly enough, is an Anglicised form of Lleudduniawn and associated with the name of Teneu's regal father.

In a twelfth-century *Life* the author tells of Teneu having a child from an illicit relationship, illicit enough for Lleudonos to have his daughter set adrift in the Firth of Forth in a coracle which was eventually cast ashore at Culross in Fiobh (Fife). There, Teneu and her infant child, a boy, were cared for by St Serf. But as St Serf lived *c*.AD700 while Teneu lived *c*.AD530 the chronology seems wrong. Teneu was influential in the proselytising of Scotland, but it is her son Cunotigern (Hound Lord) who has overshadowed his mother's work. His name has now become better known by its Anglicised pronunciation of Kentigern. It was Serf who is claimed in the story to have nicknamed the boy Munghu (Mungo), 'My Hound'. Kentigern, of course, founded his monastic settlement in Glasgow, and became chief bishop of Cumbria and Strathclyde.

The idea of pregnant women being cast adrift on the seas and then giving birth to children who invariably become great saints of the Celtic Church seems to be a popular theme with later hagiographers. Similar to the Teneu story is that of Azenor who was mother of the Breton saint Beuzec, remembered in Pembroke, Cornwall and Devon as Budoc. His *Life* was written in Brittany and tells that Azenor was thrown into the sea off Brest in a cask as a punishment for some crime. She gave birth to her son and five months later they were cast on the shore of Ireland where Azenor was rescued and her son grew up; he returned to Brittany and became bishop of Dol. It would seem that hagiographers used this idea in many saints' tales in much the same way as virgin birth in other cultures denoted the birth of a pious or holy person.

The *Annals of Ulster* record the death in AD734 of a famous abbess named after Kentigern, Kentigerna. Kentigerna was another advocate of Christianity who had a profound influence in promoting the religion in northern Scotland. She finished her life as a recluse on Inchaill-loch (the nun's island) in Loch Lomond. Contemporary sources identify her as the daughter of Ceallach Cualann, king of the Uí Mail of Kilranleagh, Wicklow, later king of Leinster (d. AD715). She was one of four sisters who took up religion.

On the death of her father, and with an argument in progress between rival claimants for the kingship of Leinster, Kentigerna persuaded her brother Comgán to accompany her to Dàl Riada in what is now Scotland where they devoted themselves to spreading the

Christian faith. Kentigerna had been married to a chieftain called Feriacus; one must presume that he was dead or that she had divorced him. She had a young child named Fáelán. According to the *Breviary of Aberdeen*, Comgán became an abbot associated with Turriff in Aberdeen. Fáelán is said to have left his mother when he was old enough and built a church at Glen Dochart in Perthshire.

Everywhere in the Celtic world, Christianity was preached, and ecclesiastical foundations were run, by families or groups of families.

Even after the Norman incursions into Wales, and the claims of Canterbury to be supreme over the Welsh Church, the *clas* system was found to be prevalent in the chapters of many cathedrals. Rhygy-farch, the son of Bishop Sulvin of St David's, succeeded his father in 1091. After his death, Daniel, another son of Bishop Sulvin, was nominated by the Welsh clergy. Jeuan, in his *Carmen de vita et familia Sulgeni*, says that Sulvin, sometimes given as Sulien, had four sons (*quatuor ac proprio nutrivit sanguine natos*). Dom Gougaud, observing this, is quick to defend his own thesis: 'But he does not say that these sons were born after their father had been raised to the episcopate or even after his entry into holy orders.' Attempts were made by the Normans, looking to Canterbury as the primacy, to suppress the *clas* system.

This is not to claim that Celtic churchmen refused to accept the concept of celibacy nor the Roman cultural concept of the inferior place of women which was then permeating the western Church. But the Celtic cultural ideas of the coequality of women and the pursuit of normal sexual relationships within the framework of the new religion were certainly in evidence for a long time. Brendan Lehane comments:

The notion of sexual restraint must have come hard to people accustomed to fairly free morality. It was not altogether new, for Christianity had only extended a practice kept by Roman Vestal Virgins, priests of Diana, and sects and religious officials in every society, of sublimating physical love in a dedication to a deity. Nor were the bishops of the Church altogether clear about their own policy. St Peter himself had been married before his conversion, and nothing conclusive remains to show whether, or how soon, or on what grounds, he broke the relationship.

The concept of celibacy, although preached as an ideal by some ascetic enthusiasts, had little currency in everyday life in the early days of the Celtic Church. At the Council of Elvira in AD305 it was decided to condemn bishops, priests and deacons who married and had children. Then at the Council of Nicaea, in AD325, clerical marriages were also condemned but not banned.

The ideal of celibacy was preached in Ireland but married bishops, abbots and other *religieux* became commonplace. The fifth-century encyclical known as the First Synod of Patrick takes it for granted that clerics 'from porter to priest' were married, making the point that it was shameful if their wives did not cover their heads outside the home. However, clergy were not to stay in the same hostel as unmarried women, nor were they to travel together in the same wagon or chariot. Oengus in his *Félire*, talking of the 350 male saints of Patrick's time, says quite clearly: 'They rejected not the services and society of women . . .'

According to Adomnán's *Life of Colmcille*, referring to the appointment of Fiacc as bishop of Leinster, Patrick is said to have made the condition that he should be 'a man of one wife only' which would indicate that some clergy married in accordance with the polygamous concepts, approved by native law, of Celtic society. The *Senchus Mór* (Patrick was one of nine commissioners responsible for drawing up this codification of the Irish law system) talks openly of married bishops. However, later stories of Patrick relate that he did not approve of such relationships: I have already mentioned that he was supposed to have investigated his own nephew, Mel, son of his sister Darerca, who was living openly with a *religieuse*. Patrick ordered them to separate in spite of their protestations. Another story, showing Patrick as an extremist, has it that a woman named Lupait, a *religieuse* of Navan, was living with a *religieux*. Patrick ordered them to separate. He was away from Armagh at the time. On his return, Lupait went to meet him to plead her case and cast herself before his chariot. Patrick simply ordered his charioteer to drive over her, thus killing her. He is even reported to have cut off the hand of Mac Nisse (Son of Nessa), whom he had appointed bishop of Condaire (Anglicised as Connor, meaning 'oak forest of the dogs or wolves'), because he was cohabiting with a *religieuse*. He is said to have issued a decree: 'Let men and women be apart so that we may not be found to give opportunity to the weak . . .' If such a decree was made, it was not very successful. Indeed, I tend to view these traditions of Patrick's celibate fanaticism with some scepticism. They are not in keeping with the cultural context of his background nor with the times in which he lived. Nor do they square with the fact that Patrick was one of the nine commissioners who approved the laws relating to polygamy, setting them down in writing. I fear that they were stories later tacked on to his traditions to support the arguments for celibacy.

There are a number of stories in the later hagiographies relating to anti-feminism that also seem rather extreme for the times. Maighnenn, the abbot of Kilmainham, vowed never to look on a woman lest he should see the Devil. St Enda of Aran would only converse with his sister, Faenche, through a veil stretched between them. As it was Faenche, then an abbess with her own mixed foundation, who persuaded Enda to give up his kingdom of Breifne and enter the religious life, his actions are somewhat bizarre.

Ciarán of Clonmacnoise refused to lift his eyes to look on his fellow female students at Clonard in case he was 'tempted'. He is said to have accepted the words of Job as his philosophy: 'I made a convenant with mine eyes; how then should I look upon a maid?' From this we must also deduce that Finnén (Finnian) ran a mixed house at Clonard. Ciarán's fear of being 'tempted', if accurately reported, says more for his own sexual repressions than for the female students of Clonard. Ciarán's problems with sexual relationships might well stem from the fact that his mother Darerca was very powerful and domineering, as was his sister Raichbe. Being raised by them might account for his anti-feminism. In fact, Finnén himself also had a sister, Rígnach, reported to be an autocrat, who was said to have taught at Clonard. If she was Ciarán's instructress then his anti-feminism might have been confirmed. The writer of Comgán's *Life* (sometimes given in Latin script as Coemgeni) comments that wherever there are women, there is sin. With such obviously sexually repressed men as Ciarán, Maighnenn and Enda in proximity to normal outgoing women, the real cause of the sin was obvious.

There is a perhaps symbolic tale given by the writer of the *Life of Brendan the Voyager* in the tenth century. Brenáinn, or Brendan, was born in Kerry c.AD486 and died at Annaghdown in 578. He was educated by St Ita. We are told that he was waiting for Bishop Erc one day when an attractive girl passed by and smiled at him. Now Brendan had obviously been brought up in the still free and

A woman's fur cap and skirt from a fifth-century BC bog body found at Huldremose in Denmark

An unidentified triune goddess from Vertillum (Côte d'Or) in the Musée de Chatillon-sur-Seine

Epona, the horse goddess, riding side-saddle. This statuette comes from Alésia

Another visualization of Epona from a relief found at Kastel in Germany, now in the Rheiniches Landesmuseum, Bonn

The goddess Artio (art = bear), who is shown seated before a huge bear to whom she offers fruit. Now in the British Museum

Relief from Alésia showing a triune mother-goddess motif. The goddesses shown here are replete with fertility symbolism

The head of an unknown Celtic female from Carrawburgh,
England. This is thought to be the head of a Celtic goddess
c. second century AD

Some bronze female Celtic
figures from a first-century BC
hoard found at Neuvy-en-Sullias
on the banks of the Loire

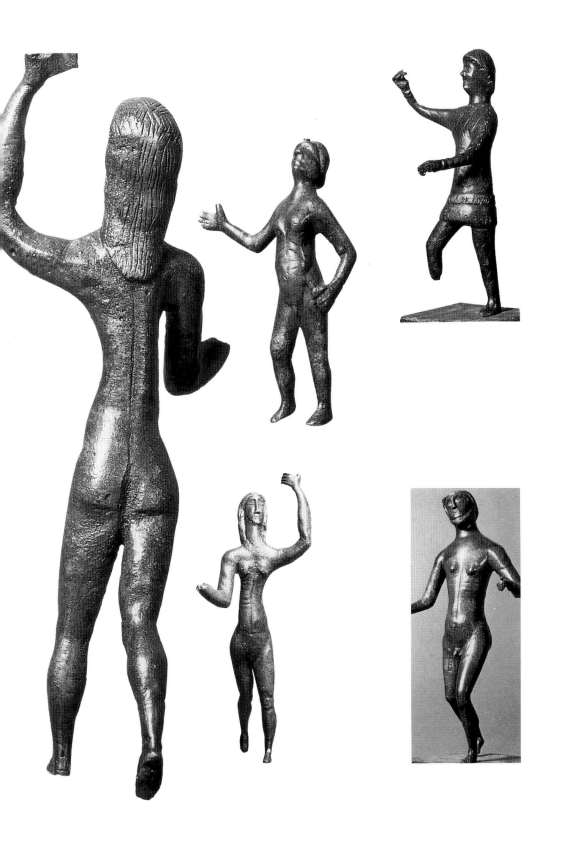

Danu (Dôn), the Mother Goddess of the Celts

A bronze statue of Epona from Dalheim, Luxembourg

A sheela-na-gig image from Kilpeck, Herefordshire, is typical of a motif that occurs throughout the Celtic world and goes back to the pre-Christian 'mother goddess'

Unknown Celtic heroine of the first century AD, from Source de la Roche, Chamalières, Puy-de-Dôme, France

A Victorian idealization of Boudicca and her two daughters

Gwenhafr, better known as Guinevere, by William Morris

Mebd (Maeve) the famous
legendary Queen of Connacht

The seal of Anne of Brittany, the last
ruler of an independent Brittany

Gráina Ní Máillie at the
Greenwich court of Elizabeth I

Countess Constance
Markievicz, Connie
Gore-Booth of Lissadell,
Co. Sligo, the first woman
MP and the first woman
to become a government
minister

Westminster's youngest MP, Bernadette Devlin (now McAliskey), helping to defend the nationalist ghetto in the Bogside, Derry

Eileen Fairweather, Roisin McDonough and Melanie McFadyean

ONLY THE RIVERS RUN FREE
NORTHERN IRELAND: THE WOMEN'S WAR

An IRA funeral in 1972. A young woman of the Cumann na mBan (republican women's group) holds the 'Starry Plough' banner while a grandmother figure reaches forth a hand to touch it. A symbolic handing on of the struggle from one generation to another ·

easy world of Celtic sexuality. What lay behind the meaning of the girl's smile? According to the hagiographer, Brendan immediately launched a physical assault on the poor girl because he saw her as an evil demon come to rob him of his chastity. Any other reasonable explanation for a girl smiling at a young man did not exist under the new Christian paradigms of sexuality. The tale seems symbolic of the changes that were happening in Celtic society.

Colmcille, however, did not seem to be worried by the presence of women for we are told that he had a female 'soul-friend' named Ercnat, the feminine form of the name Erc which means 'speckled' or 'dark red'. Ercnat was supposed to be Colmcille's embroideress and dressmaker. In fact, Colmcille was accused of fathering a child although whether the mother was Ercnat is not stated. One of the poems attributed to him alleges his innocence.

> I am being accused of a son that is not mine,
> O God act as my protector
> let there not be a legal contention about me
> because of the bright outburst of vehemence.

Colmcille's humanitarian ethics are certainly brought into question in the story of how he came to the abode of Colmán Ela at Llann Ealla, or Ela's church, now Lynally, Co. Westmeath. Colmcille had a problem. His sister, who was Colmán Ela's aunt, had two children by incest. We are left wondering whether Colmán Ela was Colmcille's son or his nephew by another sister or brother. Colmcille had baptised the two children of his sister in the faith but then discovered they were born of an incestuous relationship. We are now confused as to who the father was. Colmcille openly confesses to Colmán that he wants to 'compass their destruction without shame to myself'. This desire seems to place a heavy suspicion of guilt on Colmcille. Were the children his own? Rather than allow Colmcille to have them killed, Colmán Ela, displaying a more charitable Christianity, took the children to foster himself.

Colmcille was not the first nor the last cleric, claiming a celibate life, to be accused of fathering children, nor to contemplate murder to cover up any scandal. Moling (d. c.AD670), the founder of St Mullins, Co. Carlow, was accused of fathering a child by a married woman. When the husband demanded reparation he was killed by Moling's fellow clerics and when the unfortunate woman appeared with the baby in her arms before Moling, the 'saintly man' turned her away saying: 'I do not see anyone here who would care for the child in your arms. Take your son away. We clerics have no reason to care for the child.'

Perhaps of all people, Moling should have had more humanity and compassion for, in his ninth-century *Life*, we are told that his mother, who was named Eamhnait, had been made pregnant by the husband of her sister, a farmer of Luachair (Co. Kerry). Scared of her sister's vengeance, Eamhnait fled and, helpless and alone, was caught in a snowdrift. She gave birth to her baby and intended to kill it in her desperation but some monks from the community of St Brenáinn came and took the mother and child to look after and raise. The child was named Dairchill but was later nicknamed Moling ('Holy Leaper') because he once leapt across a river in Kerry.

Yet perhaps the story goes to prove a truism: that the experience of persecution does not necessarily make individuals – or, indeed, peoples – more humane and tolerant towards others.

Another intolerant person was St Cuimmíne of Clonfert, who is said to have refused to contemplate the idea of married *religieux*. Cuimmíne's austere and narrow attitude was responsible for one of the great tragic romances of Irish literature, the story of Liadin and Cuirithir.

While the story of Créd and Cano can be seen as an early Irish version of the Tristan and Iseult tale, itself a Celtic love tragedy from Cornwall, the story of Liadin and Cuirithir may well be said to foreshadow the historical tragedy of Héloise and Abelard of Brittany. The story is not part of Irish myth but tends to be accepted in the prehistory tales surviving in a ninth-century text. Liadin, 'Grey Lady', was a poetess of the seventh century, of the Corca Dhuibhne sept of West Munster. She was also a *religieuse*. While 'touring' Connacht, she met a poet called Cuirithir Mac Dobharchon. They fell in love and became lovers.

Liadin's religious superior was St Cuimmíne of Clonfert, who was a stern ascetic and forbade them to cohabit. He is not to be confused with Cuimmíne Fota of Magh Bíle (d. AD662), who was the author of the *Poenitentiale Cummeani*, an influential set of canon law. Cuimmíne of Magh Bíle was born, say his hagiographers, as the result of an incestuous love affair which might account for the misogynism displayed in his Penitentials. But he and his namesake of Clonfert were certainly birds of a feather. Cuimmíne of Clonfert sent Cuirithir away from the community to put an end to his relationship with Liadin. Could the reality have been that Cuimmíne was actually jealous? After all, *religieux* were still living together at this period; priests and abbots were marrying. Why would Cuirithir and Liadin take notice of the ascetic extremism of one man? Liadin finally broke free of whatever hold Cuimmíne had on her and followed Cuirithir, only to discover that he had left Ireland and no one knew where he had gone. She lay down and died of grief on the stone at which Cuirithir used to pray.

In the poem ascribed to her in the ninth-century text, Liadin blames herself for not being strong enough to disobey Cuimmíne, admit her love and elope with Cuirithir.

> *Cen áintus*
> *in gním ínus*
> *an ro-carus ro-cráidius.*

> No pleasure
> That deed I did, tormenting him,
> Tormenting what I treasure.

She ends the poem:

> Why should I hide
> That he is still my heart's desire
> More than all the world?

> A furnace blast
> Of love has melted my heart
> Without his love, it can beat no more.

The Céle Dé, Servants of God, the religious order founded by Mael Rúain of Tallaght in the eighth century, while they did not officially approve of priests having sexual unions, still accepted married couples for religious training. Certainly, the early Church generally took it for granted that priests would marry and Irish law provides for the rights of married clergy. In fact, a list of the abbots of Lusk (Lusca, in Dublin) shows that from the eighth to tenth centuries, the abbots were elected by the *derbhfine*, in the same way as a kingly succession, with sons succeeding fathers and brothers succeeding brothers. There has been a tendency to reinterpret this by claiming the abbots were 'secular abbots' and not religious at all! Indeed, eight archbishops of Armagh, prior to the enthusiastic Romaniser, Mael Maedoc Ua Morgair (Malachy), were clearly married.

Nárbhfhlaith (Noble Princess), who was a daughter of a petty king, Feradach mac Máel Dúin, was the wife of Báethchellach, the abbot of Trim, Co. Meath. She is reported to have been highly learned and knowledgeable in many of the seven liberal arts. She died in AD756. Incidentally, Báethchellach's own mother, who was a princess of Meath named Finnleacht, is regarded as an early 'saint' whose feastday is still remembered on 5 October.

The later hagiographers appear to have evolved various methods of avoiding any straightforward reference to sexual liaisons as the cause of the births of 'saints', particularly those male saints born of female saints. Typical is the story of St Creda who was the mother of Baithene, the second abbot of Iona, AD597–600, and immediate successor of Colmcille. We are told that the saintly Creda, a good and holy woman, was washing herself in a pool outside a church. On that day a thief was hiding in a tree overhanging the pool. Overcome by her beauty, the thief masturbated, allowing his semen to fall on to a bed of watercress. After she had bathed, Creda gathered the watercress and ate it. She then gave birth to Baithene, while remaining technically a virgin. However, Baithene is also recorded as a son of Creda and Brenáinn (which Brendan, alas, we do not know). The boy was fostered, in traditional manner, by Colmcille. He accompanied Colmcille into exile from Ireland in AD563.

It was not until the reforming papacy of Leo IX (1049–54) that a serious attempt was made to enforce the western clergy to accept universal celibacy. One of the prime movers of this was St Peter Damian (1007–72), a leading theologian and reformer who was left an orphan when a baby. He was the thirteenth child and his mother eventually died from child-bearing. He was raised in poverty, forced to care for pigs, until, in his late twenties, he ran off to join a community of hermits. Eventually he was ordained a priest and became cardinal of Ostia. A fanatic against all 'worldly pleasures', he even rebuked a bishop for playing chess. He was a misogynist of the first water. In his onslaught on clerical misconduct known as 'The Gomorrah Book' he called the wives of priests 'harlots, prostitutes ... [living in] wallowing places for fat pigs, resting places for unclean spirits, demigoddesses, sirens, witches ...' The irony is that his own life had been saved as a baby by the wife of a priest who had nursed him after his mother's death.

His attitudes were very influential. Leo IX ordered that wives of Roman priests should be given as slaves to the Lateran Palace, the home of the Pope. Pope Urban II, in 1189, decided that wives of priests could be taken as slaves by nobles, but when the archbishop of Reims allowed Robert of Flanders to abduct priests' wives to use as slaves, he found a revolution of married clergy on his hands and had to retract his decree. The count of Verigen, in Swabia, seizing such wives in accordance with the Pope's instructions, found his countess poisoned in her bed as a retaliation. But many wives of clergy were driven to suicide in despair at the new ruling.

The tragic affair of Peter Abelard, the Breton monk, and Héloise, in the eleventh century, is a typical and graphic illustration of the new 'forbidden love'. They have taken their place in world literature as doomed lovers in the mould of Romeo and Juliet. Abelard was of Breton nobility, born in 1079. Héloise was born in about 1100. Originally a marriage was agreed. But, with the new rules from Rome, their love become forbidden; it created doubts, guilt, and the pain of self-denial of their feelings. In 1126 Abelard became abbot of St Gildas de Rhuys on the west coast of Brittany. Héloise became prioress of Argenteuil and later abbess of the Paraclete. He died in 1156/7 and she in 1163/4.

In Ireland the last vestiges of the Celtic Church were vanishing. The reforming zeal of Mael Maedoc us Morgair (Malachy) (c.1094–1148) was setting the seal for the eventual Anglo-Norman invasion. He was changing the structure of the Church and the Synod of Cashel in 1101 was the first serious attempt to enforce clerical celibacy in Ireland. Katharine Simms, writing on 'The Legal Position of Irish Women in the Later Middle Ages' (*Irish Jurist*, 1975), points out that anyone reading the letters of Pope Alexander III, which gave papal blessing for the Anglo-Norman invasion of Ireland, would come to the conclusion that the prime object was to change the Irish marriage laws and enforce clerical celibacy.

In his second letter written at Tusculum (Frascati) on the 12th Kalends of October 1172 (20 September 1172) Alexander writes to Henry II bemoaning the 'uncivilised and undisciplined' Irish.

> . . . it appears that the aforesaid people, as perhaps has more fully come to your knowledge, marry their stepmothers and are not

ashamed to have children by them; a man will live with his brother's wife while the brother is still alive; one man will live in concubinage with two sisters; and many of them, putting away the mother, will marry the daughters.

And all from time to time eat meat in Lent; nor do they pay tithes, or respect as they ought the churches of God and ecclesiastical persons.

. . . We understand that you, collecting your splendid naval and land forces, have set your mind upon subjugating that people to your lordship, and by Divine grace, extirpating the filthiness of such abomination. We hold your purpose good and acceptable in all ways . . .

Pope Alexander was simply echoing the misconceptions of Rome when viewing the Irish law system. Many Catholic nationalists in Ireland have felt obliged to point out that the Bull Laudibiliter, issued in 1155, giving papal blessing and permission to Henry II to invade and conquer Ireland, was issued by Adrian IV, who, as Nicholas Breakspeare of Bedmond, Hertfordshire, was the only Englishman to become Pope. However, Alexander III, the former Rolando Bandinelli of Siena, confirmed the Bull and his letters congratulating Henry and 'warning' the princes and bishops of Ireland to submit to him show the clear policy of the papacy.

For some years, through the intercession of Canterbury, the papacy had tried to get the civil and canon law changed in Ireland. The Italian Lanfranc, who had rather reluctantly become archbishop of Canterbury (1070–89) and who had written a medieval 'bestseller', *Concerning the Body and Blood of the Lord* (c.1060), had been persuaded to write in 1074 to the son of the former High King Brían Bóramha, Toirrdelbach Ua Bríain, then a king of Munster and Thomond (d. 1086), complaining about the Irish laws of marriage. He says that the 'law of marriage . . . is rather a law of fornication . . .' His belief was that a man could abandon his wife at will and take some other wife who might even be a close relative of himself or even of the wife he had abandoned. Lack of knowledge of the Brehon system permeated the growing problems between Ireland and Rome.

Lanfranc's successor at Canterbury, another Italian theologian, St Anselm (1093–1109), demonstrated the same misinterpretation. Writing to the Irish clerics he says: 'It is said that men exchange their wives with the wives of others as freely and publicly as a man might exchange his horse for another's horse . . . or else they abandon them at will and without reason.' He also believed that incest was rife in Ireland with the blessing of Irish law. Obviously, the propaganda of Rome was essential in the build-up towards the Anglo-Norman invasion. It was Anselm who, perhaps, issued the first warning of Rome's support for the invasion to come when he cautioned the Irish, saying that if they failed to carry out the reforms in the laws they would 'expose themselves to God's anger as transgressors of His Laws' with inevitable consequences.

Perhaps it was in an attempt to stave off that inevitable invasion, as threatened in the Bull Laudibiliter, that the High King, Muirchertach Ua Bríain, exceeding his authority under the law, agreed at the Synod of Cashel to hand over lands to the absolute ownership of the Church. Until then such lands were under the final jurisdiction of the clan assemblies, for there was no such concept as absolute private property. Thus the first alienation of land from the people took place.

In 1152 the Synod of Kells made further attempts to enforce clerical celibacy but for the next hundred years the matter kept coming up, showing that such measures were not popular and were being ignored. The Gaelic names bear witness to continued liaisons – Ó Manacháin (Descent of the Monk), Mac an tSagairt (MacTaggart, Son of the Priest), Mac an Airchinnigh (MacInerney, McEnery, Son of the Steward of the Church Lands), and many others. The debate on clerical celibacy actually remained an issue in Ireland until the seventeenth century, when the Brehon law system was finally crushed.

Indeed, after the Anglo-Norman invasions, many of the colonists accepted the Irish language and social systems, including the law systems. We find in the fifteenth century that the concubine of the archbishop of Armagh, who had just died, refused to hand over to the Church the property and gifts he had bestowed on her, including, for good measure, his episcopal ring, horse and cup. In the same century, another archbishop of Armagh approved of raids on clergy suspected of keeping concubines.

In Wales, clergy continued to marry down to the Reformation, when of course the matter was legalised under the new ecclesiastical system. Angharad, the daughter of Uchdryd, bishop of Llandaff, one of the earliest seats of a bishopric in Wales, became a very influential lady in twelfth-century Wales. Her father's community had been founded by St Teilo, a sixth-century churchman widely venerated in Wales and Brittany, and was later famed as the place where the *Book of Llandaff* (Lan Dâv) was written. Angharad married Iorwerth ab Owain, who was one of the Welsh princes fighting the Anglo-Normans in 1171. Iorwerth was of the Gwynllwg line of princes of south-west Wales. Angharad is mentioned several times in the chronicles and her grandson Morgan ap Maredudd (d. 1294) continued to fight against the English in the years following the defeat and death of Llywelyn, regarded as the last native king of Wales.

One of the most interesting demonstrations of Welsh attitudes towards married clergy can be found in the work of the poet Iolo Goch (*c.*1320–98). He wrote a poem called *Dychan i'r Brawd Llwyd o Gaer* (Satire on the Grey Friar of Chester). A Franciscan friar from Chester had apparently made an attack on the Welsh clergy when he discovered that they still married, even if they were high-ranking churchmen. It seems that the poem was a defence of Iolo's patron, Hywel ap Madog, the dean of St Asaph (1380–97). Iolo writes of this English friar from Chester:

> . . . he was the very worst friar
> to preach his morals to a cleric;
> no one would go to heaven, he said,
> if she loved a man with a tonsure;
> that man's office is higher,
> a curse on his pate,
> if only he knew the truth.
>
> Should a cleric, preacher of love,
> not be freely allowed a wife or concubine?
>
> God the Father, true power of wisdom,
> holds the wife of a holy cleric, if she is humble,
> in greater honour in his guileless house,
> and would do more for her,
> than the keen Grey Friar
> from Chester said in his angry words.
>
> The Friar was a big strong lad,
> out of lechery he often struck a blow

furtively with his penis, if he got the chance
to play with a lovely fine girl.
May no better fate, old crooked basket,
befall the dreadful Friar
than to be caught (circle-haired thief with a wild penis,
wicked one roaming around us)
with his penis in the hot crotch
of a randy, sour Englishwoman.

Base, sombre, fervent slanderer!
Why, poor Friar from Chester,
you kite of the grave, deserving hanging,
did you falsely accuse the women,
with the soul, and prelates of the region,
of Gwynedd and Powys?

Mary Condren has observed that, in the face of Celtic cultural traditions, 'the imposition of clerical celibacy, therefore, was an extraordinary political achievement.' Celibacy of priesthood was a tool in the emergence not only of the centralised, feudal power of the papacy but of the feudal states of Europe. The move was primarily economic. St Bernard of Clairveaux identified the problem, using the Irish example, of the succession of position and power within certain family groups.

A very evil custom has grown up, by the devilish ambition of certain powerful persons, that this holy see (Armagh) should be held in hereditary succession. For they suffer none to be bishops but those who were of their own tribe and family.

Although the succession was not passed down through primogeniture, it was partially hereditary through election within the family. These families, forming political alliances, could counter the power of both monarchy and papacy. The power of these families had to be broken. To allow priests to marry and transmit property and office endangered the power of the monarchy and popes. If clergy remained unmarried then the Church also gained by receiving lands free of family claims or connections.

Therefore the biggest and most active agency in preparing the way for the feudalisation of Ireland, and, indeed, for the Anglo-Norman invasion, was the Roman Church. By the end of the tenth and beginning of the eleventh centuries Irish society was already in a state of transition from common property to several ownership. Before the rise of Mael Maedoc each clan had its own bishop and its own priests, and the diocese was merely the district occupied by the clan. The clan allotted to its clergy, for their support, certain lands, looked after by an officer who was generally a layman, an *airchinnigh*, or steward of the Church lands. It was Mael Maedoc who moved to centralise the Church and create thirty-six dioceses subject to the primacy of Armagh. It was doubtless Mael Maedoc who influenced the papacy into giving a blessing for Henry II of the Angevin empire to invade Ireland and 'enlarge the bounds of the Church, teach the truth of Christian faith to the ignorant and rude, and extirpate the roots of vice from the field of the Lord'. Alexander III wrote a letter to the Irish bishops in September 1172, ordering them, by all means in their power, to assist Henry II to keep possession of Ireland.

Within these centuries, from the first introduction of Christianity, we can see how the role and status of women have changed. At the beginning of the Christian epoch, women in Celtic society lived in a fairly egalitarian society. They were rulers, military leaders, warriors, landowners, judges, physicians, poets, teachers and priestesses. Their position was clearly defined in law. They had freedom of choice in marriage, could divorce and remain the owner of their property as well as claiming a share of joint property and sums in settlement.

With the introduction of Christianity, change came about. It was not obvious at first, for women took a leading part in the proselytising of their people for the new faith. The individualistic Celtic Church continued the social concepts of the society from which it took its roots. Clergy were married, men and women lived in mixed religious communities, ruled over by men or women with an equal hand. There are even references to women taking the role of priests and being ordained as bishops. These social attitudes, attitudes towards land ownership and the function of people in society, were an anathema to Roman Christianity. It was inevitable that the Celtic and Roman Churches soon found themselves in conflict. It was inevitable that the temporal and feudal princes of the Roman Church used the forces of Henry II's Angevin empire to finally destroy the place where the Celtic Church remained at its unreformed strongest – Ireland.

Against this background, the social freedoms that had once been the right of women were being curtailed one by one, but they would not be given up overnight.

[7]

Personal Adornment in Early Society

THIS is a good point to pause and consider what has become a contentious subject for many in the women's movement today. During the late 1960s and early 1970s, sections of the feminist movement decided to cease wearing cosmetics or following fashion as, they believed, it was a badge of subservience to men. It was a period symbolised by the 'bra-burning' of some feminist demonstrators. Make-up was something, they claimed, which had been created in a male-dominated society by which women were forced to enhance their attractiveness to men. But it is only since the last century in western Europe that cosmetics have become inextricably linked with sexuality. Body paint has, in fact, been used by both men and women for ornamental and religious purposes since prehistoric times.

In ancient Egypt cosmetics were certainly used by both sexes. In Greece and Rome also, both men and women used preparations to make themselves attractive – and not necessarily to each other. In Greece men used perfumes and scented powder. Women often applied white lead to their faces and rouge made from the root of anchusa, which produced a dark red powder. They also used this on their fingernails, mixed into a paste. In Rome too, both sexes used make-up. Lucius Calpurnicus Piso, Julius Caesar's son-in-law, wore rouge on his cheeks whenever he entered the senate building. Women used various preparations to enhance their skin, lips, eyes, hair and nails. Some of the wealthier classes brought slaves adept in the application of cosmetics.

Celtic men were certainly vain about their appearance. According to Diodorus Siculus:

The Celts are tall of body, with rippling muscles, and white of skin, and their hair is blond, not only naturally so, but they also make it their practice by artificial means to increase the distinguishing colour which nature has given it. For they are always washing their hair in limewater, and they pull it back from the forehead to the top of the head and back to the nape of the neck, with the result that their appearance is like that of Satyrs and Pans, since the treatment of their hair makes it so heavy and coarse that it differs in no respect from the mane of horses. Some of them shave the beard, but others let it grow a little; and the nobles shave their cheeks, but they let the moustache grow until it covers the mouth.

He adds that they wear 'striking' clothes with various dazzling pieces of jewellery. Some of the British Celts also painted and tattooed their bodies and Strabo adds that 'the Celtic men endeavour not to grow fat or pot-bellied and any young man who exceeds the standard measure of the girdle is punished.' In a later age it is reported that many of the male missionaries of the Irish Celtic Church were regarded with some amazement in their journeys on the European continent not only because of their different tonsure, or haircut, but because they painted their eyelids black. So make-up in the ancient world was not restricted to women, nor did it evolve, as some have imagined, as something forced on females as a means of attracting males.

How, then, did Celtic women, with their more independent role, fare in the world of cosmetic adornment? We learn not only from Greek and Roman sources but from native Celtic sources themselves that personal cleanliness and appearance were highly important to both sexes in the ancient Celtic world. We are lucky in that we not only have textual evidence but archaeological evidence. Ancient Celtic graves have revealed cosmetic grinders and we know from remains how women wore their hair, with long and elaborate hairstyles, kept in place by exotically styled pins.

Again, from the graves of Celtic women, we know that they loved jewellery: bracelets, anklets, necklaces and brooches, finger-rings and ear-rings. Depending on the woman's rank, 'hero's torcs' of intricately worked gold were also worn. The Reinheim 'princess' had a tremendous range of jewellery in her grave. Some breath-taking items were discovered in the Celtic graves at Hallstatt. And exquisite decorative mirrors are found everywhere in the Celtic world. Elaborate chain waist belts and glass bangles, usually cobalt blue in colour, were also worn from 250BC onwards.

The graves, and some 'Iron Age' bodies preserved in bogs, give information about dress and even textiles. There are a few remarkably well-preserved female garments, such as a checked (forerunner of tartan) wrap-around skirt from the fifth century BC. This tweedy, check pattern is characteristic of Celtic clothing found from Ireland through to the original Celtic homelands of central Europe.

The most extensive native material we have on personal adornment and dress comes from Ireland and we can follow a woman's daily personal routine; from comparative evidence, we can argue that this would not have differed much throughout the Celtic world. To start with, bathing was highly important in ancient Ireland for both sexes. The bath is constantly mentioned in Irish tales and people generally bathed daily and in the evening. The evening bath was a full wash while in the morning people merely washed their hands and feet. The washing of the hands and feet (*indlut*) is distinguished from the washing of the entire body (*fothrucud*). In both washing and bathing, soap was used, called *sléic* in Old Irish, which was applied with a linen cloth. Diodorus Siculus mentions that such personal fastidiousness was common throughout Gaul as well and he adds that soap (*sapo* or *sopa*) was a Celtic invention and word. The Mediterraneans, of course, bathed in oils.

It is obvious from the ancient tales that bathing was highly important, even during warfare. At the battle of Rosnaree we are told that when Conchobhar's army encamped for the night, after the day's march, 'fires were kindled, food and drink were prepared, they went into baths where they were carefully cleansed, their hair smooth-combed, after which they had supper'. The clan hostels had bath-houses and this tradition continued so that the guest house of every monastery had a bath-house for visitors. The water was always heated and in several tales, such as the story of Deirdre, we are told that it was heated by wood fires.

Men and women in ancient Ireland also went to special baths. A 'hot-air bath' was something akin to the modern Turkish bath. It was called a *tigh 'n alluis* (sweating house) and examples of such ancient bath-houses are still found in northern parts of Ireland, for example the one on Inishmurray. The bath-house was from five to seven feet long. A great turf fire was kindled inside until the place became heated. The embers were swept out and the bather entered through a small door. The door was closed, and the bather remained for an hour or so until they had developed a profuse perspiration. Then, leaving the house, the bather would plunge into a cold-water pool which was always strategically nearby. Several people bathed together. Professor Hennessy, in the *Kilkenny Archaeological Journal* (1885/6), says: 'It is remarkable that what are called Turkish baths in Ireland and Great Britain have been designated Roman-Irish baths in Germany and Bohemia. I saw baths designated *Römische-Irishe bäder* at Prague and Nuremberg in 1879.' These were medicinal baths but were also used for ritual purposes. The bathing in the *tigh n' alluis* would prepare the man or woman for the *dercad*, an act of meditation, by which Irish mystics would attempt to achieve a state of *sitchain* or peace. From a gloss on the *Senchus Mór* we are told that Fergus Mac Leide, in a rage, once killed a woman, Dorn, in such a bath by picking up one of the heated stones (*clochfothraicthe*) and hitting her with it. These 'bath stones' are referred to in many of the tales and epics.

Once out of the baths, what would be the next step in personal adornment? In ancient Ireland both men and women were fastidious over their fingernails (*igen*). In Irish law a nail rated as equal in value with a tooth for reparation should someone damage it. It was shameful to have rough or unkempt nails. Conan Maol deeply insulted Cairell, a son of Fionn Mac Cumhail, by calling him 'ragged nails' (*créchtingnech*). Well-cut and crimson-coloured nails were a mark of beauty. Women painted their nails. Deirdre, lamenting for Naoise, says: 'I sleep no more, and I shall not crimson my nails; no joy shall ever again come on my mind.' Women would also use berry juice to blacken their eyebrows. In the story of Crede we find: 'A bowl she has whence berry juice [*sugh-subh*] flows, with which she colours her eyebrows black.' *Cormac's Glossary* states that a herb called ruam (*ro-eim*) gives a red tinge to the face (i.e. a form of rouge). *Ruam* was the alder but the sprigs and berries of the elder tree, according to the *Book of Ballymote*, were also used as an artificial blush. Berry juice was also used to redden the lips. The poet Sextus Propertius (*c.*50BC–after 16BC) wrote a book of poems to his mistress Cynthia in which he criticises her for applying her make-up like a Celt, particularly using *belgicus color*, which seems to be an imported Celtic eye-shadow or blusher.

Both men and women wore their hair long, flowing down past

the shoulders – a custom denounced by Geraldus Cambrensis. This custom of long hair was also noticed a thousand years before in Celtic Gaul. The Romans thought that the Celts were unduly vain about their hair. Dio Cassius, in complete agreement with the descriptions of the women given in the Irish and Welsh sagas, says that Boudicca had 'a great mass of bright red hair' which 'fell to her knees'.

The Celtic ideal for women seems to have been blonde hair, which has lasted to recent times in traditional Scottish Gaelic love songs whose refrains refer to *nighean bhuidhe bhán* (my golden-yellow-haired maiden). Fidelma in the *Táin* possesses 'long fair yellow-golden hair, three tresses of her hair wound round her head, another tress falling behind to touch the calves of her legs'. Ammianus Marcellinus says 'almost all the Gauls are of tall stature, fair of hair and ruddy of skin, terrible for the fierceness of their eyes . . .'

The descriptions of hair in the various stories are confirmed by the figures in the illustrated manuscript books, such as the *Book of Kells*, which show the hair combed and dressed with utmost care, even the hair of priests and nuns. As late as the thirteenth-century shrine at the *Breac Moedoc*, three nuns appear on the carving with hair hanging down to the waist and not divided into fillets.

According to Dr P.W. Joyce: 'For women, very long hair has been in Ireland always considered a mark of beauty. For example, in the *Táin*, a lovely lady is described as having her yellow hair parted in four wreaths, three of them braided round her head, and the fourth hanging down to her ankles.'

Braided hair was also general among men. One test for a candidate seeking admission into the ranks of the élite warriors of the Fianna was that he should be able to run through a wood without letting the braids of his hair be caught on the branches. According to the same texts the ability to plait or braid hair was considered an important accomplishment for a young man. Combs of various makes and designs have been discovered. Indeed, women used to carry their combs in a 'comb-bag', a *ciorbholg*, an essential piece of equipment like a handbag which is referred to in the *Book of Aicill*. An assortment of binders for the hair, or forehead bands, have been found, some made of gold, silver and white bronze, others of ribbons of gold. One now in the Irish National Museum is five feet long. In fact, both men and women wore hollow golden balls at the ends of their plaited hair. One lady is described in the story of Da Derga's

Hostel as having her hair plaited with eight little golden balls. The National Museum of Ireland has many such balls dating from the early period.

The next step in the toilet was to dress. Both men and women wore underclothing, usually something of fine texture, made from wool or flax, or sometimes silk or satin, depending on one's station in life. Medb is recorded as wearing *lenti glegela* or a pure white silk shirt next to her skin. Various over-garments are described. The usual outer garment was a cloak. This could range from a woollen cloak, for winter wear, to silk and satin cloaks edged with other material or furs. Needless to say, the material and fashion varied according to the means of the wearer. The usual word for this outer garment was a *bratt* although the many Old Irish words for cloak attest to the wide variety of such garments. Figures on a relief at Housesteads, Northumberland, show that the British Celts also wore hooded cloaks. Indeed, in the first century BC to possess a *sagi*, a Celtic woven woollen cloak, was the height of fashion in Rome, says Strabo. At this time, the propagandist Julius Caesar was trying to convince his readers that the Britons did not even know how to weave.

In the *Táin Bó Fraech* there is a description of a group of women wearing purple tunics (*inar*), green head-dresses and brooches of silver. And one woman is wearing a *bratt* of purple which had five coils of plaits in it. Women often wore a parti-coloured tunic and a hooded cloak. A popular dress was of linen, commonly dyed with saffron. Most of the cloaks had hoods attached: the High Cross at Clonmacnoise shows women with this type of hooded cloak. Girdles and belts were commonly worn and even gloves (*láminn*). Many of the ancient tales describe people wearing gloves of cloth and of animal skins or furs. A lady in the 'Voyage of Maeldun' is described as wearing gloves with gold embroidery on her hands (*lámanna co n-órphill imma lámaib*). Old Irish contains four words for gloves: *láminn* (arm-end), *braccaile* (hand-case), *bracand* (given in *Cormac's Glossary* from the word *brac*, a hand) and *mana ma* (in O Cléirigh's dictionary from *man*, a hand).

The descriptions correspond with Diodorus Siculus' description of Gaulish Celtic clothing:

They wear a kind of striking clothing – tunics dyed and stained in various colours, and trousers, which they call by the name of bracae; and they wear striped cloaks, fastened with buckles, thick in winter, and light in summer, picked out with a variegate small check pattern ... some wear gold-plated or silver-plated belts around their tunics.

Finally, hats were the fashion for both men and women. Obviously, in warfare, the Celts wore helmets of various kinds. But hats of skin and even cloth were worn. In the early medieval period, married women had started to cover their heads. There are stone carvings from Entremont and a wood carving from Chamalières, around the time of Christ, which show that head-dresses or head-scarves were then a fashion among the Celts. The medieval head covering was called a *callad* or *caille*. In the story of the 'Feast of Dun na nGéid', in which a male and a female spectre arrive uninvited and devour enormous quantities of food and leave a baleful influence behind, the wife of the High King, Domhnall Mac Aedh, throws her *callad*, or hat, into the fire in a fit of despair. From this word came *caillech*, veiled, as in a nun's veil, and also *caillech*, an old woman or hag, indicating that an old woman usually wore such a headpiece. The Brehon laws refer to the woman's hat as *cenbar no caille* (head-dress) but the *Táin Bó Fraech* talks of a *cenn-barr* (head-top) being worn by a woman. In the ninth-century *Cormac's Glossary* there is an explanation that *meli* was a then defunct word for *cop-cailli* or a woman's head-dress.

It is an interesting possibility, suggested by Dr Simon James, that the way women dressed in ancient Celtic society might have depended not only on their wealth and rank but on their age and marital or maternal status. He points out that in the very early Hallstatt graves, around Asperg, mature Celtic women often have three *fibulae* (buckle, brooch or clasp) at their shoulders, while girls or younger women have one or two. At this time, the common form of dress was two rectangles of fabric (*peplos*) fastened at the sides and held at the shoulders with *fibulae*. Dr James asks whether the number of *fibulae* indicated the age or married status of the women. Certainly, the *caille* or head-dress of medieval times seemed to do so.

Footwear was generally worn by the Celts, ranging from incredibly rich leather shoes, embossed with gold plaques, as worn by the sixth-century Celtic chieftain of Hochdorf, to rough, carved wooden shoes worn by farmers. The most popular name in Ireland for shoes was *bróg*, which has come down in English as brogues, used for a type of hardy shoe. Curiously, in the early eighteenth century the English came to apply the same word to describe a strongly marked accent of English as spoken in Ireland. The logic behind this is inexplicable.

Shoes and sandals from tanned leather or bark were worn in Ireland and they bear a large number of Old Irish names. The richer classes had beautiful ornamented shoes and sandals, comparable to those found in the Celtic graves of France and Germany. In many tales we are told that people of rank wore shoes of silver or *findruine* (white bronze). Maeldun meets a lady who wears *da maelan*, sandals of silver. Diarmuid the High King meets a lady wearing two square-toed shoes (*da maelassa*) of white bronze. These shoes should not be dismissed as merely part of symbolic mythology. The Hochdorf chieftain had sandals covered with gold. Perhaps such shoes would be worn for certain exceptional occasions. The National Museum of Ireland has an ancient pair of leather shoes which are exquisitely made but permanently connected so that they could only be worn by a person sitting down or standing in one spot. Metal footwear has also been found; for example, in 1850 two dozen ancient bronze shoes were found in a single hoard in Co. Antrim. Bronze shoes, engraved with ornamental patterns, have been found bearing, in Latin, the name of St Brigid of Kildare and dated 1410. The discovery, therefore, of such metal shoes is a further endorsement of the accuracy of the old Irish records.

The final touch in personal adornment was the jewellery; again, both men and women wore it in ancient Celtic times. Perhaps the best-known piece of jewellery common to male and female was the torc, which is also known as the *muntorc* (*muin*, neck) which was seen as a mark of high office or the sign of a champion. Cormac Mac Art wears a *muntorc*; the famous statue of 'The Dying Gaul' at the Capitoline in Rome wears a torc; Celtic warriors in a second-century BC terracotta relief from Civitalba, Italy, wear torcs; while both the female warrior Scáthach and the Connacht queen Medb are mentioned wearing *muntorcs*.

Men and women wore ear-rings and the custom was noticed by Nennius in ninth-century Wales. In Ireland the word was *aunasc*, from *aue* (ear) and *nasc* (clasp).

The wife of the High King Nuada Necht is said to have had an arm covered with rings (bracelets) of gold, ready to bestow them on poets, musicians or story-tellers. The musician Cas Corach, in

Connacht, played for a chieftain's wife, and she gave him two of the *fáils* or circlets that she had on her wrists. Circlets of gold and silver seem to have been carried in early Celtic times to act as currency.

The commonest of all articles of jewellery are the brooches worn by all classes of society and both sexes. When Eugene O'Curry worked out the weight of Medb's great golden brooch, by the description given in the *Táin*, he realised that it would have weighed three pounds, so we might have to allow for some exaggeration. Macha Mong Ruadha is said to have removed her golden brooch from her shawl and, with its long pin, marked in the earth the outline for the ramparts of the palace she wanted built at Navan (Emhain Macha). It would certainly have had to be a large pin to do this. The great variety of brooches is mirrored in the numerous Old Irish words for the various types and designs. These elaborate and costly brooches continued to be manufactured in Ireland until just after the Anglo-Norman invasion. Presumably the wearing, and thus the making, of such brooches became unfashionable among the Irish when the rapacious Anglo-Normans were wandering Ireland looking for booty to seize. The famous Ulster poet, Giolla Brighde Mac Conmidhe (*c.*1180–1260), provides a last reference to their manufacture. Mac Conmidhe, incidentally, went as either a pilgrim or a crusader to Palestine about 1218–21 and on his return enjoyed the patronage of the kings of Connacht.

The most outstanding piece of jewellery, as a badge of office, was undoubtedly a diadem or crown worn by petty kings and queens and the High King and his queen. The word *minn óir* dates back to at least the eighth-century texts and describes a diadem or coronet for women of rank. In the story of the *Táin*, Cúchulainn sees a number of maidens with a beautiful woman wearing a *minn óir* on her head. He recognises her, by this token, to be Medb and so he propels a slingshot at her. It misses her head, strikes the golden diadem and breaks it into three pieces. We are told elsewhere in the same story that both Medb and her husband Ailill wear such crowns.

We are told in another story that the High King Diarmuid had a wife, Maireen Mael, who was quite bald and wore her *minn óir* to hide the fact. His second wife Mugain was filled with jealousy and hatred. Before an assembly, at Tailltinn, Mugain persuaded a *ban-cáinte*, or female poet, to ask Maireen for a present after reciting her poem. This would be the usual ritual form of asking for payment for the poem. Under the law of hospitality, no reasonable request could be refused. Mugain persuaded the poetess to demand Maireen's diadem. To Maireen's agony and shame, she did so, and Maireen was publicly exposed. However, the trick rebounded on Mugain and it was she who was disgraced by the incident.

That the High Kings wore rich crowns is shown from the High Crosses of Castledermot and Durrow, as well as in a thirteenth-century fresco painting at Knockmoy Abbey. Diodorus Siculus says:

> . . . they [the Celts] accumulate large quantities of gold and make use of it for personal adornment, not only the women but also the men. For they wear bracelets on wrists and arms, and around their neck thick rings of solid gold and they wear also fine finger rings and even golden tunics.

Strabo comments:

> To the frankness and high-spiritedness of their temperament must be added the traits of childish boastfulness and love of decoration. They wear ornaments of gold, torcs on their necks, bracelets on their arms and wrists, while people of high rank wear dyed garments be-sprinkled with gold. It is this vanity which makes them unbearable in victory and so completely downcast in defeat.

Finally, let a Celtic story-teller describe the 'ideal' Celtic woman and her adornment. Eochaidh the High King meets Étain for the first time in Professor Jackson's translation of a ninth-century text.

> He saw a woman at the edge of the spring, with a bright silver comb ornamented with gold, washing her hair in a silver bowl with four golden birds on it, and little flashing jewels of purple carbuncle on the rims of the bowl. She had a shaggy purple cloak made of fine fleece, and silver brooches of filigree work decorated with handsome gold, in the cloak; a long hooded tunic on her, stiff and smooth, of green silk with embroidery of red gold. Wonderful ornaments of gold and silver with twining animal designs, in the tunic on her breast and her shoulders and her shoulder-blades on both sides. The sun was shining on her, so that the men could plainly see the glistening of the gold in the sunlight amid the green

silk. There were two golden yellow tresses on her head; each one was braided of four plaits, with a bead at the end of each plait. The colour of her hair seemed to them like the flower of the water-flag in summer, or like red gold that has been polished.

She was loosening her hair to wash it, and her arms were out through the opening at the neck of her dress. Her upper arms were as white as the snow of a single night, and they were soft and straight; and her clear and lovely cheeks were as red as the foxglove of the moor. Her eyebrows were as black as a beetle's wing; her teeth were like a shower of pearls in her head; her eyes were as blue as the bugloss; her lips were as red as vermilion; her shoulders were high and smooth and soft and white; her fingers were pure white and long; her arms were long; her slender long yielding smooth side, soft as wool, was as white as the foam of the wave. Her thighs were warm and glossy, sleek and white, round and small, firm and white, were her knees. Her shins were short, white and straight. Her heels were even and straight and lovely from behind. If a ruler were laid against her feet it would be hard to find any fault in them, unless it should make the flesh or skin swell out on them. The right blush of the moon was in her noble face; the lifting of pride in her smooth brows; the ray of love-making in both her royal eyes; a dimple of sport in both her cheeks, in which there came and went flushes of fast purple as red as the blood of a calf, and others of the bright whiteness of snow. A gentle womanly dignity in her voice; a steady stately walk, a queenly pace. She was the fairest and loveliest and most perfect of the women of the world that the eyes of men had ever seen . . .

The description ends in the text: 'This is the maiden concerning whom is spoken the proverb: "Every lovely form must be tested by Étain, every beauty by the standard of Étain."'

We can see from the foregoing that although women in Celtic society had a position of equality, although they could be warriors and rulers and could aspire to all the professions that men aspired to, they did not lose their femininity or their sexuality. They were women who were comfortable in that role; they did not feel threatened or deprived because of their gender; they did not have to assert themselves by attempting to look and act like men. It is, I think, important to understand this point. Ammianus Marcellinus was one of the first, in the fourth century, to attempt to caricature Celtic women as being grisly, man-like Amazons, because he could not understand that a woman could still be a woman while the social and intellectual equal of man in every walk of society.

Women in Medieval History

W E are now in a period where the role of women in Celtic society was visibly changing. Nevertheless, change came slowly and women continued to occupy positions which they could not have attained in other societies. It is the purpose of this chapter to sketch some of the most interesting women who emerge from the historical canvas during the period from the so-called 'Dark Ages', an age of 'Golden Enlightenment' and development for the Celts, through to the end of the medieval period.

In seventh-century Ireland, an interesting female figure stands out: Mór Muman, the daughter of Aed Brennán (d. *c.*AD620), of the Eóghanacht of Locha Léin, a West Munster kingdom. Her story has become mythologised and is now a classic rendition of the story of the goddess of sovranty. Her death is historically recorded in the annals as taking place in AD632. The basis of the romance which grew up around her depicts the dynastic situation in the kingdom of Munster as a kingship circulating alternatively among three families, the Eóganacht Aine, the Eóganacht Chaisil and the Eóganacht Glendamnach. Mór Muman is first married to Fíngen mac Aedo Dubh (d. AD619) of Cashel, then Cathal Mac Aedo Flaind Chathrach of Glendamnach, d. AD628, and then a member of the Eóganacht of Aine. The story falls down here because the Aine branch did not succeed to the kingship until AD637 when Cuán mac Amalgado became king.

Stripped of the myths, what we have here is an historical person-age, whose father is recognised in many annals as a king of Munster. She is credited with marriage to three Munster kings. While the sovranty legend is predictable, we can be sure that the daughter of Aed Brennán was influential enough to attract a series of legends around her. Most texts agree on her marriage to Fíngen and that his rule marked a period of peace and wealth for Munster. According to the *Annals of Tighernach*:

> *In Muma*
> *re linn Fíngen maic Aedha.*
> *robdar lána a cuiledha*
> *robdar toirrtigh a treba*

> Munster
> in the time of Fíngen mac Aedo
> its store-houses were full
> its homesteads were fruitful.

It is recorded that Mór Muman was 'wise, generous and a great bestower of gifts upon the needy' and that she 'was the voice of the people's conscience at the annual *airecht* [council]'. To be so recorded, the lady must have been influential in the political decisions of the kingdom.

If one accepts the hagiographers as recounting some level of 'history', then there is no reason why many of the events that they record cannot be seriously considered as fact. We find two interesting and unusual ladies mentioned in the *Life of Mo Chua* of Balla, Co. Mayo. Mo Chua is usually an endearment form of Colmán, itself a diminutive of Colm (Dove), so we can expect problems in identifying any who bear these names. There are, for example, thirty-two saints named Colm, 234 recorded as Colmán and fifty-nine as Mo Chua. It is usually a masculine name although, confusingly, it does occur as a female one in some early records. We know that our St Mo Chua founded a monastery in the seventh century at a place then significantly known for its Druidic connection as *Ros-dairbh-reach* (the oak grove). He enclosed the walls and hence the place received its new name of Balla (walls).

Mo Chua set off to gain converts and came to a lonely coastal stretch where the cliff fell perpendicularly into the sea. The area was ruled by '*da-ban-gaisgedach*', two women champions, named Becc (Small One) and Líthgen (Lucky Birth). Líthgen has an equivalent in the Gaulish name Litogeni and there is an Irish saint of the same name whose feastday is on 16 January. These two lady warriors were very enterprising. Whenever prosperous travellers passed their way they demanded a toll. If the payment was not forthcoming they had a large basket, hung on ropes, into which they would put the hapless traveller and swing him over the cliff until he agreed to pay up.

Mo Chua's *giolla* or servant had gone on before him and when Mo Chua arrived he found his man being swung by the two intrepid ladies over the cliff because he had refused to pay up. The saint demanded his man's release but the biographer says that the two women refused until Mo Chua himself paid the toll to proceed along the road. The saint, it is reported, even had to part with his richly woven woollen *cabhal*, the hooded cloak he wore.

During the eighth century the kingship of Leinster was in the hands of the Uí Dúnlainge of the Liffey plain. The kings of Munster were continually raiding Leinster at this time and the *Annals of Tighernach* record an expedition of Cathal Mac Finguine who took great booty and hostages. In fact the king of Leinster Murchad Mac Bran and his four sons were all killed in a short space of time. At one point, the annalists seem to indicate that the people of Leinster were without a leader to defend themselves against the onslaught of the Munster kings. So they chose a young princess to lead them who 'could plan strategy and fight better than any man of the Laighin'. The young woman's name was Tuathfhlaith, whose death is recorded in AD754. Significantly, her name means 'Princess of the People'.

In the ninth century, there were certainly many women who appear to have been of an adventurous nature. There were several who bore the name Muirenn (Sea-fair), one of whom is said to have led a band of Irish travellers to Iceland and is mentioned in the Icelandic *Landnámabok* in the form of 'Myrun'. Muirenn was a popular name at this time; it was borne by Oisín's mother, several of the abbesses of Kildare, and a number of queens, so we are unable to identify the Icelandic traveller.

It is right at this point that we should refer to a Gall-Gaedhil, Aud Djúpaudga, who, while not wholly representative of Celtic culture, was part of the mixed Hiberno-Norse cultural milieu. Her father was Ketil Flatnose, a Norwegian Viking chieftain who conquered the Hebrides around AD855. He became leader of a mixed band of Gall-Gaedhil or Norse-Irish and is recorded as marrying a daughter of Cearbhaill of Ossory. Aud Djúpaudga, 'Deep-minded', was born about AD855. She was married to the Dublin king, Olaf the White, bearing him a son, Thorstein the Red, who became a king in Caithness. But she and Olaf divorced. She was said to have accepted Celtic Christianity from her mother and her 'deep-minded' epithet referred to her philosophical and theological contemplations. According to the annals and sagas, Aud returned to her home in the Hebrides and, after a while, ordered ships to be fitted out. She gathered a large group of her followers, mainly hardy Gall-Gaedhil pioneers, to voyage to Iceland. She is remembered as the founding matriarch of Iceland, especially in Laxárdal in the western part of the country.

Later in that century there appears a fascinating queen of Ireland, Gormflaith (*c.*AD870–947). She was a poetess. The daughter of Flann Sionna, High King in AD879–914, she was renowned for her beauty. She married Cormac Mac Cuileannáin, the king-bishop of Cashel, whose literary fame rests on his authorship of *Sanas Chormaic* (*Cormac's Glossary*) although some of his poems have also survived. The annalists wove a tragic romance out of Gormflaith's story. Cearbhaill Mac Muirecáin, the provincial king of Leinster, desired her and contrived to kill Cormac, forcing Gormflaith to marry him. Cormac was killed at the battle of Bealach Mughna in Kildare in AD908. Cearbhaill died the next year. Gormflaith's third marriage was for love and she became wife of Niall Glúndubh, the High King of Ireland AD914–19. He was killed fighting against the Danes of Dublin. Her son, Domhnall, was also killed and Gormflaith composed a heart-rending lament on her unhappy life which has been translated by the scholar Oscar J. Bergin:

Heavy tonight is my sighing, O God! It is heavier today than yesterday. Through grief for the son of bright Niall Glúndubh I desire to go alive into the earth.

My friends grow fewer and fewer, since I no more have sight of Niall: my fair bright ear hears nothing at which I laugh.

Dead is my father, dead my mother, dead are my two brothers, dead my fosterer, honoured and revered, dead my two foster-brothers.

Dead alas! is Dubh Chabhlaigh the just, who would set me upon a golden vat, and would give me no morsel without honey, Dubh Chabhlaigh of fair bright skin.

Dead the son of the king of Innis Gall, he the son of Amhlaeibh of Arann: Amhlaeibh's son used to be on ... my fair knee like a beloved son.

Though all these have gone from the glorious yellow-topped earth, sorer time is that dear Domhnall should be one night under the earth.

Though bitter every sickness and strife that is given to living man, the child that is born of one's fair body, that is what lives in one's mind.

Had I sent my darling to the men of Meath, the race of the upright Colmán would have guarded and kept my lad.

Alas for her who entrusts to a foolish woman the keeping of her tender child, since the protection of life should be enjoined upon a king's son or royal heir.

Woe to her who allowed the sweet-voiced lad to go into Uí Fiachrach, a land where water is plentiful, and men are unruly.

Domhnall son of Niall Glúndubh the right, son of Aed Finnliath of Febhal, son of Niall Caille – motionless! – son of noble Aed Mirdnide.

Son of Niall Frasach from Ráith Mór who bestowed honour upon poets, son of Fergal who was prince of Femen, son of hospitable Mael Dúin.

Son of Mael Fithrigh, son of Sed, son of Domhnall the generous and comely, son of Muirchertagh the Great from the plain, son of Muiredach, son of Eogan.

Son of Niall of the Nine Hostages, the festive, son of Eochaidh Muighmheadhón: the grandmother of dear Domhnall was daughter of Alpin from Scotland.

There is the pedigree of my own son, whose death darkens the sun. White was his neck, white his foot. My heart found nought so heavy.

According to Conall Mac Geoghegan (c.1600–40), compiler of the now-lost *Annals of Clonmacnoise*, Gormflaith was rejected by friends and relatives alike and was reduced to begging from door to door and trying to sell her poetry. No reason is given for this. It may well be that, while Conall was obviously repeating earlier traditions, annalists have also attempted to gloss Gormflaith's life with the traditions of the sovranty goddesses who appear as both brides of kings and old, begging hags. The annals record Gormflaith's death in AD947.

Perhaps a reason for Gormflaith falling out of political favour was that her first husband Cormac became an enemy to her father and it was on this pretext that Cearbhaill, in support of Flann Sionna, cornered Cormac at Bealach Mughna and slew him. Gormflaith hated Cearbhaill and might well have encompassed his death. The poems that have been attributed to her have been collected and translated, primarily by Professor Oscar J. Bergin, in 'Poems attributed to Gormflaith', in *Miscellany presented to Kuno Meyer* (Halle, 1912).

Gormflaith was certainly not the only outstanding woman poet of this period. Uallach, 'Arrogant', the daughter of Muimnechán, became the chief poetess of Ireland at this time. She died in AD934. It was probably not unusual to find women in such high positions at the annual assembly of bards. We have some intriguing but frustrating references to the wife of the Connacht poet Seanchán Torpéist (c.AD570–647), the successor to Dallán Forgaill as chief poet of Ireland. In one reference it is said that his wife, Brigid, was almost as renowned a poet as her husband. We know much of her husband, for he is said to have saved the *Táin Bó Cuailgne* from oblivion, and we have some of his poems. Alas, we know little of Brigid.

Welsh female poets do not appear to have achieved such public office as Uallach or to have had such reputations in legend or history. The earliest one that we know of is Heledd of Pengwern (Shrewsbury) in the late seventh century and only one poem is attributed to her. Most anthologists (male) prefer to attribute the poem as 'anonymous'. Heledd was the sister of a British Celtic chieftain, Cynddylan ap Cyndrwyn, who ruled from Pengwern, which was then in eastern Powys. His death can be traced to an Anglo-Saxon attack directly following the battle of Winwaed Field in AD655. Cynddylan was killed in an attack by Oswiu (Oswy) of Northumbria. Heledd, it is said, was moved to write a poem about the destruction of her brother's court at Shrewsbury, after which the area was settled by the Anglo-Saxons. Heledd laments over the ruins of her home.

> Dark is Cynddylan's hall tonight
> With no fire, no bed.
> I weep awhile, then fall asleep.
>
> Dark is Cynddylan's hall tonight
> With no fire, no light.
> Grieving for you overwhelms me . . .

Heledd speaks of others apart from her brother Cynddylan; she mentions Elfan, Caeawg, Cynon, Gwiawn and Gwyn, whom she describes as 'strong warriors'. Cynon, Gwiawn and Gwyn are identified as the 'seed of Cyndrwyn', so presumably they were her brothers, but who are the others? Perhaps her husband or her lover was among them?

> Dark is Cynddylan's hall tonight
> With no fire, no songs.
> My cheeks are stained by tears . . .

The only major female poet of medieval Wales whose work survives is Gwerful Mechain from the fifteenth century. It is true that we have shadowy glimpses of other female poets but they are from later periods, for example Alis (*fl.*1545), who was the daughter of Gruffudd ab Ieuan ap Llywelyn Fuchan, a poet of Llewini Fychan, Denbigh. Little of her work survives but that which does includes series of *englynion*, verses of three or four lines in strict metre with one rhyme. These are on what sort of husband she wanted, her views on her father's second marriage and so on. It has been claimed that one of the two female poets named Catrin who flourished at this period was Alis's sister. This was a Catrin who wrote an *awdl*, a long poem in traditional metre, about religion, as well as a series of *englynion*. The other Catrin is identified as the daughter of Gruffudd ap Hywel of Llanddaniel-fab in Anglesey, who wrote poems in strict metre; several of these have survived in manuscript, one on the cold summer of 1555.

It is a sad fact that no other really important female poet writing in Welsh comes along until Ann Griffiths (1776–1805), whose life we shall discuss later. Coincidentally, Gwerful and Ann, like Heledd, came from Powys. It is also sad that, excellent as these Welsh female poets are, they seem to have been totally omitted from Anthony Conran's otherwise excellent *Penguin Book of Welsh Verse*.

In order to make easier a brief survey of some of the major female personalities who appeared in the Celtic countries during the medieval period, I have decided to sub-divide the rest of this chapter into sections dealing with the constituent countries.

SOME SCOTTISH LADIES

It was in the eleventh century that the best-known Scottish queen flourished. Gruoch, daughter of Bodhe, granddaughter of Coinneach III (997–1005) of Scotland, has become famous to us as 'Lady Macbeth'. Historically, however, Gruoch in no way resembles Shakespeare's 'fiend-like queen'. Maol Callum II (Malcolm) had slain Gruoch's grandfather and his four children, including her father, in his rise to power. Gruoch, with her brother, Maol Callum Mac Bodhe, had survived and become a symbol of resistance against the new oppressive king. She married Gillecomgain, the Mormaer of Moray, a rival for the kingship, and bore him a son, Lulach, in 1031.

The following year Maol Callum II ordered Gillecomgain's fortress to be attacked. The *Annals of Ulster* record that Gillecomgain and fifty of his warriors were burnt to death when the fortress was set on fire. A grandson of Maol Callum II, MacBeth Mac Findlaech, was then elected as Mormaer of Moray. His politics were opposed to those of his grandfather and he married Gruoch, adopting her son. Maol Callum, thinking that he had finally rid himself of Moray's opposition, paved the way for his other grandson, MacBeth's cousin Donnchadh (Duncan), to succeed him. Maol Callum died in 1034.

We know that by 1040 Donnchadh had proved himself to be one of the most inept of Scottish kings. He had led the country to war several times and was several times defeated. The clans entreated MacBeth to use the Brehon system to overthrow him. Donnchadh was slain in subsequent battle (not murdered) and MacBeth placed on the throne by popular acclaim. He reigned for the next seventeen years. Fourteen of those years saw peace and prosperity in Scotland. Only in the last three years did the son of Donnchadh, brought up in England with little understanding of the Scottish Celtic laws of succession, attempt to overthrow MacBeth with an English army. This was Maol Callum a' chinn mhor (Malcolm Canmore, or Malcolm the Bighead) who was the first Scottish king to reject the Celtic law system and claim succession 'by hereditary right', the right of primogeniture.

He succeeded in killing MacBeth in 1057 but it was Gruoch's son Lulach who was then elected by the clans as king of Scotland. Maol Callum a' chinn mhor had to spend a further year fighting the Scots before he finally slew Lulach 'by stratagem' and proclaimed himself king. He was, significantly, the first king who was refused burial on

Iona, where all legitimate rulers were buried until that date. Gruoch's role in all this is a shadowy one, but what emerges from the chronicles is a picture of a wise and supportive queen who did much work in ensuring the provision of education and making grants to the religious, particularly the Culdees at Loch Leven. Indeed, MacBeth, with Gruoch doubtless accompanying him, was secure enough in popularity in the kingdom in 1050 to go on a pilgrimage to Rome. This was something no English monarch would have dared to do at this time for they would undoubtedly have been overthrown in their absence.

In 1329 Euan (sometimes 'Good John of Islay') succeeded to the petty kingship of the Western Isles. He was confirmed in his position by David II in 1344, ruling Iona, Islay, and also Coll, Tiree, Lewis, Harris, Morven, Lochaver, Duror and Glencoe. He married Áine (sometimes given as Amie), daughter of Ruaridh who was a chieftain ruling the Uists, Barra, Eigg and Rum. This lady was mother of three sons of whom the most notable was Ranald, the founder of the famous Clan Ranald. A division began to spring up between Euan and Áine which seemed to reach a head in 1355 when 'The Lady of the Isles', as she had become known, retired to the Benedictine convent on Iona.

Euan, perhaps in reaction to his broken marriage, set off to fight for the King of France against England and was taken prisoner in 1356 during the disastrous battle of Poitiers. He was imprisoned in England for a year before he was ransomed and arrived back in Scotland in 1357 where he found that Áine had divorced him.

In 1360 Euan married again to Mairghread, daughter of Robert, the High Steward of Scotland, and of another Mairghread, the daughter of King Robert Bruce. Robert the High Steward became Robert II of Scotland in 1370; he was founder of the fortunes of the Stewart (Stuart) family. Euan then relinquished his title 'King of the Isles', seemingly at the request of Robert II who, thoroughly Normanised, believed only one king should rule in Scotland; the former system of a High King and petty kings, which had really begun to disappear after the overthrow of MacBeth, vanished entirely. Euan's eldest son Ranald, by Áine, was overlooked in the succession. When Euan died it was Domnuil, his son by Mairghread, who became the new Lord of the Isles in 1380.

In folklore, Áine, the daughter of Ruraidh, was forced to retire to the isolation of the convent on Iona because of her domestic quarrels with Euan. She became a subject of contentious tales, especially as the event led to the split between Euan's two families, Áine's son having to take second place to Mairghread's son. What emerges is a side-show between two powerful women, each ambitious for her son, each seeking to found the future dynasty in Scotland – one from her convent cell on Iona, the other at the resplendent court of her father Robert II and at the court of her husband Euan, one-time 'King of the Isles'.

The most famous descendant of Euan's clan was the daughter of Ranald Macdonald of Milton and Balevannich in South Uist – Flora Macdonald. Although she is out of the period we are discussing, a detour into the eighteenth century will be forgiven to examine this amazing Celtic lady. Her real name was Fionnghal (Fair One) but she has become known by the Anglicised form, Flora. She was born in 1722 and was only twenty-three years old when Prince Charles Edward landed in Scotland in an attempt to regain the lost throne of his grandfather, James II (James VII of Scotland). Flora's father had died and her mother had remarried to Hugh Macdonald of Armadale in Sleat, who was a Hanoverian supporter. Nevertheless, he had a certain sympathy, as did most Scots, for Charles Edward because the Stuarts had promised to sever the unpopular union between Scotland and England.

Flora's close friend was Lady Mairghread Macdonald, a fervid Jacobite and friend of Charles Edward. Following the terrible slaughter and defeat of the Scottish army at Culloden, Flora discovered that Charles Edward was hiding in the area. With another Jacobite friend, Lady Clanranald, Flora concocted a plan to disguise him as her Irish maid 'Betty Burke'. The Clanranalds were later to be arrested and transported to London for trial and execution. Flora, with 'Betty' and Neil Mac Eachain (whose son was to become one of Napoleon Bonaparte's favourite generals – Marshal Macdonald, Duke of Taranto), began the journey to Skye. English military patrols arrested them at one point but, thanks to Flora's clear-headed control, they did not recognise the prince. He had to hide in Rossinish while Flora organised more clothes and a ship. Then, on 28 June 1746, they set out for Waternish on Skye. The Hanoverian militia, spying the boat, opened fire on it but they escaped.

There were several more days of adventures and escapes before Flora escorted Charles Edward and Neil to Portree from where they were to cross to Raasay on the next stage of their journey to the final exile of the Stuarts.

Flora Macdonald was eventually arrested and taken in chains to London on 8 November 1746. She was imprisoned on the prison ship *Royal Sovereign* in the Thames until 6 December. Conditions on this ship, as on the other prison hulks which had been requisitioned for the 'Scottish rebels', were intolerable. The death rate was high. For example, on one transport ship on the journey from Scotland to London, 157 prisoners out of a total of 564 died in the appalling conditions. More died while awaiting trial; even more were executed or died during transportation to the colonies. Only nine succeeded in making escapes from London. Of the first forty-nine prisoners to be brought to trial, seventeen were executed on Kennington Common, ritually hanged, drawn and quartered as prescribed by law. Heads were placed on spikes along Fleet Street. Execution followed execution, including those of several Scottish peers, while the remaining prisoners were transported as cheap labour to the New World colonies. In January 1747 nearly a thousand prisoners, including women and children, were ordered to be transported to the Americas.

It was against this background that twenty-four-year-old Flora Macdonald waited in the dark hold of a prison ship on the Thames to hear her fate.

On 6 December she was removed to the Tower of London. She must have been acutely aware of the number of women who had been executed within these forbidding grey stone walls. In the meantime, Flora's stepfather, playing much on the fact that he had been loyal to the cause of the Hanoverians, managed to stir up sympathy for Flora and in July 1747, after nine months' imprisonment, she was released into the custody of Lady Primrose. A year later Flora was allowed to return to Scotland. She was nearly drowned on the crossing back to Skye when her boat floundered in rough seas.

At Armadale she found that she was welcomed as a heroine. In January 1750, she married Alex, son of The Macdonald of Kingsburgh, who had helped her escort the prince through Skye. They left for America and during the next sixteen years they had ten children. Curiously enough, during the American War of Independence Flora and her husband chose to support the English, although many of her fellow Scottish prisoners in London who had been transported, together with their children, were eagerly serving the fledgeling republic and had formed a Scottish Brigade of the American Revolutionary Army. Her husband became a brigadier in George III's colonial forces between 1774 and 1779. He was wounded in the fighting and, when the independence of the American colonies was recognised, Flora returned to her native Skye where she died, aged sixty-eight, in March 1790. 'Her name will be mentioned in history,' commented Dr Samuel Johnson, 'and if courage and fidelity be virtues, mentioned with honour.'

Certainly, no survey of Celtic women could fail to mention her name, although it is sad that she is only known to us by the Anglicised name of Flora Macdonald and not by her real name of Fionnghal Ní Dhòmhnuil.

SOME MANX LADIES

Aufrica was always a popular female name among the Manx from the early Christian period and seems to derive from a form of Euar, the Manx for 'yew'. It was a name borne by the wife of Olaf I (*c*.1103/1113–1153), king of Man and the Isles. One of the daughters of Aufrica and Olaf, Reynilt (Ragnild), married Somhairle, or Somerled of Argyll, who contested the throne of Godred II of Man between 1158 and 1164. Somhairle and his son Dugal were able to wrest control of the Western Isles, which were then part of the Manx kingdom. The name Aufrica was also borne by the daughter of Godred II, who was to marry John de Courcy (1177–1205), 'Conquestor Ultoniae', in 1180. It is this Aufrica who became a strong force in the politics of the area.

De Courcy was a Norman knight from Somerset who decided to set out to conquer the Ulster kingdoms on his own account with a band of young knights and followers. He had arrived in Ireland in 1177, five years after Henry II's 'conquest', and by 1 February he had captured Dún Phádraig (Downpatrick), the strategic hill fort which gave its name to Co. Down (Dún) and which was capital of the petty king Ruaraidh Ua Dúnshlaoibhe (Dunlevy), who was killed in 1201. Downpatrick was the site of an influential religious centre. By coincidence, the papal legate, Cardinal Vivian, who had arrived there to bless the Ulster army of Ua Dúnshlaoibhe, had just landed from the Isle of Man where he had married Fionnghuala (Fair Shoulder), the daughter of the king of Cinel Eoghain, Melaghlin Mac

Lochlainn, to Godred of Man and the Isles. Fionnghuala became known in Man as Fingola (sometimes Phingola) and she was obviously Godred's second wife, the stepmother of Aufrica.

Melaghlin Mac Lochlainn now came to the support of the beleaguered Ua Dúnshlaoibhe and a large army took the field against de Courcy on 24 June 1177. The archbishop of Armagh, Bishop Ó Caráin, the bishop of Down and many other clerics, with the most sacred relics of Armagh, appeared to support the native army. The Anglo-Normans slew the clergy as well as the Irish soldiers. Battle followed battle until de Courcy was being hailed as 'Princeps Ulidiae'. He was to rule the Ulster kingdoms for twenty years in spite of the claims of the descendants of Ruaraidh, until 1272, to be 'kings of the Irish of Ulster'.

De Courcy married Aufrica in 1180, according to Professor Edmund Curtis, 'with the Norman instinct for "happy marriages".' He thus allied himself with the Norse-Gaelic world in the north, and dreamed of a feudal principality in Ulster allied with the kings of Man and the Hebrides, and the semi-Gaelic earls of the Galloway in Scotland. But de Courcy obviously did not want to pay homage to the Angevin emperor, Henry II, and was therefore deemed by King John, whom Henry had made 'King of Ireland', to be a dangerously ambitious rival. De Courcy was eventually pushed into a contrived quarrel with the de Lacys. He was captured and imprisoned. No more is heard of him after 1219.

Looking more deeply into the story, we find that Aufrica was playing an important role in the intrigues of this drama. She appears in occasional references, helping her husband create a new Ulster and bring in Benedictines and Cistercians to Antrim and Down to replace the former Celtic foundations. Castles were raised at Downpatrick, Dromore, Coleraine, Newry, Dundrum and Carlingford, as well as the impressive Carrickfergus Castle and abbey.

Aufrica's first language was Manx Gaelic, almost indistinguishable from Ulster Irish at the time, and doubtless she was bilingual in Norse. She became proficient in Norman French and was 'a lady of much pleasing wisdom, but stern in justice'. According to one source, while her husband was away attacking Donnchadh Ó Cearbhaill, king of Oriel (Airghialla, a kingdom founded in the fourth century across the borders of Connacht and Ulster) Mac Lochlainn's army attacked Downpatrick. Aufrica is said to have personally directed defences and driven them off.

It may well be that a child of Aufrica married into the de Lacy family which had instigated de Courcy's overthrow. An Egidia de Lacy married Richard, Lord of Connacht, whose granddaughter bore the name of Aufrica. In 1292, we find this Aufrica de Connacht claiming to be the rightful monarch of the kingdom of Man and the Isles. Thus this Egidia de Lacy could only have been daughter or granddaughter of the original Aufrica de Courcy.

The last independent king of Man and the Isles, Magnus, had died in 1265. He had no immediate heirs but left his kingdom to Alexander III of Scotland to rule as suzerain monarch. England, in the person of Edward I, decided to put in their claim to take over the small strategic kingdom and for the next century Scotland and England fought over it while the Manx tried to retain their own independence against either side.

Two women claimed the kingship of the Isle of Man at this time. In July 1291, Moirrey (Mary), the daughter of Ragnall II (d. 1249), asked Edward I to respect her claim. She had married a Norman knight in Alexander III's service named de Waldeboef. In 1305 her grandson, John de Waldeboef, was still trying to establish his claim to the kingship. Alas, little is known of this Moirrey except that she must have been a strong-minded lady to attempt to establish her claim at a time when Edward I was successfully intervening in Scottish domestic affairs as 'The Hammer of the Scots', having also already claimed jurisdiction over the Manx.

Edward must have been bemused when, a year later, the previously mentioned Aufrica de Connacht demanded to be recognised as queen of Man and the Isles. In 1306 Aufrica granted her rights to the kingship to 'the noble and potent man Simon de Montecute', presumably by right of marriage to him. His descendants obviously succeeded in asserting their authority over the Island for William de Montacute ruled there from 1333 to 1344 and his son, bearing the same name, from 1344 to 1392.

Lauon, the sister of the wife of Ragnall II of Man and the Isles, was married to Ragnall's brother Olaf in 1214. Olaf established himself as petty ruler of Lewis. He persuaded his nephew, another Ragnall, bishop of Sodor and Man, to dissolve his marriage so that he could marry Cristina, daughter of Ferkkar of Ross. Ragnall's wife, in Man, was deeply incensed at the dishonour done to her sister. She sent a secret letter in 1223 to her son Godred Donn in Skye asking him to kill Olaf for dishonouring Lauon. Godred Donn failed and was in turn seized on Iona where he was blinded by Olaf as punishment.

There was only one major religious house for women on the Island until the dissolution of the monasteries in 1541 and this was the Priory of St Mary, in Douglas. We know that there was at least one interesting prioress, Cristina, who was prioress in 1408. She was recorded as a fierce critic of John Stanley, appointed King of Man and the Isles in 1405 by the blessing of Henry IV. Stanley's heirs and successors were to rule the Island on the service of paying homage and two falcons to all kings of England on their coronation. The title of 'King of Man' was changed to 'Lord of Man' during the time of Thomas (1504–21), when the concept of petty kingships under a suzerain king fell into disuse. Alas, we do not know what form Cristina's criticism of the new English kings of the Island took.

At the time of the dissolution we know that there were only three sisters left at St Mary's with their prioress Margaid (Margaret) Egliston. Margaid was certainly a lady who saw a main chance. Edward (1521–72) of Man accepted the Reformation. He sent his comptroller, Richard Calcott, to take over the religious houses on the Island and sell their properties. Richard Calcott decided to buy the former nunnery of St Mary's himself and Margaid, freed from her vows by the Reformation, promptly married him. Calcott built his new bride a splendid residence on the site with stones from her former religious house.

While we are dealing specifically with Celtic women, perhaps it would be churlish not to mention that one of the most determined of the Stanley 'Lords of Man' was a 'Lady'. Although she falls outside our period and was more French in culture than Celtic, she is worthy of notice. Charlotte, the wife of James I (1627–51) of Man, was, in fact, of a Breton family, de la Tremouille. James naturally sided with the Royalist side in the English Civil War. As well as his estates and residence on the Island he had a Lancashire estate, Lathom House. In 1643 he left Charlotte there to hasten to Man where the Manx, under Illiam Dhone Christian, an ancestor of Fletcher Christian of the famous *Bounty* mutiny, had risen up in support of Parliament. The support for Parliament was seen as a means of ridding the Island of the Stanley overlordship. Early in 1644 Lord Fairfax for the Parliamentarians laid siege to Lathom House for eighteen weeks. The siege was then left to Colonel Alexander Rigby, who demanded an immediate surrender. Charlotte was in charge of the defences and replied through an intermediary: 'Tell that insolent rebel he shall have neither persons, goods nor home. When our strength is spent, we shall find a fire more merciful than Rigby; and myself, children and soldiers, rather than fall into his hands, will seal our loyalty in the same flame.'

Her words did not have to be put to the test because Prince Rupert relieved Lathom House. Charlotte joined James in Man and there they lived until 1649 when, after the execution of Charles, Parliament demanded that James surrender the Island. He refused and on 15 August 1651 sailed to England with 300 Manx troops loyal to him to join Charles, now claimed by the Royalists as Charles II, at Worcester. Before leaving he made Charlotte his deputy, 'willing and commanding all officers in commission or otherwise to be obeying, aiding and assisting you upon your command'. The Islanders were divided although some of the Manx militia on 23 September 'offered to take oaths of faithfulness to be true' to Charlotte and her government. Meanwhile, James had been captured after the battle of Worcester, tried and executed by Parliament.

Colonel Duckenfield was sent to the Island. He quickly did a deal with the Manx led by Illiam Dhone and then went on to Castle Rushen where Charlotte was holding out. The summons to surrender was the first news of her husband's death. This news caused some of her soldiers to desert and so, on 31 September, she deemed further resistance was useless. Charlotte, who had been legally 'Lord of Man' following the death of her husband, surrendered on condition that she, her children, friends and servants were allowed to leave the Island. She was, in fact, the last Royalist leader to submit to the English Parliamentarian forces outside Ireland. Her son was restored to the Lordship of Man at the time of the Stuart Restoration and marked the beginning of his rule with the execution of the Manx leader Illiam Dhone; Illiam Dhone's cousin Edward died in prison. In spite of Illiam Dhone and Edward becoming folk heroes among the ordinary Manx, the Stanley family, hated by many ordinary Manxfolk, remained as Lords of Man until 1736 when the title passed through the daughter of James II (1702–36) of Man, Amelia Anna Sophia, who had married James Murray, second duke of Atholl. The duke died in 1764 and his daughter, Charlotte, married a cousin, John Murray, who also became the third duke of Atholl. Charlotte and John decided to sell the Lordship of Man to the British Crown for £70,000.

SOME WELSH LADIES

In the Welsh chronicles, such as *Brut y Tywysogion* (Chronicle of the Princes), there are many references to prominent Welsh women. Alas, the majority of names are usually given only as the mothers, daughters or wives of those in high position. Yet their very role makes them fascinating. We know of Esyllt, the daughter of Cynan ap Rhodri, the king of Gwynedd (d. AD836), who married an adventurer from the kingdom of Strathclyde named Gwriar. Her son, Merfyn Fryach (the Freckled), became king of Gwynedd, AD825–44. So here we have a clear example of a claim of kingship through the female line – not for the first or last time in the Celtic world. Merfyn married Nest, sister of Cyngen ap Cadell, the last of the kings of Powys (d. AD855). Cyngen died on a pilgrimage to Rome.

The son of Merfyn and Nest, Rhodri ap Merfyn, was able to claim Powys as well as Gwynedd by a claim through his mother's line. He married Angharad, sister of Gwgon ap Meurig, king of Ceredigion and Ystrad Tywi, and thus, in effect, became the first king of a united Wales; he was known as Rhodri Mawr (the Great), and died in AD878. Therefore, the very unity of Wales had been achieved through the female lines of kingship and not the male lines. As Professor David Walker points out: 'None of the marriages could create a hereditary claim.' Professor Walker means this in the English sense but that was not the Celtic way. They provided a sound basis in Celtic law for a successful take-over of power.

It is a pity, then, that we do not know just what role such women as Esllyt, Nest and Angharad played in the politics of the time. The union through the female line even continued under Hywel ap Cadell, or Hywel Dda, 'the Good' (d. AD950). He married Elen, daughter of Llywarch of Dyfed (d. AD904) and niece of Rhodri ap Hyfraidd, which brought him a claim over Seisyllwg and Dyfed. The union of the Welsh kingdoms was completed by the time of his death. Elen had died in AD929, the year Hywel had gone on a pilgrimage to Rome. Hywel was the first king to strike coins for the united Welsh kingdom. How much of a part did Elen play in this achievement, in Hywel's policies against the powerful, growing empire of Wessex which achieved the union of the Anglo-Saxon kingdoms in AD937? Was she influential in Hywel's decision to form a commission to gather and codify the Welsh law system? Alas, the references to her are all too brief.

Brief, too, are the glimpses of another twelfth-century Welsh lady, also named Angharad, the wife of Gruffudd ap Cynan, king of Gwynedd. Her death is recorded in 1162. She was the daughter of Owain ap Edwin. She was the mother of three sons, Cadwallon, Owain and Cadwaladr – 'and many daughters', adds the chronicler. The way the chronicler rhapsodises over her means that she was a woman of some importance and influence. She had 'yellow-gold hair, large eyes, of fine shape and queenly figure, with strong limbs and well-made legs, with the best of feet, and longer fingers and thin nails. She is kindly with a healthy appetite with food and with drink. She is eloquent, wise and prudent, a woman of good counsel and liberality of mind and purpose; merciful to her people of Gwynedd, charitable to the needy and, in all decisions, a woman of justice.' One is left in some frustration, wanting to know exactly what she did to win such praise from the chroniclers.

Some Welsh women do appear in firmer form from the pages of the chronicles in the early twelfth century. It is from this period that emerges the figure of Nest, a lady who seems almost an equal to the mythical Medb of Connacht. She was acclaimed 'the most beautiful woman in the country' and was the mistress of a king and wife successively of two powerful Norman lords. Men killed for her, went to war for her and were outlawed for desiring her. Through her large family she supplied the seeds of the great Norman families who were to take part in the initial Anglo-Norman invasion of Ireland and expropriation of the great estates there.

She was the daughter of Rhys ap Tewdwr Mawr, king of Dyfed in South Wales. Rhys had been slain in battle in 1090 fighting the Norman invaders of his kingdom. His young daughter was eventually sent to the court of Henry I (1100–35) as a hostage for the good conduct of her people. Henry I, attracted by her good looks, had an affair with her and she bore him a son, Henry FitzHenry. Her brother Gruffydd ap Rhys had been taken into exile into Ireland where he grew to manhood. The Normans were colonising the former kingdom of Dyfed and establishing a colony of Flemish soldiers intermixed with English settlers in what is now Pembroke. Nest returned home to find the kingdom of Dyfed under Norman tutelage. Walter FitzOtho and Gwladus, a princess of Gwynedd, had a son, Gerald of Windsor, who held Pembroke Castle for Henry I. Perhaps on the percept that if you can't join them, marry them, Nest married Gerald in 1109 and bore him five children.

Then, one night, she was abducted in brutal fashion by her own cousin Owain ap Cadwgan, who had become besotted by her. The chronicle of *Brut y Tywysogion* for that year records the abduction in exciting fashion.

Cadwgan ap Bleddyn prepared a feast for the chiefs of the land. And he invited to the feast which he had made, his son Owain from Powys. And that feast he held at Christmas in honour of God. And when that feast was ended, and Owain had heard that Nest, daughter of Rhys ap Tewdwr, wife of Gerald the Steward, was in the castle . . . he went with but a few men in his company to visit her as a kinswoman.

And kinsfolk they were: for Cadwgan ap Bleddyn and Gwladus, daughter of Rhiwallon, Nest's mother, were first-cousins, and Bleddyn and Rhiwallon, sons of Cynfyn, were brothers by Angharad, daughter of king Maredudd.

And after that, at the instigation of God, he came of a night to the castle and but few men with him, about fourteen, after having secretly made a hole under the threshold unknown to the keepers of the castle. And then he came to the chamber in which Gerald and Nest, his wife, were sleeping. And they raised a shout around and about the chamber in which Gerald was, and kindled tapers and set fire to the buildings to burn them. And when he heard the shout, Gerald awoke, not knowing what to do. And then Nest said to him, 'Go not out to the door, for there thine enemies await thee, but follow me.' And that he did. And she led him to the privy which adjoined the chamber. And there, as is said, he escaped by way of the privy hole.

And when Nest knew that he had escaped, she cried out from within and said to the men who were outside: 'Why do you cry out in vain? He whom you seek is not here. He has escaped.' And after they had entered, they searched for him everywhere. And when they did not find him, they seized Nest and her two sons and daughter and another son of his (Gerald) by a concubine, and they sacked and plundered the castle. And after burning the castle and collecting spoil, and having intercourse with her, Owain returned to his land. But Cadwgan, his father, was not at that time present in the land, for he had gone to Powys to pacify those who were in disagreement with Owain and who had forsaken him.

And when Cadwgan heard of that deed, he was indignantly

grieved because of the rape that had been committed upon Nest, daughter of Rhys, and also for fear lest king Henry should be enraged at the injury to his steward. And then he returned and sought to restore Gerald the Steward to his wife and his spoil from Owain, but he did not obtain them. And then in guile, Nest was speaking to Owain thus: 'If thou wouldst have me faithful to thee and keep me with thee, have my children escorted to their father.' And in his infatuation and love for Nest, Owain released Gerald's two sons and daughter and sent them to Gerald.

Eventually Owain was forced to flee to Ireland with an angry Gerald in pursuit, aided by his Norman friends. Owain's father, Cadwgan, lost his lands as punishment for the actions of his son but eventually he persuaded Gerald to return them on condition Owain did not return to Wales. However, Owain, a contrary individual, did return. He tried to inveigle his way back into favour by fighting against his fellow Welshmen who were then fighting the Anglo-Normans led, in fact, by Nest's own brother Gruffydd ap Rhys. But in 1116, Gerald the Steward and an army of Flemings from Rhos caught up with Owain near Carmarthen. In the ensuing skirmish, Owain was killed.

Gerald himself died soon afterwards and Nest remarried to Stephen, the constable of Cardigan Castle. To him, Nest bore another son. Thus Nest was the progenitor of three families, all of whom were to take part in the Anglo-Norman conquest and settlement of Ireland – the FitzHenrys, FitzGeralds and FitzStephens. The Welsh branch of the FitzGeralds eventually adopted the name Carew from Carew Castle, four miles east of Pembroke, which was part of Nest's dowry when she married Gerald. Gerald Cambrensis was a grandson of Nest, his mother being Nest's daughter Angharad who married William de Barri, who was not only Gerald Cambrensis's father but the progenitor of the famous Irish Barry family of Co. Cork. Gerald's brother, Philip de Barri Mór, was called Mór, 'Great', to differentiate him from other de Barris, and thus become the ancestor of the Barrymore family. Philip expropriated the biggest estate in Cork to be seized by the Anglo-Normans.

Gruffydd ap Rhys, Nest's brother, had been brought up as a political exile in Ireland. He returned to Dyfed around 1112–15 and spent some time with Nest at Pembroke. Then he launched a Welsh uprising against the Anglo-Normans, starting with attacks on Arberth and on the castle of Richard FitzPons at Bychan. He was initially successful. It was not until 1137 that Gruffydd was killed in battle. Just before this time, Gruffydd's wife, Gwenllian, makes an appearance in history. Gwenllian takes her place with Boudicca as one of the most popular Celtic female warrior heroines.

There is some confusion about her origins as Gwenllian was a popular name in medieval Wales. The Gwenllian who was wife to Gruffydd ap Rhys has been identified as one of two possible people. In some texts she is given as one of the two daughters of Bleddyn ap Cynfan, Cunydd and Gwenllian. But the Gwenllian who was Bleddyn's daughter is more often recorded as wife of Caradoc ap Gruffydd ap Rhydderch who was slain a generation before at the battle of Mynydd Carn in 1088. The second Gwenllian is identified in other texts as the daughter of Gruffydd ap Cynan, the king of Gwynedd. This seems to be more feasible.

Gwenllian emerges as the equal of her determined and ambitious sister-in-law, Nest. Following the death of Henry I in 1135, a general uprising was planned in South Wales against the Norman castle. Gruffydd ap Rhys had gone to finalise the plans with Gwenllian's father, the king of Gwynedd. In his absence, a large force of Normans attacked Deheubarth, his home territory. Gwenllian raised what fighting men she could and led a counter-attack which drove the Normans back to the castle of Cydwedi (Kidwelly). Here the Normans, under Maurice de Londres, fortified themselves. Gwenllian and her forces now made an attack on Cydwedi but were driven off and took to flight. Gwenllian was killed, fighting a rearguard action, at a spot just north of the castle later known as Maes Gwenllian (Gwenllian's field) in 1136. She had managed to drive off the initial surprise attack and give her husband time to prepare his forces. Her name became a rallying call for the Welsh in much the same way as Boudicca was a symbol to their Iceni ancestors.

Gruffydd ap Rhys and Gruffydd ap Cynan launched a new offensive. Both men were killed in the following year. In spite of their deaths, the war against the Anglo-Normans continued. In these subsequent wars, an uncle of Strongbow, Richard FitzGilbert, was slain at Crickhowell. In the year of Gruffydd's death the Anglo-Normans received their biggest check when the Welsh won a decisive victory at Crug Mawr, two miles from Cardigan. Perhaps there was justice in the fact that Gwenllian and Gruffydd's son, Rhys ap Gruffydd (d. 1197), captured Cydwedi Castle, where his mother had been killed, and managed to retain it. He finally made a peace with Henry

II at Gloucester in 1175 and was rewarded with the title of Justiciar of Deheubarth. In 1176 Rhys organised the first eisteddfod that we have any record of. This was held at Christmas at Aberteifi (Cardigan) Castle and it was proclaimed throughout Wales, Ireland and Scotland.

Rhys also had a sister named Nest, who is not to be confused with his famous aunt. This Nest married Ifor ap Meurig, who had also fought the Anglo-Normans and whose son Gruffydd attended the peace council in Gloucester in 1175. Rhys had a second sister, Gwladus, who married firstly Seisyll ap Dyfnwal of Gwent. In spite of the agreement at Gloucester, the Anglo-Normans burnt his fortress and killed Gwladus' sons, Gruffydd and Cadwaladr. Gwladus herself was taken prisoner. She was ransomed and later married Caradoc ap Iestyn, lord of Neath and Afan, whose stronghold was at Aberfan. Caradoc seems to have conducted his affairs with more political acumen than Gwladus' first husband and their descendants held the lands until the thirteenth century. When Rhys' own daughter, named Gwenllian after her grandmother, died in 1190, the chronicler noted that she was 'the flower and beauty of all Wales'.

Gwenllian, incidentally, was also the name borne by the sister of the last independent king of Wales, Llywelyn ap Gruffydd ap Llywelyn. After Llywelyn's death Edward I pressed on with his conquest of Wales, refusing to negotiate with Llywelyn's brother Dafydd, who had assumed the kingship, and who was eventually captured in 1283. Dafydd was taken to Shrewsbury, sentenced to death and hanged, drawn and quartered. Gwenllian, whose mother had been Eleanor, the sister of Simon de Monfort, who had died when Gwenllian was born, was also taken prisoner. With her, Edward I was a little more merciful. He simply consigned her to a convent at Sempringham; according to the *Brut y Tywysogion* 'she was made a nun against her will'. Edward wanted to be sure there were no future claimants to the throne of Wales. In this he did not succeed for there were uprisings in Wales against the English conquest down until the Tudor period.

We should, at this point, mention a lady who became queen of Wales and one of the most interesting and influential women in the country, although strictly speaking, she was not a Celt. Joan (1195–1237) was the daughter of King John. When Llywelyn ap Iorwerth, or Llywelyn Fawr (the Great), the king of Wales, became resigned to Norman power and accepted John and his Angevin empire as having suzerain rights over the Welsh kingdom in 1204, part of the settlement included a marriage agreement. John's daughter Joan was married to Llywelyn in 1205. She learnt Welsh and became known to them by the Welsh form of Joan, Siwan. Siwan, as queen of Wales, proved a remarkable woman and was chief counsellor to Llywelyn. She negotiated affairs of state with her brother John in 1211 on behalf of Llywelyn and later with her half-brother Henry III in 1225, 1228 and in 1232.

Siwan remained very much her own person but in 1230 she had a brief affair with William de Braose, a young Marcher lord. Llywelyn had him hanged and Siwan was imprisoned for a short time. But Llywelyn and Siwan were reconciled within a year and they established a Franciscan friary at Llanfaes, on Anglesey, in thanks. On her death Siwan was buried there and her tomb and effigy are still to be seen. Saunders Lewis, the major Welsh poet and playwright, wrote a play about the relationship of Siwan and William de Braose. *Siwan* (1955) is considered as one of his finest works.

An ironic touch to this story is that Gwladus Ddu (d. 1251), the daughter of Llywelyn Fawr and a former wife of his, had married Reginald de Braose in 1215. When Reginald died in 1228, the young William had taken over the estates. Gwladus, however, had then married Ralph Mortimer (d. 1246). It was this marriage that made the Mortimers, subsequently the Dukes of York, the direct descendants of Llywelyn Fawr. This enabled David Powell (1552–98) in his *Historie of Cambria, now called Wales* (1584) to give a Tudor propaganda twist to history by asserting that Elizabeth I was not only rightful monarch of England but also rightful queen of Wales as the descendant of Gwladus Ddu.

Elizabeth I was not the only powerful Tudor woman of her period. She had a distant relative who has become known in history as 'The Mother of Wales'. This was Catrin of Berain (1534/5–91), who was head of an intricate web of family connections which dominated Welsh life. She was the granddaughter of an illegitimate son of Henry Tudor, who became Henry VII. She became the owner of the Tudor family home at Penmynydd in Anglesey.

Catrin married four times: firstly, John Salusbury of Llewenni, Denbigh (d. 1566); secondly, Sir Richard Clough of Denbigh (d. 1570); thirdly, Maurice Wynn (d. 1580); fourthly, Edward Thelwall of Plas-y-Ward, Denbigh (d. 1610). Catrin's eldest son Thomas

Salusbury was executed for his complicity in the plot to assassinate Elizabeth and place her cousin Mary, Queen of Scots on the throne. The plot was organised by Anthony Babington in 1586. Catrin seemed to move from Catholicism to Protestantism and through her various marriages obtained great financial and political power in Wales. Among several poets who sang her praise was William Cynwal (c.1588) who wrote:

> Catrin wych, wawr ddistrych wedd
> Cain ei llun, cannwyll Wynedd.

> Splendid Catrin, like the brightness of foam
> Fine her aspect, the candle of Gwynedd.

Lucas de Heere painted her portrait wearing a locket said to contain a lock of the hair of Richard Clough, the only one of her husbands that she is reputed to have really loved.

SOME IRISH LADIES

Most Irish schoolchildren would be able to tell you that Diarmait Mac Murchada of Uí Ceinnsealaigh, otherwise Dermot Mac Murrough, Lord of Hy Kinsella, King of Leinster and the Foreigners, who died at Ferns on 1 May 1171 after a reign of forty-six years, was the 'traitor' who invited Henry II and his Anglo-Normans to invade Ireland and thus commence the centuries-long unhappy relationship between Ireland and England. Nothing is ever that simple, though the immediate cause of the invasion was, in fact, the personalities behind the tussle for the office of High King. Between 1156 and 1166 there were two candidates for the position – Muirchertach Mac Lochlainn of Ailech and Ruaraidh Ua Conchobhair of Connacht. Reduced to a very simple storyline, Diarmait Mac Murchada supported Mac Lochlainn but it was Ua Conchobhair who emerged triumphant. Ua Conchobhair's supporters chased Mac Murchada out of his kingdom and he left Ireland in August 1166, in an attempt to interest Henry II in helping him regain his position. Henry II was busy consolidating his Angevin empire, which covered England, Normandy, Anjou, Poitou and Aquitaine, with claims over Scotland, Wales and Toulouse. He was not interested at that time in an invasion of Ireland but Mac Murchada was able to recruit a band of mercenaries led by Richard FitzGilbert de Clare, Earl of Pembroke, nicknamed 'Strongbow', a grandson, as we have seen, of Nest. Among the inducements Mac Murchada promised Strongbow was the hand in marriage of his daughter Aoife, implying that this would mean that Strongbow could inherit the kingdom when he died. However, the Norman law of primogeniture did not have currency in Ireland. Strongbow apparently did not realise this.

A small force landed in Ireland early in 1169 but was defeated by the forces of the High King. However, in May 1169 Strongbow landed with a larger force of 200 knights and 1200 men-at-arms. First Waterford and then Dublin fell to them. Mac Murchada died and Strongbow, who had married Aoife, now claimed the kingship of Leinster by hereditary right. The Mac Murchadas ignored this and the *derbhfine* of the clan promptly elected Muirchertach Mac Murchada, the dead king's nephew, as the king.

Strongbow and his Norman adventurers were now beset by the combined Irish armies commanded by the High King. Strongbow appealed for help to Henry II, recognising him as his suzerain lord. There was little doubt that had Strongbow been able to secure a conquest of Ireland on his own account then he would have set himself up as king independently of Henry II. Henry arrived in 1171 with 500 knights and 4000 men-at-arms.

On 6 October 1175, the Treaty of Windsor was agreed in which Ruaraidh Ua Conchobhair formally recognised Henry II as his suzerain and declared himself his liege man. Perhaps because he had failed in promoting the commonwealth of the people of Ireland, in that he had been unable to turn back the foreign invasion, Ruaraidh resigned the High Kingship immediately and then his provincial kingship in 1186. He and his heirs could no longer claim the High Kingship but they reverted to their title of kings of Connacht.

Ruaraidh stood down to allow his son, Conor Maemoy, to be elected to the provincial kingship. Conor Maemoy tried to defend his people from the rapacious Normans as they spread across Ireland. He was killed in 1189. His son, Cathal Carraig, claimed inheritance but Ruaraidh's brother, Cathal Crobhderg (of the Wine-red Hand) was *tanist*, and therefore heir. We are told that Cathal Crobhderg's mother, Gerróc (*gerr*, short) was the prime instigator in making her son claim the office of king of Connacht. But there was never to be a High King of Ireland again and Ruaraidh Ua Conchobhair, the last High King, ended his life in 1199 in pious obscurity in the abbey of Cong.

Against this dramatic background of the Anglo-Norman invasion several other notable women played key roles and their stories demonstrate the complexities of history where nothing is ever black and white.

Der Bhfhorgaill, Anglicised as Dervogilla, was the daughter of Murchadh Mac Lochlainn, a claimant for the High Kingship. She was married to Tigernán Ua Ruairc of Breifne who, in spite of his wife's parentage, was constantly at war with Mac Lochlainn on behalf of Ua Conchobhair. Tairrdelbach Ua Conchobhair, who had succeeded Domhnall Mac Lochlainn as High King in 1121, had reigned for thirty-five years. Potential heirs were jockeying for position. It seems that it had been Tigernán's own mother, Ailleann, who had an influential hand in the politics of the marriage. She had suggested to Der Bhfhorgaill's mother Mór, daughter of Muirchertach Ó Bríain, the former High King (d. 1119), a lady whom the annals called 'Chief Queen of Ireland', that the marriage of their son and daughter would be in the best interests of their families.

The event that was to change the face of Ireland was when Der Bhfhorgaill was abducted by Diarmait Mac Murchada. But the story was not simply that an ambitious provincial king abducted the wife of his rival as some mad, youthful folly. The event took place in 1152 when Der Bhfhorgaill was aged forty-four and Diarmait was forty-two. It was obvious that Der Bhfhorgaill had been married to Ua Ruairc against her own wishes, as a matter of politics. But Der Bhfhorgaill was already in love with Diarmait, her father's friend and supporter, who often visited his court. They had carried on their affair for some years.

The details come down to us in an amazing Norman French chronicle poem written in about 1200 entitled 'The Song of Dermot and the Earl', consisting of 3500 lines. The anonymous poet's source is known. Muiris Ó Reagáin, born in 1125, had become Diarmait's *latimer* or chief interpreter and it is thought that he helped Fionn Mac Gormain, bishop of Glendalough, in compiling the *Leabhar na Nuachonghbhala* (or *Book of Leinster*) commissioned under Diarmait's patronage in 1150. It is believed that Muiris either wrote his own version of the life of Diarmait, which was then translated into Norman French, or simply dictated the information to the Norman chronicler.

> King Diarmait often sent word
> To the lady whom he so loved
> By letter and by messenger
> Often did the king send word
> That she was altogether, in truth,
> The thing in the world that he most loved.

When Tigernán Ua Ruairc was defeated in battle by Muirchertach Mac Lochlainn (Der Bhfhorgaill's brother) and Diarmait Mac Murchada, with the unlikely assistance of the now elderly High King, Tairrdelbach Ua Conchobhair, the time seemed right for Diarmait to take Der Bhfhorgaill to his kingdom. It seemed that Ua Conchobhair had momentarily turned on Ua Ruairc for getting a little too ambitious. Diarmait now arranged to meet Der Bhfhorgaill at Drumahaire, Co. Leitrim.

> . . . Where the lady had sent word
> That she would be ready.

Ironically, the year of the 'abduction' was the same year in which a synod was held at Kells, chaired by Cardinal Paparo, at which the Church was to condemn concubinage and 'irregular unions'.

Der Bhfhorgaill lived with Diarmait for one year before Tigernán Ua Ruairc, having made his peace with Ua Conchobhair, marched an army into Leinster, recaptured Der Bhfhorgaill and made off with a lot of Diarmait's cattle and wealth. However, Diarmait and Der Bhfhorgaill had a child, a daughter also called Der Bhfhorgaill, who eventually married Donal Mac Giolla Mocolmoc, lord of Uí Dunchada.

Tairrdelbach Ua Conchobhair died in 1156. His wife Tailltu Ní Mael Lochlainn was, in fact, sister to Der Bhfhorgaill and her influence had helped change Tairrdelbach's attitude to Ua Ruairc at the time of his alliance with Diarmait and Mac Lochlainn. Tairrdelbach's death was the start of the conflict for the High Kingship between Der Bhfhorgaill's brother Muirchertach Mac Lochlainn and Ruaraidh Ua Conchobhair. It was Muirchertach Mac Lochlainn who was now acknowledged as High King. Even Ruaraidh Ua Conchobhair accepted the decision and formally acknowledged him in 1159.

Perhaps Diarmait might have reclaimed Der Bhfhorgaill now, but it seemed that she was no longer interested in Diarmait or the unfolding political scene. She threw herself into endowing the Church and gave money to the new abbey at Mellifont near Drogheda in 1157. In 1167 she became the prime mover in building a new convent at Clonmacnoise.

It was in 1166 that Muirchertach Mac Lochlainn was overthrown in a *coup d'état* led by Ruaraidh Ua Conchobhair and Tigernán Ua Ruairc. Diarmait was suddenly without friends in high places. Tigernán Ua Ruairc could not forgive Diarmait for having abducted his wife. It was this private grudge that was another factor in shaping Ireland's destiny. Tigernán Ua Ruairc marched into Diarmait's Leinster kingdom and destroyed his capital at Fearna (the place of the alder trees) or Ferns. Diarmait was defeated and banished. This is the point at which he began his recruitment of Anglo-Norman mercenaries in an attempt to wrest back his kingdom. We know, alas, the wider results.

And what of Der Bhfhorgaill, 'the Beautiful Queen'? In 1186 she retired to the monastery at Mellifont where she ended her days. She died in 1193 at the age of eighty-five. Let us leave the final words of the story to Muiris Ó Reagáin, Diarmait's confidant: 'She was a fair and beautiful lady entirely beloved of Diarmait.'

Another influential lady at this time was one of Diarmait's own daughters named Aoife, 'Radiant'. Diarmait had initially married Mór, the only daughter of Murtough Ó Tuathail, lord of Uí Muiredaigh (southern Kildare). Mór was the sister of Laurence Ó Tuathail (St Laurence O'Toole, 1130–80) who was to become Ua Conchobhair's ambassador to Henry II during the negotiations which resulted in the Treaty of Windsor in 1175. He was canonised in 1226. Mór lived through the tragic and momentous events of her life as Diarmait's principal wife (*cetmuintir*) in silence. No drama or scandal is associated with her. Of the two daughters she bore Diarmait, the elder was Orlaith, 'Golden Sovereignty', sometimes Anglicised as Urlacam. She married Donal Ó Bríain of Thomond, becoming the mother of Domhnall Mór Ó Bríain, the king of Thomond. Orlaith's younger sister Aoife was to marry Strongbow. It is interesting to note that Der Bhfhorgaill named her daughter by Tigernán, Orlaith. It seemed a popular name at this time and the High King, Brían Bóramha, had a sister and niece of that name.

In 1155, in fact the year before he abducted Der Bhfhorgaill, Diarmait married a second wife, which was accepted under the law. This was a political marriage to Sadb, daughter of Cearbhall Mac Faelain of Dési. Sadb (Sweet) was the second most popular girl's name in medieval Ireland and Brían Bóramha had a daughter of that name. The first recorded Sadb was a goddess, daughter of Bodb Dearg, turned into a fawn by the Dark Druid, and Otherworld mistress to Fionn Mac Cumhail. Sadb Subhair (of the Pleasant Speech) was recorded as the daughter of the legendary Medb and Ailill of Connacht.

Of Diarmait's daughters, it is Aoife that claims our close attention. By all accounts Aoife was very beautiful. Giraldus Cambrensis tells us that she was possessed of 'exceeding beauty'. Diarmait, determined to secure his kingdom, had promised to give her in marriage to Strongbow. But during the initial arrival of mercenaries in Ireland in 1167 Diarmait also offered her to FitzStephen and FitzHenry. What Aoife's wishes were is not recorded. When Strongbow arrived, however, Aoife was still free to marry and the promised wedding took place. They had a child named Isabella. Strongbow died in 1177 from gangrene of the foot. Aoife raised Isabella and she eventually married William Le Mareschal, Henry's Earl Marshal of Ireland, who under Norman law had succeeded to Strongbow's possessions. It was now the fashion for the Norman knights to make strategic marriages with Irish princesses to reinforce their claims, made under their laws but not Irish law.

Hugh de Lacy married Róinsech (Rose), the daughter of Ruaraidh Ua Conchobhair; William de Burgh married a daughter of Domhnall Ó Bríain by Orlaith, Aoife's sister, and so forth. Aoife's daughter Isabella had five daughters who were progenitors of many of the great Norman houses in Ireland. Even Elizabeth I of England could boast a direct descent, through her mother Anne Boleyn, from Tadhg Ó Cearbhaill, chief of the Eile (Ely) Ó Cearbhaill, whose daughter married the third earl of Ormond (Butler or Le Botiller) in 1405.

It is significant that the Norman invaders of Ireland felt that intermarriage with the daughters of the main kings and chieftains of those they had conquered gave them a justification for their claims to Irish titles. Perhaps the old concept of the sovranty goddesses of the Celts had survived and was accepted by the invaders.

In the mid-thirteenth century there emerged the inspiring figure of Étain, the daughter of Fínghin Mór Mac Carthaigh. The Mac Carthaighs had been deposed from the kingship of Cashel. Fínghin raised an army and destroyed six of the Anglo-Norman garrison castles built on the Cork coast. One chronicle describes how Étain commanded part of her father's army in her own right. William de Dene commanded the Anglo-Norman feudal army. The Irish and the Anglo-Norman armies met at Callann near Kenmare on 24 July 1261. Never had the Anglo-Normans suffered such a defeat since their arrival in Ireland. The army of the Mac Carthaighs overthrew them. Eight Norman barons, twenty-five knights, including the haughty John FitzThomas, who had been given Munster as a fiefdom, were slaughtered with thousands of their men-at-arms. The Irish had won a most spectacular victory.

However, Milo de Courcy later managed to slay Fínghin by trickery at Rinn Róinn near Kinsale. Étain was now joined by her uncle Cormac and during the next year they faced the new Anglo-Norman army led by the Justiciar, Richard de la Rochelle, and Walter de Burgo. Although Cormac Mac Carthaigh was slain in this battle, the Anglo-Normans again suffered such heavy losses that they retreated not only from the battlefield but from all south-west Munster. The victorious Irish had reclaimed the kingdom of Desmond, in southern Munster, for another generation. As Professor Edmund Curtis writes: 'For centuries not a single English settler dare now set foot in the country of the Mac Carthys and O'Sullivans . . .'

Étain Ní Carthaigh flits all too briefly across this fascinating page of history, keeping up the warrior tradition of her ancestors.

Again in the thirteenth century we have reference to Éabha Ruadh Ní Murchú leading her clan into battle. To give herself a more frightening aspect, she wound iron bars into her long red tresses. 'Red Eva' Mc Murrough, as she is given in English records, was the chieftainess of a Tyrone sept. A descendant of 'Red Eva', the daughter of an Ó Murchú who migrated to France and became a shoemaker, was the mistress of Louis XV – Marie Louise Murphy. She was a favourite model of the artist François Boucher.

In the fifteenth century there lived Máire Ní Ciaragáin, sometimes given as Maria Kerrigan, ruler of a sept in Fermanagh, who led her clan into battle against the English and won their respect with her reputation that she never took any English prisoners. Conversely, Mór Ní Cába, who died in 1527, achieved her place in history with a different reputation. The annals call her 'the nurse of the learned and destitute of Ireland'. Mór apparently endowed Irish bardic colleges and hostels for the sick and needy at a time when their provision under the old Brehon system was under threat by attempts to suppress the native law system and institutions. Yet another lady named

Mór was Mór Ní Cearbhaill of Munster (d. 1548) who married James 'FitzJohn' FitzGerald, the thirteenth earl of Desmond (d. 1558). At this time, few of the Anglo-Norman colonists (the 'Old English') could speak English and, indeed, the FitzGerald Desmonds were at the forefront of insurrection against England. The Kildare branch of the family had been decimated by English troops after a failed insurrection in 1534. They were now totally intermarried with the native Irish ruling families. When James succeeded to the earldom in 1540, his wife Mór Ní Cearbhaill is recorded as privy to his 'rebellions against the king' and is said to have raised the sept of her clan against the earl of Ormonde's troops. She was eventually killed in the fighting but, frustratingly, we know no further details.

The most famous female Irish leader was a lady who has become known by the Anglicised phonetic form Granuaile from Gráinne Mhaol (of the Cropped Hair). Gráinne Ní Máille, sometimes totally Anglicised to Grace O'Malley (c.1530–1603), was called 'a nurse of all the rebellions in Connacht' by Sir Richard Bingham. To Sir Henry Sidney she was 'a most famous feminine sea-captain'. To Lord Justice Drury she was 'a woman who has overstepped the part of womanhood'.

Gráinne's father was Eoghan Ó Máille, chieftain of the Mayo clan. She was married at the age of fifteen to an Ó Flaithbheartaigh (O'Flaherty) of Connacht – he was Donal an Chogaidh (of the Battles). Donal was *tanist* or heir apparent to Donal Crone, The Ó Flaithbheartaigh of all Iar-Connacht. By him, she had three children, Mairead who was to marry a Richard Burke, Murrough na Maor (d. 1626) and Eoghan (killed 1586). What started her in her career is uncertain but even while her children were young, Gráinne found herself commanding 200 fighting men and three fast raiding ships, in control of the seas along the Connacht coastline, and also in command of trading missions south to Munster.

Two events happened in 1558: the twenty-four-year-old Elizabeth Tudor became Queen of England, and, with a new regime, Elizabeth's governors in Ireland started to interfere in local matters. They helped Murrough-ne-doe overthrow Donal Crone as The O'Flaherty and thus Donal an Chogaidh was also deposed as *tanist*. This interference must have shaped Gráinne's dislike of the English imperial administration. Not long afterwards, the Joyce family attacked Donal's fortress on the shore of Lough Corrib. It is said that Donal was killed after a spirited defence in which the Joyces gave him the new nickname of Donal an Cullagh (Cock) but, when he was killed, Gráinne continued the defence and the castle was named Caisleann-an-Circa, the 'hen's castle', after her.

She returned back to Uí Maille territory, to a castle at Beal na Chléir dominating Cléir (Clew Bay). She continued to lead her own men in controlling the coastal waters and seeking tribute and booty from any English ships she found. It has been said that she was elected by her *derbhfhine* as chieftain of her clan, because her brother, Donal, whose fortress was at Cathair na Mart (Westport) was not qualified to stand for the succession being under the age of seventeen years, the *aimsir togu* or 'age of choice'. Certainly Gráinne was now undisputed commander of the fleet of ships which the O'Flahertys used to dominate the seas around Connacht, even to Munster. So the interesting point is that she continued to have the allegiance and support of her late husband's clan.

In 1566 she married again. Her husband was Risteard-an-Iarain Bourke – Iron Richard Bourke, on account of the armour he wore. He was a chieftain of the Mayo sept of the MacWilliam Iochtar branch of the family. The Bourkes (de Burgo), a family of Norman origin, were credited with building Galway (town of the foreigners). He was *tanist* to The MacWilliam. Curiously enough, a Gráinne Ní Maille had married a Thomas Bourke (de Burgo) a century earlier and an inscribed chalice of 1494, with their names, is kept in the National Museum of Ireland. According to accounts Gráinne married Risteard under the Brehon law which allowed the couple a year's trial marriage.

Their main seat was now Carraig an Cabhlaigh (Carrickahowley, or Rockfleet Castle), Co. Mayo. In 1567 their son Tibbot-na-Long was born, Anglicised as Theobald. Tibbot-na-Long meant 'Tibbot of the Ships', the legend having it that he was born on shipboard while Gráinne was off on one of her raids. By this time, the English administration had come to hear of Gráinne. Sir Henry Sidney, who met her, wrote: 'This was a notorious woman on all the coasts of Ireland.'

In August 1573, the Earl of Essex invited the chieftain Brían Ó Néill and 200 of his lesser chieftains to a banquet to discuss peace. When the Irish retired for the night, Essex's soldiers burst in on them and slaughtered men, women and children alike. Praising this act, Elizabeth I, in a letter dated 11 April, told Essex that he was a 'great ornament of her nobility'. On 22 May, however, Elizabeth wrote to

Essex ordering him to make peace with the Irish leaders on the least dishonourable terms that he could obtain. We do not know what had changed Elizabeth's mind.

The peace was not lasting, as Elizabeth's commanders continued to expand their personal holdings in Ireland and slaughter any who stood in their way. The first Elizabethan governor of Connacht, Sir Edward Fitton, sent a Captain William Martin and a small fleet of ships to capture or destroy Gráinne. On 8 March 1574, this force surrounded Gráinne in her stronghold at Carraig an Cabhlaigh. Gráinne turned the attempted siege into a fierce attack on the English and by 26 March she had sent Martin and his men scurrying back to the safety of Galway.

Legend takes over when it is claimed that at this time, in 1575, Gráinne was invited to London to meet Elizabeth of England. Of the many stories about this event, one says that Gráinne was pregnant when she set out on the voyage to London. *En route* Gráinne gave birth to her son who was promptly dubbed Tibbot-na-Long. Another story is that Gráinne arrived at court with the child and Elizabeth, much taken with the baby, promptly conferred on him an order of knighthood. As romantic as the story seems, it is legend. It was not until 1593 that Gráinne made her famous trip to Elizabeth's court at Greenwich.

What was happening during the late 1570s was that Gráinne's career had taken a sudden plunge. In 1577 she had been captured during an expedition against the Earl of Desmond and imprisoned in Limerick. She was in Limerick for eighteen months and then transferred to Dublin Castle. She was, however, back in Connacht in 1579, against the background of brewing insurrection. By 1580 Gráinne's husband Risteard had been elected as The MacWilliam but on 30 April 1583 he died, of natural causes. *The Four Masters* record his passing as that of 'a plundering, warlike, unquiet and rebellious man'.

Gráinne now claimed her rights to his property under Brehon law and installed herself at Carraig an Cabhlaigh. It was then that a new governor of Connacht arrived from England, Sir Richard Bingham, who was to prove Gráinne's most implacable foe. He took her son Tibbot-na-Long as a hostage. Even so, Gráinne was deeply involved in insurrection against England, in spite of the fact that Elizabeth of England had actually sent Gráinne a conditional pardon on 4 May 1588. On 7 February 1589, it is recorded that John Browne, Sir

Richard's sheriff, with 250 men-at-arms, marched on Gráinne's castle. Gráinne's son-in-law, Richard 'The Devil's Hook' Burke, met him and demanded Browne withdraw. He did not and there was fierce fighting before the English force had to withdraw.

It was in 1593 that Gráinne showed herself to be an astute politician. Tired of Sir Richard Bingham's continued attempts to destroy her and bring Connacht firmly under the English heel, Gráinne decided to bypass him and make a direct appeal to Elizabeth herself, pledging allegiance and asking that she take her authority directly from Elizabeth. Intrigued, Sir William Cecil, private secretary to Elizabeth, sent Gráinne a questionnaire, the answers to which provide a fascinating life history as well as comments on social conditions in Ireland at this time.

In July 1593, Gráinne set out with The O'Flaherty for London. At the beginning of September, Gráinne entered Greenwich Castle. According to Anne Chambers:

> . . . the details of the meeting of these two women, each outstanding and unique in her own special role as ruler and leader and alike in their personal characteristics, must unfortunately remain in the realm of fantasy and legend. Curiosity must have been a motivation for them both, curiosity about each other. Elizabeth, as a ruler in a male-dominated preserve, must have marvelled at how 'Grace', without the supporting facilities of state that she herself enjoyed, could successfully lead and govern so effectively and perform all the exploits for forty years credited to her by Elizabeth's own Irish deputies and governors.

Elizabeth I is said to have ordered an Irish phrase book to be printed for her use so that she might say a few words in Irish to Gráinne. However, it is recorded that the main interview was conducted in Latin, in which Gráinne was fluent.

Elizabeth was a few years younger than Gráinne. Tradition has it that when these remarkable women were introduced, Elizabeth held her hand out for Gráinne to kiss, but Gráinne was much taller than the English queen and so Elizabeth had to hold her hand up to her. We are told that Gráinne considered the meeting to be one of equals.

One interesting story has a ring of truth. It appears that Gráinne, during the audience, wanted a handkerchief. A lady-in-waiting to Elizabeth passed her a small square of cambric and lace. Having used it, Gráinne threw it into the fire. Elizabeth informed her that it was meant to be put in her pocket and later washed. Gráinne was amazed and declared that in Ireland they had a higher standard of hygiene than to pocket a soiled cloth.

The result of Gráinne's visit to Elizabeth was that Elizabeth wrote to Richard Bingham and basically told him to 'lay off' his harassment of Gráinne and her family and to ensure Gráinne had 'some maintenance for her living the rest of her old years'. Elizabeth said that Gráinne had given her various promises and assurances 'that she will fight in our quarrel with all the world'.

This is an appropriate moment to mention another powerful Celtic lady who could well have been a witness to Gráinne's meeting with Elizabeth I. Blanche Parry (c.1508–c.1593) was from Brecon in Wales. In 1565 she was appointed 'Chief Gentlewoman of the Queen's Most Honourable Privy Chamber and Keeper of Her Majesty's Jewels'. It was an office that made Blanche Parry one of the most influential women in the land, in spite of the fact that she remained a steadfast Catholic. She also remained unmarried and is reported to have become blind in her last years. At her death, she owned extensive lands in Wales.

Gráinne returned to Mayo about 19 September. But Bingham proved reluctant to implement his queen's commands. Gráinne's reputation as a leader had been immensely increased by her visit to London. Bingham finally had to release Tibbot-na-Long, and Gráinne's brother Donal was also released from an English prison.

But the situation in Ireland was becoming increasingly tense with The O'Neill and The O'Donnell, princes of Tyrone and Tyrconnell, building up new Irish armies in the north and preparing a great offensive against the English. With Gráinne at large, commanding the sea routes and calling Connacht to take part in the uprising, Bingham realised that the situation was exceedingly dangerous. As Lord President of Connacht, Bingham was responsible for some of the worst atrocities carried out by the English in Ireland during the period. One massacre resulted in a thousand unarmed prisoners slain in one day after their surrender to his troops. Bingham captured Gráinne and was about to have her executed but she escaped through the aid of her son-in-law, Richard Burke, and fled to Ulster where she stayed under the protection of The O'Neill. Bingham was recalled to London and imprisoned for aggravating the situation.

The wars of resistance against Elizabeth's empire resulted in the great Irish defeat at Kinsale in 1601. It must have been a bitter blow to Gráinne. She returned to Connacht. She is reported to have died in 1603, the same year as Elizabeth, and reputed to have been buried on Inis Chléir, Clare Island, in Clew Bay, Co. Mayo. Others claim Burrishoole Abbey as her final resting place. The exact circumstances of her death remain a mystery.

Gráinne did not live to see the start of James I's ruthless new colonial policy with its enforced clearance of people from the land and their replacement by colonists. Neither did she witness the sad flight of The O'Neill and other princes of Ireland into exile in France, Spain and Italy. The O'Neill died in exile in Rome in 1616 and his tomb is in San Pietro in Montorio, Rome. The new policy of James led to the start of the Ulster Plantations whose legacy is still with us today.

Gráinne Ní Máille emerges as one of the most powerful personalities (male or female) in Irish history. She has become immortalised as a symbolic national figure, standing along with the goddess Éire, Caitlín Ní Houlihan and Roisín Dubh as the personification of the Irish passion for freedom. Numerous songs and poems have been written about her. One of the most popular songs has the verse:

> *Tá Gráinne Mhaol ag teacht thar sáile,*
> *Oglaigh armtha lei mar gharda;*
> *Gaeil iad féin 's ni Gaill no Spainnigh,*
> *'S cuirfid ruaig ar Ghallaibh*

> Gráinne Mhaol is coming over the sea,
> With a guard of young soldiers,
> They are Irish, not English or Spanish,
> And they will rout the English.

> *Oró! Sé do bheatha 'bhaile!*
> *Oró! sé do bheatha 'bhaile!*
> *Oró! sé do bheatha 'bhaile!*
> *Anois ar theacht an tSamhraidh.*

> Ho there! Welcome home!
> Ho there! Welcome home!
> Ho there! Welcome home!
> Now our summer has come to us!

It is of passing fascination that at a concert in New York's Carnegie Hall, on 3 November 1962, with the Clancy Brothers and Tommy Makem, the audience enjoyed what was probably the first Irish 'sing-along' performed in that concert hall. And the song was about Gráinne Ní Máille, 'one of the most remarkable women in Irish history': surely a unique tribute. And during the last two centuries a number of novels, some pure fantasy, have appeared on her life and more particularly on her legend. It is ironic that it is to the English state papers that we turn to learn the facts of her life rather than to the Irish records.

Although we are now out of the period we are discussing, it would be wrong to leave without a mention of just one more powerful Irish woman in the mould of Gráinne who lived a generation after her.

Máire Rua Ní Mhathúna (Red Mary, c.1615–86) was the daughter of a chieftain of the sept of Ó Mathúna of Co. Clare. She married Dónall Ó Nualláin of Dysert O'Dea (O'Dea's Hermitage) between Ennis and Corofin, the site of the famous battle in 1318 when Muircheartach Ó Bríain defeated the army of Richard de Clare and slew him, halting the Anglo-Norman advance into Munster for a further generation. Máire bore Dónall four children. When he died five years later she married Conchobhar Ó Bríain of Leamaneh (Léim an Eich, the stallion's leap) Castle, which stands south-east of Kilfenora, Co. Clare. She bore him five children. In 1651 Conchobhar was fighting against the Cromwellians and was mortally wounded and carried back to the castle. Máire Rua now took command of its defences. She was a woman of courage and determination with, we are told, striking red hair. When her castle fell to the Cromwellians, Máire Rua attempted to save the estate from confiscation by the English by marrying a Cromwellian officer named John Cooper in 1653. She thus ensured that her children continued as The Ua Bríains of Dromoland, whose most famous descendant was William Smith O'Brien (1803–64), the Member of Parliament for Ennis who turned to revolutionary politics and led the ill-fated Irish uprising of 1848.

Many legends have grown up about Máire Rua which distort her character, claiming that she had a dozen husbands, was a robber who hanged people whom she disliked from the walls of her castle, and kept hundreds of male lovers disguised as maidservants. Perhaps the unkind tradition arose because of her manipulative marriage to an English officer as a means of preventing the confiscation of her estates.

[9]

Celtic 'Witches'

No examination of the history of women during the late medieval period, in any section of western Europe, can ignore the great witch persecutions. They were conducted under the auspices of the Christian Church as a means of asserting its dominance over independent-minded women whom they saw as heretical. The 'witch hysteria' had little effect in the Celtic world generally. Only in one Celtic land did it have very destructive results and that was the Anglicised areas of Scotland. The 'witchcraft' hysteria which spread throughout Europe resulted in 300,000 executions between 1484 and 1782, the overwhelming proportion of those victims being women.

The First Synod of Patrick, the fifth-century encyclical which is attributed to the ecclesiastical rules drawn up by Patrick, Auxilius and Iserninus, but which may well have been drawn up in the following century, has this to state about witches:

A Christian who believes that there is such a thing in the world as an enchantress, which is to say a witch, and who accuses anyone of this, is to be excommunicated, and may not be received into the church again until – by their own statement – they have revoked the criminal accusation and have accordingly done penance with full rigour.

The early Celtic Christians were, therefore, quite clear that no such being as a 'witch' existed. It is true, however, that in early Irish and Welsh literature, female Druids had become reduced in the stories to witch-like figures, as had their male counterparts, able to perform feats of magic and enchantment. But, of course, as I have discussed at length in my study *The Druids*, the male and female 'saints' of the early Church also used magic and feats of enchantment which were always superior to the feeble efforts of the Druids. Witches and wizards were no more than characters in stories for entertainment.

However, from the tenth century, Rome began to fan the flames of intolerance against any that did not accept its dogma by claiming them as heretics and therefore witches or warlocks, engaged in all sorts of perverse practices. Pope Gregory IX in 1233 issued the first papal bull to encourage the persecution of 'witches'. But it was Pope Innocent VIII, in his notorious bull *Summis desiderantes* in 1484, who gave justifications and instructions for the start of a pitiless persecution. This was supported by the publication in 1489 of *Malleus Maleficarum* by Jacob Sprenger and Heinrich Krammer, a publication which became the witch-hunters' 'Bible'.

I do not think it possible to examine the attempted 'witchcraft' persecution in Ireland unless we first examine the social attitudes in Ireland, particularly the attitude of women from the settler communities. In Ireland, certainly as late as the fourteenth century, the natives were trying to cling to the liberal philosophies of their ancestors, now much modified by Roman Christian attitudes. The settlers, the 'Old English' or Anglo-Irish, as they were to become known, were trying to live in two cultural worlds, following their own imported values while also copying the less restricted social attitudes of the natives.

Nowhere is this more clear than in the changing position of marriage in Ireland. In fact the law on marriage was being redefined and clarified during the twelfth and thirteenth centuries. The differences between the native Irish and the settlers formed a division that was reflected by the ecclesiastical laws. Among the native Irish (*inter Hibernicos*), the upholding of the Brehon law system was the subject of much criticism from the hierarchy of the Church. As Art Cosgrove has demonstrated, attacks by the ecclesiastic hierarchy on the marital behaviour of those who upheld the Brehon system were frequent during the eleventh and twelfth centuries. The Brehon system continued to take no notice of canonical prohibitions and the traditional marriages survived the coming of the Anglo-Normans.

Polygamy continued even among the Irish aristocracy and men and women continued to have a succession of spouses. Pilib Mág Uidhir, lord of Fermanagh (d. 1395) had twenty sons by eight mothers. Toirdhealbach Ó Domhnaill, lord of Tir Conaill, around the same period, had eighteen sons by ten different ladies. Archbishop Bole of Armagh, writing to Pope Paul II in July 1469, claimed that several of the Irish aristocracy 'are living in incestuous relationships, because they can rarely find their equals in nobility, with whom they can fittingly contract marriages, outside the degrees of consanguinity and affinity.'

Aedh Ó Conchobhair of Kildare, in 1448, sought a dispensation because, prior to his marriage to Onora Ní Ghiolla Phádraig, he had had a relationship with her sister and also her cousin, related in the third degree of affinity, thus, under ecclesiastical law, invalidating the union. These affairs were generally unknown to all but those involved. The bishop of Kildare was able to absolve Aedh, dispense the impediments created by his behaviour and permit him and Onora to contract marriage again.

The frequency with which dispensation from the impediments of canonical regulations on consanguinity and affinity was sought, however, is an indication that the aristocratic Irish were turning from the Brehon system to the new ecclesiastical laws. Perhaps this could have been a 'knock-on' effect of the influence of the settlers, the Anglo-Irish, among whom the canonical concepts of legitimacy under primogeniture determined hereditary concepts.

What is interesting, however, is that a large number of such cases were being brought by Irish women who wished to 'reclaim' their husbands. In 1397 Una Ní Conchobhair claimed that her husband Manus Ó Cathain had replaced her with a concubine without any court judgement. Caitlín Ní Dochartaigh claimed that her husband Manus Mac Giollagáin ignored a decision of a court in Derry and was openly consorting with other women.

Art Cosgrove maintains that the best illustration of the attitude of Irish men towards the ecclesiastical courts and canon law on marriage is the case of Muirchertach Ruadh Ó Néill, The Ó Néill of Clanaboys of Antrim and Down (1444–68). He had married Mairéad, daughter of Maghnus Mac Mathghamhna. He deserted her for a woman named Rose White. When brought before an ecclesiastical court he claimed that his marriage was invalid because of a tie of affinity, since he had previously had a sexual relationship with Mairéad's first cousin Medbh. In support of this, he had a witness in the person of Aine 'new Owhityll', a fifty-year-old woman. The name might be an attempt to render into English phonetics the Irish name Ní Amhlaoibh.

She stated that Muirchertach had been a prisoner of Medbh's father. During his captivity, Muirchertach was often in bed with Medbh. The witness even said that she had shared the same bed. But the court refused to accept this evidence and took the view that the story had been fabricated. The case continued for two years and in December 1451 the archbishop of Armagh decided that the marriage between Muirchertach and Mairéad was valid. The Ó Néill was ordered to leave Rose White and return to his wife.

Muirchertach clearly felt that the canonical laws could not be ignored. The fact that he had spent time and money defending himself is proof of this. Yet he was certainly acting in accordance with the Brehon laws. His dilemma is typical of the changing concepts of the period.

The colonial secular legal system did not present any challenge to ecclesiastical law in the same way as the native Brehon system did. Therefore, the colonial administration from the outset tried to prevent the settlers from adopting the language, laws and attitudes of the native Irish – with a remarkable lack of success prior to the seventeenth century. In 1366 the famous Statutes of Kilkenny were instituted in which the preamble chides the settlers for deserting their own language and using the Brehon law.

The settlers continued to be absorbed into the Irish national culture. A de Burgo, who became bishop of Clonfert in 1541, could neither speak nor understand English. In that same year, the address of an English emissary from Henry VIII had to be translated into Irish so that the assembled Lords and Commons of Ireland, gathered in the Irish Parliament, could understand it. Few of them apparently understood English.

Nevertheless, there is evidence that many settlers did defer to ecclesiastical law in marriage. The Dublin municipal administration of 1351 had pre-empted the Kilkenny Statutes by forbidding marriage between colonists and natives, describing the native Irish as 'enemies of the king'. Kilkenny was not so subtle, simply forbidding intermarriage solely on ethnic grounds, prohibiting 'alliance by marriage . . . concubinage or by caif [*coibche*]'.

Colonial courts did exist and often people with native Irish names did make appeals to them for redress of grievances arising from marital problems. In Cork in May 1307, a wine merchant from Youghal named John Don, who married a woman called Basilia, went on a business trip. In his absence a Stephen O'Regan visited his house and slept with his wife 'for the whole time that John was abroad'. This also happened during a second trip and John Don found out. John devised a plan to catch Stephen and Basilia 'red-handed'. He pretended that he was going to Cork on business but stayed at another house in Youghal. Stephen and Basilia dined together and went to a tavern to indulge in a drinking session. They attempted to buy the silence of the tavern keeper for five shillings. They then went off to bed.

The tavern keeper alerted John Don, however, who, with a group of armed men, proceeded to his house to capture the couple. Alarmed by the approach of the armed men, O'Regan made an attempt to escape but was caught. John Don's men bound him and then castrated him.

O'Regan then brought his case before the colonial secular courts, who supported his claim of assault against John Don. O'Regan was awarded £20 damages, a rather large sum, and John Don had to pay a fine of £3 6s 8d (5 marks) to the court or face imprisonment. A week later in the same court John Don was awarded £2 for damage caused by Stephen O'Regan in his house.

How John Don treated Basilia is not mentioned.

Mostly, however, such cases were brought before ecclesiastical courts by settlers. Almost all the evidence of such legal actions is found in the Armagh registers. Suits to enforce marriage contracts, pleas for annulments on a variety of grounds, and other matters were brought before the Armagh diocesan courts. Annulments on degrees of consanguinity or affinity were often made. Other pleas for annulment were based on allegations of pre-contract marriages which disbarred one or other of the parties from making a second marriage under canon law.

One interesting case referred to by Art Cosgrove occurred in 1481 and concerned a marriage of thirty years previously. Thaddeus Carpenter sought the annulment of his marriage to Juliana Maynaghe on the grounds that she had already been married to Roger Sarsfield. A number of witnesses were brought forward to say that they had attended the marriage of Juliana and Roger Sarsfield. Roger had then left for England but Juliana remained behind. Juliana then married Thaddeus Carpenter some time prior to 1467. So they had been together at least fourteen years before Thaddeus sought an annulment.

Jeneta Sarsfield, Roger's sister, came forward to testify that Roger had still been alive five years before when she had received a letter from him. Thaddeus received his annulment for it was the policy of ecclesiastical courts to uphold the first marriage contract even if the second contract had been enacted under canon law.

Where ecclesiastical law and Brehon law merged was in the demand for substantiation should claims for annulment be made on the grounds of impotence. Such was the case when Anisia Gowin claimed, in February 1521, that her marriage to Nicholas Conyll should be nullified because of impotence. The court ordered that she was 'to spend the night with Nicholas in the same bed, without any disturbance'. Nine men had to carry out an examination of Nicholas and report their findings to the court. The evidence was that Nicholas was certainly not impotent.

The marriage practices among the settlers did not differ markedly from elsewhere in Latin Christendom. Among the natives, however, the conflict between Brehon and canon law continued. According to Dr Cosgrove:

> Nevertheless, the clash between two quite different concepts of marriage and its function in society continued throughout the middle ages. The problem was that women regarded as concubines by the church often enjoyed the same legal and social status as wives in Gaelic society, and the children of such women were accorded the same rights as those of the canonically recognised wife.

Even among many of the settlers, marriage was still widely held to be a personal matter subject to private contract between the parties. The aim of the Church was to have all marriages publicly celebrated as, it claimed, this was a safeguard for the contract. How did the law know that a man and woman were united unless the matrimonial bonds were public? Under Brehon laws the marriage contracts were more clandestine and their provisions more free for both partners than under the ecclesiastical laws. The evidence is, therefore, that many of the settlers found life more equitable under the Brehon system. Women, in particular, sought a greater independence of thought and action by appealing to the native language, law and customs. As Peter Cherici states: 'And in many Anglo-Irish households, women behaved with a fierce independence regarded as scandalous by visitors from England.'

Even after the Anglo-Norman invasion, the holders of the Primacy of Ireland at Armagh until 1303 had Irish names. After that either English-born or English men took over the hierarchy of the Church in Ireland. It was inevitable, therefore, that 'witchcraft' should raise its head because women in Ireland were not behaving in the way the Roman-orientated English ecclesiastics expected them to behave. The concept of witchcraft and the female witch was a direct attempt to curb the behaviour of women whose lifestyles and attitudes were deemed contrary to Roman Christian practices and doctrine. In fact, Pope John XXII in 1316 had made it absolutely clear that witchcraft was to be equated with heresy, so anyone acting contrary to the dogma of Rome was a witch.

In 1317 Richard de Ledrede, a Franciscan friar who had been appointed bishop of Ossory, set up an inquisition to discover the evidence of witches in Ireland. De Ledrede, with papal approval, could bring force to bear against any vestiges that remained of Celtic Christianity, and against the native laws where they were in conflict with the doctrine of Rome. To do this he picked on women as vulnerable victims to make examples of – those women who continued to adhere to the uninhibited sexual attitudes of Celtic society.

Obviously, he needed to choose, for his main example, a woman of some standing in society. He could victimise as many women of the 'native order' or lower classes as he wished without disturbing the attitude of the middle and upper classes. But his purpose was to frighten the Anglo-Irish and Irish ruling classes into total submission and subservience to Rome.

He found his victim in 1324 in the person of an Anglo-Irish noble, Dame Alice Kyteler (Kettle) of Kilkenny. It appeared that she had been married four times and three of her husbands had died of natural causes while the fourth was insane. His insanity was blamed on a potion administered by Dame Alice. Her first husband, William Outlawe of Kilkenny, had been a wealthy banker, as was her son by that marriage. Her second husband was Allan le Blund of Callan, her third husband was Richard de Valle while her fourth was Sir John le Poer. Dame Alice had therefore married into some of the most influential Anglo-Irish families in the land and was wealthy and well connected.

Bishop Ledrede was in his element and had drawn up six charges. These were based on the evidence of several of Dame Alice's friends and from three of her children who had been taken into custody by members of his inquisition and 'interrogated'. Threats and physical pressures doubtless brought forth the desired response. Charges that she had poisoned her husbands, conjured spirits by sacrificing nine red cocks and nine peacocks, and had a demon lover named Roibín Mac Art, were made.

Peter Cherici comments:

> It was possible that Alice knew and practised the traditional herbal medicine of the Celts which the friars would regard as sorcery. And if Robin Mac Art was her Celtic paramour who came to her bed chamber at dusk and left at dawn, the friars might perceive him as the demon *incubus* of Christian mythology.

De Ledrede wrote to Roger Outlawe, Prior of the Preceptory of Kilmainham and Chancellor of Ireland, demanding the arrest of Dame Alice. But presumably Roger Outlawe was a relative. Certainly Dame Alice's son William Outlawe and another relative, Sir Arnold le Poer, Seneschal of Kilkenny, persuaded the Chancellor to put opposition in the way. De Ledrede decided to act on his own, charging Dame Alice and accusing her son, William Outlawe, of heresy for good measure. Stephen le Poer, Bailiff of Overk, doubtless on the instructions of Sir Arnold, then arrested Bishop de Ledrede and lodged him in Kilkenny jail.

The bishop of Ossory replied by ordering the cessation of all the religious services in his diocese. After seventeen days the bishop was released and went to St Canice's Cathedral, in Kilkenny, to sing a *Te Deum*. De Ledrede tried to have Dame Alice's son arrested again, having discovered Dame Alice had wisely fled to Dublin. Being summoned to Dublin to answer why he continued to charge Dame Alice, De Ledrede found support from the Vicar-General and Archbishop of Dublin. Dame Alice now had to flee from Ireland.

De Ledrede resorted to sheer vengeance and arrested Dame Alice's household; after questioning they all confessed and claimed Dame Alice as their leader. William Outlawe was accused again of heresy. Outlawe finally ended up in prison. But Dame Alice's Irish maid, 'Petronilla of Meath', was tortured and then burnt at the stake, the only occasion when ritual torture to secure a confession of witchcraft was recorded in Ireland. Poor Petronilla was flogged on six separate occasions until she confessed that she was a mistress of the black arts! On Sunday, 3 November 1324, Petronilla of Meath was ritually immolated in Kilkenny. 'This was the first instance of the penalty of death by fire being inflicted in Ireland for heresy.' While there is no official record of what happened to the other five women and seven men who constituted Dame Alice's household, it is stated that 'some of them were publicly burnt to death; others, confessing their crimes in the presence of all the people . . . were solemnly whipped through the town and the market place . . . others were banished . . . others who evaded the jurisdiction of the Church were excommunicated . . .'

Sir Arnold le Poer was himself accused of heresy by de Ledrede and placed in Dublin Castle but was treated so well by the Chancellor, Roger Outlawe, who had now been appointed Justiciar, that the enraged bishop of Ossory also accused him of heresy for good measure. Le Poer died in prison in 1331 but a committee of clerics cleared Roger Outlawe of any heresy.

As if in poetic justice, de Ledrede was eventually accused of heresy himself by his Metropolitan Alexander de Bicknor. He appealed to the Holy See and set off to Avignon to see the Pope. In 1339 he was back in office but in 1349 he was once more charged with heresy. He managed to regain his office in 1356 and remained as bishop until his death in 1360. He was buried in St Canice's Cathedral. The house of Dame Alice is still the oldest in Kilkenny and was restored and reopened as Kyteler's Inn, an odd memorial to such a persecuted woman.

The intent behind the bishop's persecution was to stop the Anglo-Irish adopting the more liberal Irish lifestyle. It was, however, left to Edward III of England, in 1366, to pass specific laws forbidding the Anglo-Irish to adopt the Irish language, obey the Brehon laws or accept Celtic sexual paradigms. These laws became known as the Statutes of Kilkenny. Then in 1586 the Irish (Colonial) Parliament passed a law against witchcraft bringing the laws of the settlers into line with English law. Apparently this had been prompted by more witch trials in Kilkenny in 1578 when thirty-six persons were executed, including two females and a Negro. One wonders what the unfortunate Negro was doing in Kilkenny at that time.

However, the case of Petronilla of Meath seems to be the only case of a native Irish woman being burnt as a witch. Other cases concerning settlers occurred in Ireland, such as that of Florence Newton in Youghal in September 1662. Although the sentence is not recorded, Florence was probably burnt or ritually strangled. Another case involved a woman in Co. Antrim in 1698, who was strangled and burnt after being found guilty. Most of these witches appeared among the Protestant settler population, such as Mary Dunbar of Island Magee, Janet Mean of Braid Island, Jane Latimer of Carrick-fergus, Margaret Mitchell of Kilroot, Catherine McCalmont, Janet Liston, Elizabeth Sellar and Janet Carson of Island Magee, all charged in the eighteenth century.

In Wales, the same enlightened attitudes tended to prevail although folk tales speak much of famous witches, and while there are records of prosecutions of witches between 1563 and 1736, very few resulted in executions. Stories of witches such as Sal Fawr of Clydau in Pem-broke, Beti Ty'n Twll of Capel Celyn in Merioneth, Meri Berllan Piter of Aberarth, Cardigan and many others are retold in folk tales. The evil they were said to possess could only be undone by Y Dyn Hysbys (The Wise Man). These men could be clerics, medicine men or men born into a family of hereditary shamans and magicians. Such men were popular in rural Wales but demonstrate that the 'wise' male must dominate and control the 'evil' female. However, there were only two instances of 'witch burning' at this time, in Llandewi Brefi.

The most famous 'witch' in Welsh tradition, conjured to frighten children, was 'Mol Walbee' or Maude de St Valerie (d. 1210), the wife of William de Braose, Lord of Painscastle, Radnor. Although Giraldus Cambrensis praised her for her godliness, the Englishman William Camden presented her to the world as an evil, designing woman and claimed that the wailing of the waters of the River Wye at night was caused by the spirits of those she had drowned in its waters. There is no basis for the slanders against Maude. Poor Maude met her end in Windsor Castle when King John had her and her young son captured and imprisoned there because of some alleged slight to his reputation. Maude and her son were starved to death.

The Scots, sadly, were not as lucky as their Irish and Welsh sisters and brothers in escaping the witch persecutions, mainly because the Reformation there had introduced new attitudes which not only saw heresy as dangerous but instituted a belief in the literal truth of the Bible and saw 'witches' as consorting with a very real Devil. The zeal of the new Protestantism resulted in the majority of ritual executions during the persecutions, some 100,000 in Protestant Germany alone. 'Thou shalt not suffer a witch to live,' says Exodus 22.18, while Deuteronomy 18.10–12 states:

There shall not be found among you any one that maketh his son or his daughter to pass through fire, or that useth divination, or an observer of times, or an enchanter, or a witch.

Or a chamber, or a consulter with familiar spirits, or a wizard, or a necromancer.

For all that do these things are an abomination unto the Lord; and because of these abominations the Lord thy God doth drive them out before thee.

The persecution of those whose behaviour was 'out of step' with the perceived religious norms was no longer a Catholic monopoly. The French Protestant reformer, Jean Cauvin (John Calvin, 1509–64), living in exile in Geneva, spoke out against witches. It was one of the few occasions this founder of the religious system that gave birth to Presbyterianism found himself entirely in agreement with Rome. The Scot, John Knox (1505–72), twice visited Calvin in Geneva and Knox introduced his ideas into Scotland. He set the tone of the Scottish Reformation by publishing six tracts including his infamous *Blasts of the Trumpet Against the Monstrous Regiment of Women*, in 1558.

Things might not have been so bad for the Scots except that the Anglicised monarch James Stuart ('Jamie Baggy-Breeks'), James VI, had nearly been overthrown by a plot devised by the Earl of Bothwell in 1590. James, who had a passing interest in 'witchcraft', came to believe that the plot was aided by 'witches'. James had been a pupil of George Buchanan (1506–82), who was a supporter of Knox and believed implicitly in the Mosaic text on witches. He undoubtedly instilled this into his pupil. James soon found a number of victims in North Berwick. A local schoolmaster, Dr John Fian, was supposed to be their leader. He and Agnes Sampson were forced to confess after being tortured, and their trials took place between 1590 and 1593. The result was that the 'witch conspirators' were publicly burnt.

James was delighted and set himself up as an 'expert' on the subject. He wrote *Daemonologie* (1597), attacking earlier works which were more sceptical on the existence of 'witches'. In particular he felt a rage at Reginald Scott's *Discoverie of Witchcraft* (1584) which denied the existence of witches. With the king's authority and blessing, a new sport developed in Scotland. Hunt the witches! It was soon to transfer to England when James VI of Scotland became James

I of England. No sooner had he been enthroned than he ordered the English public hangman to burn all copies of *Discoverie of Witch-craft*; the following year, 1604, he had the English Parliament pass a new Witchcraft Act whose terms were more severe and harsher than any previous law.

James's *Daemonologie* was to be the theoretical basis of the terrible persecution of primarily women by the Protestant Christian movement during the seventeenth and eighteenth centuries. His bellicose and misogynous opinions gave licence to the terrible tortures and executions meted out during those years. Between 1590 and 1650 some 3000 Scots, the vast majority women, were ritually executed as 'witches'.

Curiously, the only example of a 'witch' execution in Brittany appears to have been that of a male. Gilles de Rais (1404–40), 'a most valiant knight at arms', had fought with Joan of Arc against England. After Joan's execution, the Church turned its unwelcome attentions on him and, probably having a rather short Celtic temper, he physically attacked the priest who had come to interrogate him. He was arrested, tried by the inquisition, and found guilty of heresy, pederasty, sorcery and the murder of a hundred children. Contrary to these accusations, de Rais seems to have been a pious and honourable man. He was highly regarded by his fellow knights and he had lavishly endowed the Chapel of the Holy Innocents at Machecoul. His mistake was supporting Joan of Arc. Being a noble he was executed by hanging at Nantes.

Good fortune had it that the excesses caused by James in Scotland passed by the other Celtic countries with few if any major 'witch' persecutions.

[10]

Sex and Poetry

D URING the preceding pages it has become clear that Celtic
men and women, initially, had few problems regarding their
sexuality. Celtic women were relatively free from the taboos
and repressions suffered by their Greek and Roman sisters and, likewise, Celtic men were neither inhibited nor repressed in their self-
expression. I stress that I am speaking generally and in the context
of the times they lived in. The Celtic world was certainly not some
earthly paradise where sexual problems did not exist. Again, it should
be remembered that society was in a state of flux and that the limiting
and suffocating controls of western Christianity were slowly getting
a stranglehold on Celtic society.

It would not be right to produce a book on Celtic women without
reference to the rich corpus of love poems and, indeed, erotic poetry
which are written in the Celtic languages. In both Irish and Welsh,
particularly, there was a great flourishing of courtly love poems in
medieval times. By this time only vestiges of the former free sexual
attitudes could be seen in this poetry, but those very vestiges are
remarkable.

According to Seán Lucy, introducing his *Love Poems of the Irish*:

Irish love poetry is remarkable for its range, its richness and its
freedom, and this is true of it in all its kinds. Epic or romantic
tale, courtly lyric or country song – all these kinds of Irish verse
give us a treatment of love which is notable not only for its passion
and beauty but also for its realism and its honesty.

However, most of the poets producing these works do appear to
be male. There are some interesting exceptions and we have already

233

touched on female poets like Heledd of Powys, Alis of Lleweni Fychan, the Catrins of Denbigh in Wales, Brigid wife of Senchán Torpéist, Gormflaith and Uallach of Ireland. Of these female poets Gwerful Merchain of Powys is unique. She wrote not only love lyrics but powerful erotic pieces. So far, no equivalent school of such erotic poetry has been found in Irish. This may well be to do with the sudden Irish reticence in the nineteenth and early twentieth centuries in translating this type of poetry. Be it remembered that the famous *Cúirt an Mheadhon Oídhche* (The Midnight Court) by Brían Mac Giolla Meidhre (Brian Merriman, *c.*1747–1805) was frequently banned by the Church authorities. Good translations of Irish love poetry are, indeed, few in number. Frank O'Connor has made a disproportionate number of them. According to Lucy: 'He seems to have had a particular fondness for love poetry, and his translations of the courtly love poems are particularly fine, showing both intensity and variety of feeling.'

We have already dealt with some works by the identifiable female poets of Ireland. From the male poets we can deduce how women were viewed in their eyes. An eighth-century verse is typical of the idealised love lyric:

> No better blessing
> A girl who pleases the senses.
> With her, you can leave your home,
> Leave your friends,
> Sailing together on the first ebb tide

But the bulk of surviving love poems, if we discount those recorded in the stories of the myths, are of the school written after the arrival of the Anglo-Normans and are described as medieval 'courtly love' verses. One poem, some advice to lovers, was identified by Frank O'Connor as probably belonging to the period just before the Anglo-Norman invasions because of its epigrammatic astringent irony:

> To live a happy life with your wife
> Do not be impatient,
> Feel fortunate to be with her,
> Feel fortunate when she leaves you alone.
>
> Be joyous when you are alone at work,

> Be joyous when you join her in bed,
> Be equally sad or happy
> If you learn that she is living or dead.

More in the tradition of the courtly love poem is one which dates from the thirteenth century, which is not ascribed to any particular poet. The following translation was made by the sixth earl of Longford:

> If now you hate me, as you say,
> Can you forget so soon
> How you and I, the world away,
> Once lay and watched the moon?
>
> Can you forget the day when cool
> Seemed to our love the sun,
> The day that we –? But I'm a fool,
> Besides, that day is done.
>
> Can you forget you stroked my hair?
> Moist palm upon my brow,
> Red mouth, soft breast – You do not care.
> All that's forgotten now.
>
> Have you forgotten too, my flower,
> How often you would tell
> How God ne'er made until that hour
> A man you loved so well?
>
> Can you forget your love for me,
> Whom now you do detest?
> But that's all one, those times are gone.
> No doubt 'tis for the best.
>
> If each could learn as well as I
> To profit by my pain,
> There's ne'er a man beneath the sky
> Would ever love again.

Another thirteenth-century verse was brilliantly translated by Frank O'Connor:

Love like heat and cold
Pierces and then is gone:
Jealousy when it strikes
Sticks to the marrowbone.

It is not until the eighteenth century that we find a major piece of Irish love poetry that is clearly identified as being by a woman poet. Eibhlín Dubh Ní Chonaill (*c*.1748–*c*.1800) was the daughter of Domhnall Mór Ó Conaill of Derrynane, grandfather of Daniel O'Connell, known in Irish history as the 'Liberator' because of his work for Catholic emancipation. Eibhlín wrote *Caoineadh Art Uí Laoghaire*, which is now considered one of the finest works in Irish poetry. It is a lament composed on the death of her husband, whose name is Anglicised as Art O'Leary.

She had married Colonel O'Leary, who had newly returned from the Irish Brigade of the Austrian army. She had eloped with him against her father's wishes and they had set up home at Macroom in Co. Cork. O'Leary found it hard to readjust to life under the English Penal Laws, which deemed him a 'non-person', after the freedom of Europe. He was not allowed to own a sword nor a horse worth more than £5. Colonel O'Leary had returned moderately wealthy and with a good horse. He immediately began to suffer abuse. Imagine what it was like for a Northern American Black arriving in a Southern American slave-owning state in 1860. The same attitudes and intolerance would have applied. An English neighbour called Morris demanded his horse, offering him £5. Under law, he could not refuse to hand it over. But Colonel O'Leary was not used to the servile ways which his countrymen had to adopt to live under the English system. He challenged Morris to a duel for this insult and Morris, no doubt surprised by this 'uppity mere Irishman', immediately had him outlawed for such effrontery.

The English soldiers came for him but Art and Eibhlín held them at bay, besieged in their house in Macroom. Eibhlín loaded the guns for her husband as he beat them off. He escaped to go into hiding but was ambushed and shot dead. His riderless, bloodstained mare came trotting back to Eibhlín and brought her to where her husband lay dead. As a footnote, Morris was shot dead in Cork in 1773 by O'Leary's brother. Two years later Eibhlín's nephew Daniel O'Connell was born, who went on to campaign for an end to the worst aspects of the Penal Law system.

Eibhlín's lament for her husband has been translated several times, by Seán O Cuív, Frank O'Connor and Seán O Tuama. Daniel O'Corkery in *The Hidden Ireland: A Study of Gaelic Munster in the Eighteenth Century* (Dublin, 1924), says of her poem:

> The note of this whole poem is headlong impulse. Scarcely once does the keening abate in swiftness, in wildness, or in grip, if one may use this word of so intimate an outpouring of grief. While one reads it, it is impossible to think of the matter as having been gathered, sifted, arranged; yet had Eibhlín Dubh searched a whole year for the one ending that should be more Gaelic than any other, that should more surely than any other, pierce the hearts both of O'Leary's kinfolk in Iveleary and her own kinsfolk in Iveragh, she could not have bettered this ending that we know. The poem is living with the breath and stir of that still Gaelic-speaking corner of Ireland.

In the opening verse Eibhlín talks of how she fell in love with Art at first sight, how she left her home and eloped with him, 'that was no bad choice, you have given me everything'.

> *Do chuiris gan dearmhad*
> *Párlus d'á ghealadh dham*
> *Rúmana d'á mbreacadh dham,*
> *Bácus d'á dheargadh dham,*
> *Bríc d'á gceapadh dham,*
> *Rósta ar bhearaibh dham,*
> *Mairt d'á leagadh dham*
> *Cóir mhaith leaptham dam*
> *Codladh i gclúmh lachan dam.*

> You did not forget
> To have parlours painted for me,
> Rooms decorated for me,
> Ovens heated for me,
> Loaves fresh baked for me,
> Cattle slaughtered for me
> A bed made for me,
> So that I might sleep in feather down.

The poem ends with the verse:

> *Stadaidh anois, d'bhúr ngol*
> *A mhná na súl bhfliuch mbog*
> *Go bhfagaidh Art Ua Laoghaire deoch*
> *Roimh é dhul isteach 'sa sgoil,*
> *Ní h-ag foghlaim léighinn ná port*
> *Ach ag iomchar cré agus cloch.*

> Cease your weeping now
> Women of the soft, wet eyes,
> Till Art O'Leary drain his cup
> Before he enters the dark school
> Not for music or learning
> But to prop the earth and stone.

According to Corkery:

> ... the people ... needed no instruction as to what sort of school
> was referred to in those lines; they knew it for a bardic school;
> furthermore, they were aware why that word 'school' has risen to
> the lips of the keening woman; they knew it was because of the
> sense of darkness, silence, mystery, aloofness that overwhelmed
> her to think of the bed in which Art O'Leary was to sleep for
> evermore.

The inhospitable earth of Ireland was symbolically the last remaining
'school' England had left the people.

Courtly love poetry was also being produced in Scotland in Scottish Gaelic and yet the first poem we find ascribed to a female poet,
in the fifteenth century, also introduces a very free, erotic element.
The poet is identified as Sibáel Cambeul, Anglicised as Isobel Campbell, countess of Argyll. She was a member of the family of chieftains
of the Campbell clan who first emerge in Scottish history in the
thirteenth century. Her poem was called 'Parted Lovers':

> There is a young man who is my lover,
> King of Kings, may he be successful in entering my chamber!
> Would he were here now
> stretched on my breast

with his muscular body
against my soft skin

Courtly 'love poetry' also flourished in Welsh. This was usually a
preserve of male writers. The works are often typical male boasts of
conquests, such as the poems of Hywel ab Owain Gwynedd (d. 1170)
in his 'Boast of Women':

> A duress that much worries me, has come my way
> And longing, alas, can't be avoided,
> For Nest, fair as apple in blossom,
> For Perweur, heart of my sin;
> For Generys the virgin, who'd not calm my lust –
> May she not achieve chastity!
> For Hunydd, matter till doomsday,
> For Hawis, the custom I'd choose.
>
> I had a girl of the same mind one day;
> I had two, their praise is greater,
> I had three, and four, and fortune,
> I'd five of them, their white flesh lovely;
> I had six, and sin not avoided –
> Clear white they sought me on top of a fort;
> I had seven, and the toil persisted;
> I'd eight, to pay for the praise I sang them –
> To keep tongue quiet, teeth do well!

There is an anonymous fifteenth-century poem imploring a woman
not to become a chaste *religieuse*.

> A pious, dark-eyed maiden
> Has with loving made me pine.
> If for another's profit
> I'd loved, God, I'm lacking wit!
> Women, I love, what's all this –
> You don't like Spring birches?
> You, that eight stars go to tint,
> Won't let your beads be silent?
> A saint of a religious,
> Kind to the choir, not to us?

Enough of bread and water,
For God's sake, and cress abhor!
Mary! With these beads have done,
This monkish Roman religion!
Don't be a nun – Spring's at hand.
And cloister worse than woodland.
Your Faith, my fairest truelove,
Goes quite contrary to love.

There was also something of a unique literary flourishing in Wales during the fourteenth to seventeenth centuries in an outpouring of poetry which dealt explicitly with sex and which was quite different from the vast corpus of 'love poetry'. Dafydd Johnston says: 'The principal common factor seems to be the desire to shock by the deliberate flaunting of accepted conventions of decent restraint in treating sexual matters.' Almost all the poetry is in the strict metres of the bardic tradition, the *cynghanedd* and the metre of the *cywydd*, the couplets of seven-syllable lines with end-rhymes alternately stressed and unstressed.

Almost all this 'erotic' poetry was written by men with one clear, notable exception. The poems seem to be a reaction to the 'courtly love' poetry of medieval times, popular through European culture. While the courtly love poetry offered an exalted ideal of female perfection and the honourable behaviour of the male lover, this poetry portrayed a 'wham, bang, thank you, ma'am' attitude. It is clearly derived from male fantasy, which the Christian Church did more than its fair share to promote. The idea was that women had a more lascivious nature than men and that their sexual desires were insatiable. As Dafydd Johnston says: 'The belief formed the basis for the practice of rape both in literature and in real life. If the girl refused to yield, then only her deceitful nature could be stopping her from confessing her desire, and so it was acceptable to take her by force'.

Some of the poems rebound on the male poets. In many of them the poet, in pursuit of sexual intercourse, is made to look absolutely foolish by the female victim. Tudur Penllyn, writing in the fifteenth century, has his amorous attentions spurned at knife-point in 'Ymddiddan Rhwng Cymro a Saesnes' (A Conversation Between a Welshman and an Englishwoman). And Dafydd ap Gwilym (*fl.* 1350–80), in a poem entitled 'Y Ferch yn Ymladd yn ôl' (The Girl

Fights Back) has his forceful seduction turned back very fiercely.

> *Ymguro, ymdaro dig,*
> *yno – gwae brydydd unig –*

complains the disconcerted Dafydd.

> We struggled and exchanged blows angrily,
> then – poor old lonely poet –
> the gentle girl scratched my nose
> and my face, love's misery.

> She was cunning, she bashed me on the head,
> it's quite true, with her closed fist.
> The girl did pull my hair
> like a foreigner . . .

Dafydd ap Gwilym seems, from his poetry, to be in constant 'hot water' with women. In his poem about 'The Women of Llanbadarn', he laments:

> Plague take the women here –
> I'm bent down with desire,
> Yet not a single one
> I've trysted with, or won,
> Maiden, wife or crone,
> Not one sweet wench my own!

However, from Dafydd's poetry, two interesting loves appear from real life. Dyddgu, a dark-haired lady to whom he composed nine *cywyddau*, strict-metre poems, was the unattainable object of his desire and was, in fact, the aristocratic daughter of Ieuan ap Gruffudd ap Llewelyn of Tywyn in Ceredigion, a descendant of the king Tewdwr Mawr ap Cadell. The other woman, in opposition to Dyddgu's remote and virginal role, was Morfudd. She was the subject of thirty *cywyddau* written by the poets, and it appears that Dafydd finally eloped with her though she was already married.

While there is still some scholastic debate as to whether Morfudd was a composite character in Dafydd's mind or whether she really existed, the probability is that she really existed. Her father's name is given as Madawg Lawgam in one poem. Another says she

descended from Ynyr Nannau, the founder of the Vaughan family of
Nannau in Merioneth. Dafydd describes real places and real people in
his poems about her. Even after she married and became a mother
Dafydd continued to court her. Other poets, such as Ifan Môn and
Llywelyn ap Gutun ap Ieuan Lydan, mention a tradition that Dafydd
finally eloped with her and his family had to pay a fine to her husband
in compensation.

Against the sexual pretensions of these male poets we have a
counterblast from a woman poet. We have already mentioned Gwerful Merchain of Powys (fl. 1462–1500). She is the only female poet
of medieval Wales from whom a substantial corpus of poetry has
survived. One of her poems suggests that she kept a tavern. The
subject of her poetry varies but her 'erotic' poetry represents only a
small portion of her work. A poem on 'Christ's Passion' has been
especially praised. Her poem 'I Wragedd Eiddigeddus' (To Jealous
Wives) has been interpreted by Dafydd Johnston as 'a subtle but
clear proclamation of female sexuality'.

> What sort of manner is it for a person,
> it does no good whatsoever,
> most strange, grievous kind of manner,
> particularly calamitous vice,
> that wives, hindering kind of attitude,
> swift frown, are excessively jealous?
> What nature, troublesome image,
> pure instruction, causes them to be so?
> Gwenllian said to me –
> the hoary old song was wanton in days gone by –
> that it is not love, wanton languishing,
> which turns towards gold yonder;
> the love of noble wives
> is for good cocks – bitter omen.
>
> Believe me, angry cry –
> every big-cocked lover is after me –
> no virtuous wife will give,
> the silly girl, her prick and her pole,
> if it follows a cunt in field,
> it wouldn't go one inch from her fist,
> not freely, she would not allow it,

nor basely, not for any price;
she would not make a deal with anyone
condoning adultery.
It is grievous, fine craft,
that the girl is not ashamed,
that the big prick means more to her
than her people, any day,
and eight of her family, and her father,
and her fair treasure and her adornment,
and her mother, I doubt not,
and her brothers, loud clear praise,
and her cousins, form brothers in the faith,
and her relatives and her sisters.
It's a bad state of affairs that a cock
completely deprives a woman of her senses.

Calumny is an unpleasant thing,
envy is the matter which causes it.
In my land there is some blight
and jealousy, abundant burden,
in every market, bad arrangement,
about her cock, violence and ill-will.
Despite giving eighteen
of the lord's cows, and the plough oxen,
and giving, however much the need,
rash summons, all the sheep,
a shapely girl prefers,
some say, to give the buildings and the land,
and would sooner give her good cunt,
beware, than give her cock;
sooner give her pan from her kitchen and her provisions
and sent her trivet than her fine rare post;
sudden in her haste, sooner give her dress
and all her possessions than give the prick.

I did not sing my satire,
God's truth, in any part of this poem,
to anyone, of the comeliness of the faith,
who wants a bigger than average cock.

Dafydd Llwyd of Mathafarm (c.1395–c.1486) was said to have been a would-be lover of Gwerful. He sent his friend, the poet Llywelyn ap Gutun, as his intermediary, but it seems he was rejected. Among Dafydd's poetry, elegies and love poems, are a group of fiercely pro-Welsh poems presumably in support of Owain Glyndwr's uprising against English rule.

There is a possibility that some of the poems which have not been attributed to an identified author might have been the work of women poets. Indeed, Dafydd Johnston suggests that one poem attributed to Dafydd ap Gwilym might, in fact, have been written by a woman for its style is far removed from Dafydd's style. The poem 'Ymddiddan Rhwng Mab a Merch' (Conversation Between a Boy and a Girl) concerns an inexperienced young boy asking a girl for sexual intercourse. The following is Dafydd Johnston's translation.

> Dexterous girl with slender waist,
> grand of manner with fine eyebrows,
> I request your leave in secret
> for Jesus's sake to make love to you.
> May I, pleasant is my greeting,
> have leave to lie with you girl?
>
> What good would it be to you, pale lad,
> to have it unless it were kept secret?
>
> By my faith, fine girl famed as a lover,
> I would keep it secret for ever to get to do it.
> I don't know what to do,
> or how to go about it.
>
> Lift my dress, seek openly,
> as if from under my navel,
> and put your knee between my knees –
> if you bring one put them both.
>
> What is, sprightly treasure,
> my feeble [syfal] cock won't stand up?
>
> What happened, great masculinity,
> to the words you spoke just now?

Like the sun they faded away,
or empty husks with the wind.
Devil take your women today,
or your mistress or any girl in your life,
or your way between my two thighs.
or your favour, you're a cold lad.
So take your thin little cock
and seek companionship in a bed of fleas.

And God's curse on you girl,
you ill-tempered wild-arsed bitch.

The word *syfal* (feeble) is, apparently, not attested elsewhere but
Dafydd Johnston believes its meaning is clear. He goes on to say:

> . . . one should not discount the possibility that it is the work of
> a woman. This is a poem which not only shows the boy's preten-
> sion in proposing intercourse and then being unable to perform,
> but also exposes the inconsistency of his attitude towards the girl
> as he accused her at the end of being 'wild-arsed', i.e. randy, the
> very quality which he had previously hoped to find in her. As the
> girl's sexuality becomes a threat the boy resorts to moral condem-
> nation to preserve his self-respect.

The work of Gwerful Mechain shows clearly that a woman could
and did write erotic poetry in Welsh at this period. Dafydd Johnston
comments on Gwerful:

> It is true that Welsh strict-metre poetry was an almost entirely
> male tradition, but Gwerful Mechain is a very important exception
> which proves that it was possible for a woman to compose in the
> strict metres and to talk openly about sex. In a sense Gwerful's
> very existence as a poet was a challenge to the male-dominated
> bardic establishment, and the element of challenge is most promi-
> nent in her erotic poems. They challenged social prejudices which
> held that women should not openly admit to their sexuality. They
> challenged male poets who presented a respectable picture of the
> female body, and who saw women merely as objects of men's lust
> . . . Gwerful's poems offer an image of an aggressive woman which
> is very different to the tranquil passivity of the courtly love idea.

245

The poem 'Cywydd y Cedor' (The Female Genitals) is apparently a reaction to the male poets' lustful descriptions of the female. Specifically, it was said to have been written in response to a cywydd by Ieuan Dyfi, an archetypal 'love-poet' from Aberdyfi, Merioneth. He addressed most of his poems to his lover Anni Goch but, chauvinistically, his poems harp on the deceit of women down all the ages. Once again the basic translation of Gwerful's counterblast to Ieuan is by Dafydd Johnston, with some minor word-changes for clearer comprehension.

Every foolish drunken poet,
boorish vanity without ceasing
(never may I warrant it,
I of great noble stock)
has always declaimed fruitless praise
in song of the girls of the lands
all day long, certain gift,
most incompletely, by God the father;
praising the hair, gown of fine love,
and every such living girl,
and lower down praising merrily
the brows above the eyes;
praising also, lovely shape,
the smoothness of the soft breasts,
and the beauty's arm, bright drape,
she deserved honour, and the girl's hands.
Then with his finest wizardry
before the night he did sing,
he pays homage to God's greatness,
fruitless eulogy with his tongue;
leaving the middle without praise
and the place where children are conceived,
and the warm vagina, clear excellence,
tender and fat, bright fervent broken circle,
where I loved, in perfect health,
the vagina below the smock.
You are a body of boundless strength,
a faultless court of fat's plumage
I declare, the vagina is fair,
circle of broad-edged lips,

it is a valley longer than a spoon or a hand,
a ditch to hold a penis two hands long;
vagina there by the swelling arse,
song's table with its double in red.
And the bright saints, men of the church,
when they get the chance, perfect gift,
don't fail, highest blessing,
by Bueno, to give it a good feel.
For this reason, thorough rebuke,
all you proud poets,
let songs to the vagina circulate
without fail to gain reward.
Sultan of an ode, it is silk,
little seam, curtain on a fine bright vagina,
flaps in a place of greeting,
the sour grove, it is full of love,
very proud forest, faultless gift,
tender frieze, fur of a fine pair of testicles,
a girl's thick grove, circle of precious greeting,
lovely bush, God save it.

The work of Gwerful Mechain is clearly unrestricted, untrammelled, by any male dominance. She is able to meet the male poets on their own pretentious grounds and shame them. There is a scene from a movie that comes to my mind: a Greek movie entitled *The Travelling Players* (1972), directed by Theodoros Angelopoulos, about the vicissitudes of a travelling theatre company in Greece during the Second World War. The Italians have invaded. Food is scarce and olive oil, the basis of Greek culinary preparation, is even scarcer. One of the young girls of the company, in desperation, decides to sell her body to an Italian soldier for a bottle of olive oil.

The young, handsome Italian soldier, bedecked in his fine uniform with polished boots, confidently and proudly enters the dingy bedroom. The girl takes the bottle of olive oil and stands passively by the bed. Self-assured, the soldier, wearing his superior smile, begins to undress, removing his uniform. Eventually he stands naked before her, smiling, poised, cocksure. She simply stares at him, stares at his naked body, his genitals, a deep expressionless stare. There is no excitement on her features, she views him merely as an object. The young man slowly loses his poise, he begins to blush, to grow nervous, and eventually brings both his hands forward to protectively cover his genitals from her dispassionate appraisal. He has been put into the place of an unsure, naughty little boy, this proud, boastful warrior, by the indifference of the girl. She has seen through his finery, his uniform, the outward veneer that creates his character, to what is underneath. A silly, impertinent male. In such a way does Gwerful Mechain disarm the boastful poets for she recognises their bragging sexual fantasies for what they are.

Epilogue

HISTORY inevitably becomes a story of individual endeavour, sometimes connected by a general theme, sometimes not. It is therefore very easy to pick certain individuals who emerge on to the historical canvas over the centuries and use them to form whatever tradition we wish to establish. This is not the case with the story of women in early Celtic society because, while we rely on the stories of individuals as illustration, we can place them and their lives against a native law system and show them to be part of a cultural environment, a particular society. But, by the late medieval period, there can be little doubt that the role of Celtic women had been utterly changed.

I began this study by posing some questions, as devil's advocate, asking whether particular events occurring in later Celtic history might be the result of a certain tradition. It would, undoubtedly, be viewing things with rose-tinted spectacles to answer those questions in affirmative terms.

Was, for example, *Párliament na mBan* truly an echo of a tradition of women's coequal place in ancient society? I think not. The author was a male and a priest at that. He was Domnall Ó Colmáin, priest of Chnuic Rátha (Knockraha, Cork), who was tutor to the son of Sir James Cotter, a Cromwellian settler. Dr Brían Ó Cuív has suggested that he first composed the work in 1670 and revised it in 1703. So how valid is it as an expression of ancient ideas of sexual equality? It is hard to say for, certainly, the theme and morals of *Párliament na mBan* would not have been out of cultural 'synch' with an earlier Irish literary period.

Nor, for that matter, would that other work to which some scholars genuflect, *Cúirt an Mheadhon Oídhche* (The Midnight

Court). This classic, to which I have referred in the previous chapter, has become one of the most widely translated works in Irish. It relates how the poet falls asleep and awakes in the midnight court of Aiobheal, queen of the fairies. There he is made to answer, on behalf of his fellow men, a number of complaints from women – the calculating habits of men who will marry old hags for money, the celibacy of the clergy, who above most men can support a wife. The poet, in David Marcus's amusing translation from the Irish, comments:

> Another thing I'd like to mention
> That's beyond my comprehension –
> Whatever made the Church create
> A clergy that is celibate?

But the poet goes on to wryly observe that not all the clergy are celibate in the eighteenth century.

> We know that some are tough old terrors,
> Who would never mend their errors,
> Frozen fogies who believe
> God blundered when he fashioned Eve;
> But others secretly admit
> They think her nature's choicest bit!
> There's many a house that didn't begin
> To prosper and smile till the priest dropped in,
> And many a woman could toss her head
> And boast of the time he blessed her bed;
> Throughout the land there's ample proof
> The Church is anything but aloof,
> And many a man doesn't know that he
> Has a son with a clerical pedigree.

The story is earthy, humorous but very pertinent. When the male poet is about to be beaten, for man is truly guilty as charged by women, he awakes. No work in the Irish language has been so hypo-critically treated as this, no work banned so often or regarded as dangerous. Yet, indeed, *The Midnight Court* would certainly not have been out of place in early Irish literary society.

One woman complains of the lack of young male lovers, that men are not even getting married in the area until they are old. The woman reproaches:

> By the time they're ready to take a wife
> They're not worth taking to save their life,
> They're stiff and shrunken and worn and weak
> And when they mount you they wheeze and creak.

And again:

> Fat chance there was of a night's high jinks
> With such a fossilised old sphinx;
> What passion could a girl entice
> From thighs as stiff and as cold as ice,
> A hulk that a furnace couldn't heat,
> A bag of bones, devoid of meat?

Ireland has produced many women who bestrode the state of history. Yet Irish history has tended to present a male-dominated picture, and it is only in recent decades that feminist historians have rescued these women from relegation to footnotes on the pages of history. For example, having read the story of Gráinne Ní Máille, could one think it possible that a study on the Elizabethan period in Ireland could fail to make reference to her? Cyril Falls' *Elizabeth's Irish Wars* (1950) does not mention her; while Richard Berleth's study of the period, *The Twilight Lords* (1979), dismisses her in one line.

Anna Wheeler of Cork, co-author of *An Appeal of One Half of the Human Race, Women, against the Pretensions of the Other Half, Men, to Retain them in Political and thence in Civil and Domestic Slavery* (1825), one of the most revolutionary statements of women's rights, is often ignored even by historians of the Left. In fact, most works that mention the book ascribe its authorship solely to Anna's common-law husband William Thompson of Roscarbery, Co. Cork. Anna and William did not believe in the 'economic institution of marriage'. Thompson's revolutionary socialist theories and his pioneering work, especially his concept of the theory of 'surplus value', were acknowledged by Karl Marx in *Das Kapital*. Anna, alas, receives little mention at all from those who genuflect to Thompson.

Little has really been written about Mary and Lizzie Burns from Keady, Co. Armagh. Mary became common-law wife to Friedrich Engels (1820–95), the socialist philosopher and collaborator of Karl Marx. She accompanied him on a tour of Ireland in 1856, interested him in learning the Irish language and encouraged him to write a 'History of Ireland' which, sadly, remained unfinished. She died of a heart attack on 3 January 1863. Some time later Engels took up with Mary's sister Lizzie, who was a supporter of the Irish Republican Brotherhood (the Fenian movement) over which Marx and Engels played an actively supportive role.

Helen Blackburn (1842–1903) from An Bheal Inse (Valencia), Co. Kerry, is another pioneer who receives hardly any credit in studies of how the franchise for women was secured. She wrote *Women's Suffrage: a Record of the Movement in the British Isles* (1902) and was one of the great pioneers of women's rights. One has to dig deep to find out about the work of Margaret Gillespie (1878–1954) from Boyle, Co. Roscommon, who is better known under her married name of Cousins. She became treasurer of the Women's Franchise League and was one of six Irish delegates to the Parliament of Women at Caxton Hall, London, in 1910. She was imprisoned in Holloway for her suffragette activities. She went to India and formed the Women's Indian Association in 1917. Imprisoned by the British authorities there, she went on to become the first woman magistrate and on independence the Indian government recognised her work for Indian freedom.

Irish women from all periods and in all roles have tended to be forgotten in the onward flow of male-dominated historical interpretation. Hardly known in either Irish or Spanish history is the story of Lucy Fitzgerald, wife of a Captain Patrick Fitzgerald of the Ultonia (Ulster) Regiment of Spain's Irish Brigade.

She was a Florence Nightingale figure over a generation before 'The Lady With the Lamp'. When Bonaparte invaded Spain, the Ultonia Regiment were defending the fortress of Montjuich, protecting the town of Gerona in Catalonia. The French besieged the town for eight months. During that time Lucy sought permission from the Spanish High Command to organise a women's unit of the Ultonia Regiment, which was designated the 12th Company but known as the 'Company of Saint Barbara', the patron saint of gunners and miners.

The purpose of the company, made up of wives or the soldiers of the regiment, was to take ammunition and food to the troops and then care for the sick and wounded. Lucy was elected as their commandant. Through the long days of French shelling and attacks, which took a regular toll of soldiers, civilians and the gallant Irish women alike, Gerona refused to surrender.

Lieutenant General the Marquise Laurent de Gouvion St Cyr was sent to reduce the town with 33,000 troops. The Ultonia Regiment's strength was only 600. Its commander was Colonel Anthony O'Kelly of Roscommon. In August 1808, O'Kelly was told that if the town continued to resist it would be reduced without mercy. Once the French broke in, everyone would be killed. O'Kelly called the townspeople together and put the facts to them. Their decision was sent back to the French. 'This town has taken its decision and we shall defend it!'

The French started their final assault. A diarist recorded:

In the square of San Pedro were the Irish women of the company of St Barbara, noblest of their sex, who only moments before were filing under a rain of shells, bombs and grenades to administer to the needs of the defenders; with the silent eloquence of example more persuasive than any words, they communicated their spirit and courage to the soldiers, in their arms they carried the wounded to the blood-covered floors of the hospital. Certainly Gerona was that day the abode of heroines.

Lucy Fitzgerald's last report to Spanish headquarters was dated 10 August 1809. It is in the *Archivo General Simanacas* in the *Archivo del Regimento Infantera Morteros 120 – Ultonia No 59*.

All ranks behaved with distinction. They administered untiringly to the needs of the defenders at the various points of attack. They brought much needed water and brandy to the fort of Montjuich and carried back the wounded on litters and in their arms. Despising the dangers of shells and bombs which aimed about them without stop, they displayed heroic zeal, charity and supreme courage. Lucy Fitzgerald, Commandant. August 10. 1809.

It reads as an epitaph. Yet Lucy Fitzgerald with modesty neglected to mention her own heroic role. The regimental flag of the Ultonia Regiment is now the town flag of Gerona, an acknowledgement to that heroic defence. By their defence against Napoleon, the Ultonia Regiment of the Irish Brigade, and Lucy Fitzgerald's company of St Barbara, not only forced Napoleon to engage a large part of his army of occupation in Spain in attempting to reduce Gerona, but ultimately provided an example to Spain which prevented it from being submerged under the empire of Bonaparte. When the Irish Brigade of Spain took part in the attack on Napoleon's army at Badajoz their rallying cry was 'Ultonia!' (Ulster!) Perhaps it should have been 'Lucy Fitzgerald!'

Women writers, artists and revolutionaries, actresses and *religieuses* almost poured out of Ireland from the late seventeenth century onwards. For example, the world of the seventeenth-century theatre in London was certainly male-dominated so far as playwrights went, yet a working-class girl from Co. Tyrone succeeded in becoming one of the most successful writers of comedy plays. Susanna Freeman (1667–1722) started her career as a domestic servant, but ran away and made her way to England. Both her first and second husbands were killed in duels. Susanna had mastered several languages and in order to camouflage her Ulster accent she affected to speak English with a French accent.

She began writing and her play *The Perjured Husband* opened in Windsor with a special performance at the castle which Queen Anne's French chef, Monsieur Joseph Centlivre, attended. They were soon married and as Susanna Centlivre she became one of the most popular playwrights of the day. Her house in Spring Garden Street (now demolished) near Charing Cross became a meeting place for intellectuals. She lies in St Martin-in-the-Fields with a simple inscription: 'Here lies Susanna Centlivre (née Freeman) from Ireland. Playwright. 1st December, 1722.'

One must not forget the large number of *religieuses* who have travelled the world not only as missionaries, but as teachers, doctors and nurses. Mary Catherine McAuley, foundress of the Congregation of Our Lady of Mercy (1778–1841), and her sisters founded a nursing order in Dublin which devoted itself to the 'service of the poor, sick and ignorant'. The order not only fought illness and poverty in Ireland, dealing with the epidemic of Asiatic cholera in 1832, but was able to build hospitals in England, such as in Bermondsey, in Southwark, London, where the sisters' community became the first Catholic religious house to be founded in England since the Reformation. The order was also the first women's organisation to furnish a group of nursing volunteers for the Crimea during the war (1853–56).

Dr Evelyn Bolster, in her remarkable study *The Sisters of Mercy in the Crimean War* (1964), says:

> That Florence Nightingale was an administrator of no mean ability cannot be denied, yet her methods of dictatorship, intrigue and personal vendetta have unhappily bespattered the early days of nursing reform . . . Of course, if the end justifies the means, there can be no criticism of Florence Nightingale. If, on the other hand, one believes that totalitarianism is never justified, there is much in Florence Nightingale's administration which calls for criticism. Viewed from this angle, history calls for a new approach to certain aspects of the Crimean campaign and for a vindication of the Sisters of Mercy.

Certainly, the role of the Irish Sisters of Mercy was grossly misrepresented by Florence Nightingale and all those who have subscribed to her mystique. The evidence is that Florence Nightingale was no white angel but a complex personality, authoritarian in the extreme and prejudiced.

When the British Army Medical Department collapsed, and the fifteen Sisters of Mercy volunteered their services as nurses in the Crimean military hospitals, they were accepted by the British government. But racism inevitably raised its head and Florence Nightingale and her administration often blamed their own incompetencies or mistakes on these Irish nuns. 'The real mistake we made in the selection of these ladies (between ourselves) is that they are Irish,' wrote Sidney Herbert on 5 March 1855, to Florence Nightingale. Dr Bolster's account of the racism suffered by the Irish nurses at the hands of Florence Nightingale makes for very sad reading.

The work of collecting the stories of individual women, as well as those of women's movements and organisations, has been proceeding during the last few decades as an awareness has seized society. Not the least significant is the story of the part Irish women have played in the struggle for their own country's independence, as demonstrated in Margaret Ward's seminal *Unmanageable Revolutionaries: Women and Irish Nationalism*.

As Margaret Ward explains, women have played a coequal part in that struggle. But in spite of such organisations as the Ladies'

Land League, Inghinidhe na hÉireann and Cumann na mBán, women have never been seen as an independent force in Irish political history nor accorded their proper place. In spite of their tremendous input into the political life of Ireland, apart from the emergence of a few notable political individuals such as Constance Markiewicz and, latterly, the Irish President, Mary Robinson, they have usually been excluded from positions of influence.

Times are now changing, but changing slowly. At this time, Ireland is unique in the countries of Europe in having no civil divorce. The referendum of 1986 on divorce, with a 64 per cent turn-out, produced a 63 per cent vote against divorce: an example of the influence of the Catholic Church. In 1990 the Irish Family Planning Association was fined in the Dublin District Court for selling contraceptives in the Virgin Megastore in central Dublin. And abortion remains illegal, as does information on the subject and pregnancy counselling. A 1983 referendum actually caused the insertion of a clause into the Irish constitution guaranteeing the equal right of an unborn child to life. During the 1980s some 4000 Irish women were forced to seek terminations in Britain every year. This anti-abortion legislation was highlighted in February 1992 when a fourteen-year-old Dublin girl, raped by the father of her girlfriend, became pregnant. Because the rape became the subject of police proceedings, the High Court forbade the girl to travel to Britain to have a termination of the pregnancy. The High Court's ruling was misinterpreted by foreign press and media, who thought the ruling had been made on the grounds of the illegality in Ireland of abortion. It was, however, a misjudgement of the court in the circumstances; it was corrected almost immediately by the Irish Supreme Court's ruling which overturned the High Court but opened up the anti-abortion issue again. Women under modern Irish law, which is simply an inheritance by the Irish state of colonial English law without the modifications made to it by England since 1921, are in a far worse position, so it seems, than their ancestors under the Brehon laws of 2000 years ago.

In the Isle of Man, the 1881 Women's Suffrage Act, like male voting qualifications at that time, applied only to property owners and thus enfranchised only 700 women. The law was amended in 1892 to allow women occupiers to vote. Only in 1921 was universal adult suffrage granted in the Island, and women became eligible to stand for election to the Manx Parliament. As we have seen, it was not until 1933 that the first woman was elected. Between 1933 and

1978 only seven women had served in the House of Keys, prompting local Celtic League activists to form a group called Equality versus Exploitation (EVE) which pointed out that the issue of a Manx government women's suffrage postage stamp on the Island was of little meaning when discrimination against women continued.

An article on 8 June 1979 in the *Guardian* claimed that, outside the Arab Emirates, one was unlikely to find women so repressed as in Wales. The article demonstrated such racist attitudes towards the Welsh that had it applied to any other ethnic group, such as Asians or West Indians, it would never have been published. Perhaps it was accepted because Plaid Cymru's seats in Parliament had just been reduced to two in the General Election of that year and the referendum on a Welsh Assembly on 1 March had resulted in only 11.9 per cent voting 'yes'. It was therefore 'Welsh-bashing time' again among the English press and media.

Nevertheless, there was an element of truth in the article. In another article, 'The Social Status of Women in Wales', Ifan Lloyd criticised the national movement in Wales, which, he said, might be expected to be strongly supportive in word and deed of women's emancipation but seemed to be ignoring such questions.

His argument was that when women were given the franchise, and the right to be elected, in the Patagonian Welsh colony of Y Wladfa in 1867, it was not due to the Celtic cultural inheritance from the philosophies of the Laws of Hywel Dda. It was the result of the Nonconformist movement in Wales of the eighteenth century. Women had played a prominent and vital part in the movement as counsellors (*cynghorwyr*) who directed the Methodist societies (*seiadua*) and travelled the countryside organising. Among these forceful women in the new religious movement were two who deserve a special mention.

Madam Sidney Griffith, the wife of the squire of Cefnamwlch, persuaded the preacher Howell Harris (1714–73) that she was a prophet. David Williams, in *A History of Modern Wales* (1950), says: 'She was a formidable woman, given to visions, and Howell Harris had great faith in her oracular utterances on such occasions.' He accompanied her around the country until her husband disowned her and Harris and his own wife separated. She died in 1752. She was, however, a powerful voice in the new religious revival.

There was also the work of Bridget Bevan of Laugharne, the heiress daughter of John Vaughan of Derllys Court and wife of the

Carmarthen boroughs' Member of Parliament, Arthur Bevan. She was a fashionable woman and became known as 'Madam Bevan'. She threw herself into Griffith Jones' 'circulating schools' movement in Wales, trying to educate Welsh children and adults, and providing a reading public for books in Welsh. Between 1737 and 1791 no fewer than 158,237 pupils had passed through the schools in addition to unregistered adults attending night schools. When Mrs Bevan died in 1779 and left £10,000 to continue the work, lawyers contested her will and her estate remained in Chancery for thirty years.

At the time, Ann Griffiths, who has been described as 'the greatest Welsh woman poet', was writing her religious poetry. She was born Ann Thomas in 1776 in the parish of Llanfihangel-yng-Ngwynfa in Powys. Her family were well off, her father being a small-time poet and ardent churchman. Ann's mother died in 1794 and so, at the age of seventeen, Ann became the mistress of the household, looking after her father and her four siblings. In 1796 she converted to Methodism. Her hymns and letters to friends won her literary recognition among a later generation. Her father had died in 1804 and she married Thomas Griffiths of Meifod. A daughter was born in July 1805, but the child died after two weeks and Ann died soon afterwards. In 1806 a collection of her hymns was put together and published as *Casgliad o Hymnau*. According to Saunders Lewis her longest hymn '*Rhyfedd, rhyfedd . . .*' (Strange, strange . . .) is 'one of the greatest religious poems in any European language'.

Many critics claim that Mary Owen (1796–1875), of Ynysyma-erdy, Briton Ferry, Glamorgan, took on Ann's role as one of the foremost religious poets at this time. Her collection of hymns, *Hymnau ar Amryw Destunau* (1839), contains many that are still popular in Wales today.

But in the nineteenth century things were changing for the Nonconformist movement. The radical Methodist movement became the Calvinist Methodist Church of Wales (now the Presbyterian Church of Wales) in 1811 and the role of '*cynghorwyr*' became a male preserve as clergymen took command.

One should not pass over the period with the idea that only a few women succeeded in Welsh life, and then only by excelling in religious works. There are many women who achieved distinction in other ways.

A woman who wound up with a reputation for excelling in areas where the male boasted his superiority was Marged uch Ifan, or

Margaret Evans (b. 1695), who lived at Penllyn, near Llyn Padarn, Llanberis, in Caernarfon. She was claimed to be a crack shot, the best hunts*man* and fisher*man* of her day. In addition, she was a champion wrestler, a blacksmith, a boatbuilder, a maker of harps and an excellent fiddle player. Thomas Pennant in his *Tour of Wales* (1778–81) recounted how he went to see this formidable lady but could not find her at home. He adds that she married 'the most effeminate of her admirers' in order, he cynically explains, 'to maintain the superiority which nature had bestowed on her'.

But of course, like the Irish, Welsh women achieved distinction during the eighteenth and early nineteenth centuries mostly in the field of literature, both in the Welsh language and in the English language. Jane Brereton (1685–1740), who wrote under the name 'Melissa', was born in Mold, Flint, and contributed her poetry in English to that arch-bastion of male superiority, *The Gentleman's Magazine*. She was married to the dramatist Thomas Brereton but after his death in 1722 she settled in Denbigh. Four years after her own death a volume of her poems was published as *Poems on Several Occasions*.

Samuel Johnson was friendly with several Welsh ladies who had succeeded in making a literary reputation. Anne Penny was born Anne Hughes at Bangor, Caernarfon (*c.*1729–80). She published several volumes of poetry in English starting with *Anningait and Ajutt* (1761) which she dedicated to Johnson. Another friend of Johnson was Hester Lynch Piozzi (1741–1821). Hester was born at Bodfel, near Pwllheli, as Hester Salusbury. Aged twenty-two she married Henry Thrael who introduced her to the London literary scene, and her friends soon included Oliver Goldsmith, David Garrick, Joshua Reynolds and Samuel Johnson. Johnson accompanied her and her husband on a two-month tour of North Wales in 1774. Henry Thrael died in 1781 and in 1784, against Johnson's advice, she married Gabriele Piozzi, an Italian music teacher. They set up home at Bachegraig, near Tremeirchion.

Hester had achieved a literary reputation, publishing numerous studies on politics, history and even a survey of civilisation since the time of Christ. She was described as a pretty, vivacious woman who was a compulsive conversationalist and proud of her Welsh heritage. Her marriage to Piozzi was a happy one and after he died in 1809 she continued with her vast range of interests until she died and was buried at Tremeirchion in 1821. Yet another of the Welsh women with whom Johnson associated was Anna Williams (1706–83) from Pembroke. She went to London when she was twenty-one with her father, the inventor Zachery Williams. She wrote poetry but, after an operation on her eyes in 1752, became blind. Johnson helped her write down her later compositions, which were published in 1766 as *Miscellanies in Prose and Verse*.

Julia Ann Kemble (1764–1838) is better known as Ann of Swansea or Julia Ann Hatton. She was one of the children of Roger Kemble and Sarah Wood, founders of a successful company of strolling players. Her sister was Sarah Kemble Siddons, while her brother was John Philip Kemble who became manager of both Drury Lane and Covent Garden. Julia did not follow the family into the theatre. She married twice but both husbands died and she earned a living by running a dancing school in Swansea. She wrote a play called *Zaffine or the Knight of the Bloody Cross* which became a success, and followed this with a dozen novels and two collections of verse, becoming one of the most successful writers of her day.

Almost contemporary with her was Felicia Dorothea Hemans (1793–1835) who lived at Gwrych, near Abergele. Without formal education, she published her first volume of poems at the age of fifteen years. She married a Captain Alfred Hemans in 1812 and bore him five sons before they were separated six years later. She then devoted herself to literature; her play, *The Vespers of Palermo*, was greeted with great acclaim in London and Edinburgh. Sir Walter Scott, William Wordsworth and Lord Byron were counted among her admirers and friends. Her best-known poem is 'Casabianca' which begins with the now famous line 'The boy stood on the burning deck . . .' Generations of schoolchildren have had to learn it and, as a result, her reputation has suffered as her better works have been all but ignored. She spent the last years of her life in Dublin.

Sarah Jane Rees, known as 'Cranogwen' (1839–1916), from Llan-grannog, Cardigan, launched one of the first Welsh language magazines for women, *Y Frythones*, which ran from 1878 to 1891. She wrote poetry, collected in a volume called *Caniadau Cranogwen* (1870), was founder of the Temperance Union of the Women of South Wales, and an advocate of the women's movement generally.

Rhoda Broughton (1840–1920) from Denbigh was unusual in having a mountain in Antarctica named after her – Mount Rhoda. Her novels, in English, displayed an extraordinary freedom of speech and were highly popular in her day. Her first novel, *Cometh up as a Flower* (1867), made her name synonymous among English readers with audacity. No woman novelist had dared to speak frankly about emotions and her mocking humour anticipated the more free, feminist expression of the later decades of the century.

Amy Elizabeth Dillwyn (1845–1935) from Swansea became one of the most powerful voices for women's rights in industry and public life. Her father owned the Dillwyn Spelter Works which, on his death, she took over as one of the first female industrialists. Her progressive attitudes were made clear in her forays into literature and her first novel, regarded as her best, *The Rebecca Rioter* (1880), was set against the famous social disturbances against toll-gates and road trusts which threatened the traditional communities of Wales.

There are, of course, numerous modern women writers in both Welsh and English, but it would be wrong to pass through a genuflection to Welsh literary women without a mention of Kate Roberts (1891–1985), novelist, short-story writer and literary journalist, who is now regarded as the twentieth century's most distinguished prose writer in Welsh. Born in Rhosgadfan, near Caernarfon, Kate Roberts studied Welsh at the University College of North Wales, Bangor, before becoming a schoolteacher. She began writing for *Baner ac Amserau Cymru*, then the leading Welsh newspaper. She produced work on a variety of subjects, literary, political and domestic. Many of her novels portray life in domestic settings from the woman's experience. Her novels are part of an austere Welsh landscape, full of repressed emotions and tragedy.

Yet her books for children are entirely different, though filled with social observation without sentimentality. Politically, she was a feminist and an ardent member of Plaid Cymru, seeking self-government for her homeland. She was a regular contributor to *Y Ddraig Goch*, the party newspaper. Although some of her work has been translated into English, one of the greatest of Welsh writers tends to be generally unknown outside Wales.

But all these ladies, from the seventeenth century onwards, are the exception rather than the norm.

To the inevitable question – What happened to change the role of women in Celtic society? – Margaret O'Hara and Bernadette Bulfin say that the move away from the tribal community and the rise of the 'state' provide an answer. They argue that 'this descent into serfdom and civilisation ... in the Celtic lands began with the twelfth-century Norman invasions and was completed in Ireland

with the conquests of the seventeenth century. The Celtic codes were
then replaced with English law of the period which was even harsher
than medieval law. Under the new system torture could be used to
extract confessions for several hundred capital offences, and a land-
lord could confiscate common lands and throw people off their farms
to beg if he decided grazing was more profitable than farming.'
Nowhere was this 'ethnic cleansing' by powerful landlords, with the
connivance and blessing of the government, more horrendous than
among the remaining Scottish Gaelic-speaking areas of Scotland in
the eighteenth and early nineteenth centuries, the period of the
notorious 'Highland Clearances'. Ian MacCodrum (c.1693–1779)
sums up the attitude in a lament:

> Look around you and see the gentry
> With no pity for the poor creatures,
> with no kindness to their kin.
> They do not think that you belong to the land
> and although they leave you empty
> they do not see it as a loss.
> They have lost their respect
> for every law and promise
> that was made . . .

It is no surprise that under such a system, where men and women
were reduced to penury and, indeed, no more than a form of economic slavery, the cultural paradigms were quickly altered. Man the
slave asserted his lost independence by asserting control over his
wife. It was part of this general loss of freedom that women became
'the slaves of the slaves'. Indeed, this was the phrase used by the
Irish Marxist philosopher and historian James Connolly, executed
for his part in the 1916 Uprising. In his arguments for women's
emancipation, he said that colonisation and the rise of feudal
capitalism had reduced women in Ireland to domestic bondage.
It was not until the seventeenth century that the majority of the
English settlers in Ireland began to distance themselves from the
native language and culture. When, at the end of the eighteenth
century, it was observed that the Irish language had been chased into
the countryside among the rural population and workers, it was,
curiously, many of the Anglo-Irish who rallied to the preservation
of the language. Among them was Charlotte Brooke of Co. Cavan

(*c.*1740–93), perhaps ironically an ancestor of the fanatical Unionist, Sir Basil Brooke, later Viscount Brookeborough, who was one of the leading architects of Partition in Ireland. Charlotte devoted time and money to recreating interest in Irish and was connected with *Bolg an tSolair*, the earliest Irish language magazine, published in Belfast. The native Irish intelligentsia and law system had finally been smashed by the end of seventeenth century. As the political independence of the Irish was eroded, the old systems and ideas were changed. Aspirations of political independence under the old Celtic system had ended with the Tudors.

In all the other Celtic lands, the native systems had been forcibly changed. Internal dynamics, whose seeds had been planted from England, had created a two-nation situation in Scotland with the concept of 'Highland' (Celtic) and 'Lowland' (Anglicised) cultures. Ironically, it was a woman who did more than most to create such a change. Margaret of Scotland (canonised by a grateful Roman Church) was born in 1045, the granddaughter of the Anglo-Saxon king Edmund Ironside (d. 1016). Her brother Edgar Aetheling was the Anglo-Saxon 'pretender' to the throne occupied by William the Conqueror. After the Norman conquest of England, Edgar and Margaret had found political refuge in Scotland. She married the king Maol Callum a' chinn mhòr (Malcolm III). His first wife Ingibjorg of the Orkneys had died giving birth to his third son in 1067. Margaret was deeply religious according to the uses of Roman liturgy and took with her to Scotland her own Anglo-Saxon confessor, Father Turgot, who later wrote her biography. She was reported to be horrified at the Celtic rituals which were still being used in the Scottish Church, and even the fact that the Scottish Gaelic language was spoken at the Scottish court was a matter of distaste to her. She protested that Gaelic was used in the churches of Scotland where Mass was celebrated in the vulgar tongue 'with I know not what barbaric rites.'

Margaret instigated a debate on the state of the Scottish Church, inviting three Benedictine monks from Canterbury to argue the merits of a complete change from Celtic to Roman custom. Bishop Fothudáin of St Andrews, the primacy of Scotland, was replaced by Margaret's own confessor, the Saxon Turgot, who proceeded to impose Latin in the Church.

Some historians, in order to bolster the idea of the English language having an older currency in Scotland than it has, have gone so far as to claim that Margaret imposed English in both the court and the

Church. However, on the overthrow of Edmund Ironside, the last Anglo-Saxon king before the Danish succession in England, his son Edward the Outlaw fled to Hungary and lived in exile until invited to return in 1057 by the restored Anglo-Saxon monarchy in the person of Edward the Confessor. Edward the Outlaw had married Agatha, a German-speaking Hungarian princess. It is specifically stated that Margaret's brother Edward Aetheling was not considered a serious candidate for the English throne by the Witenagemot (English parliament) because he could not speak English, having been born and raised abroad. If this is so, it seems unlikely that his younger sister, Margaret, had any fluency in the language. It was certainly Latin and not Anglo-Saxon, the contemporary form of English, which displaced Scottish Gaelic as the language of the Scottish court, Church and eventually administration.

Nevertheless, it was Margaret who, exerting her influence over Malcolm III, instigated such reorganisations and persuaded the Scottish court and Church to begin the changes which led to the alienation and marginalisation of Gaelic, once the lingua franca of all Scotland, to its present minority position. The recession of Gaelic to north-western Scotland is a story which has still to be written. Because of the language shift, it has been the subject of much prejudice and misinformation. In fact, Gaelic only died out in south-western Scotland, in Galloway, as recently as the eighteenth century. Robert Burns was a child when the last native Gaelic-speaker of his area, Carrick, a lady named Margaret MacMurray of Cultzeon near Maybole, is recorded as having died.

The ruling élite of Brittany had become French in attitudes even before the defeat of the Breton armies in 1488. In Cornwall, the Cornish language and its cultural ideas were swiftly in retreat, although Cornish did not disappear as a generally spoken community language until the late eighteenth century. Even while the Celtic languages still existed as the languages of the majority in the Celtic countries, the old Celtic social concepts had been changing and the values of the conquerors were being accepted. Of course there were anachronisms, echoes of the past which continued to be enshrined in the languages.

In Irish, as example, the male Anglicised names beginning Mac and Ó could not be used for women. Mac means 'son of' and Ó 'grandson or male descendant of'. A woman, customarily, could not take the name of her husband but retained her own name, being Ní, 'daughter or descendant of'. Indeed, it is incongruous that a woman, marrying a MacSweeny, 'the son of Sweeny', could not call herself Mrs MacSweeny nor could she change the gender of her name for she would be no descendant at all of Sweeny. Similar linguistic differentiation is made in the Brythonic Celtic languages. It was not until the sixteenth century, after the Acts of Union, that a system of fixed surnames was imposed in Wales for administrative purposes. As in Irish, it was incorrect for daughters to be called *ab* or *ap* (the equivalents to 'son of') but the use of the old form of *ferch* or *ach/uch* (daughter) is extremely rare now. This linguistic demarcation is a faint resonance of the more equal attitudes between men and women whereby a woman did not become the possession of her husband to the extent of automatically having to take his name.

According to Peter R. Cherici it was only in the eighteenth century that 'Celtic sexual attitudes underwent their final transformation, aligning themselves more closely with the practices and beliefs common to Western Europe.'

In Celtic society as a whole, as a purely Celtic social order disintegrated and reformed under the influence of the new definitions of sexuality approved by western Christendom, and with a law system based on wealth, power and male dominance, the unique sexual philosophies also began to fade from memory. Yet they still exist, in myth and folklore and, to a large extent, in the surviving codifications of the native law systems. However, these are now much intermixed with Roman Christian dogma. I do not mean this in any narrow sectarian sense, as I have previously pointed out, but only in a cultural sense. I speak of the early Christian movement which evolved in Rome under Paul of Tarsus and his followers which, as opposed to eastern attitudes, is to be found as the fundamental basis behind all of western Christianity including the Protestant offshoots of the faith.

Originally, as we have seen from Greek and Roman observations and from the corpus of Celtic mythology and law, the pre-Christian Celts had a sexual ethic which was different to that of their fellow Europeans. Their sexual relationships did not carry any burden of guilt or social disgrace. Men and women were not ashamed of the natural functions of their bodies and regarded them as pleasurable and even divine in a religious sense. As Celtic society came under the political and cultural sway of the Roman empire, and then under Christianity emanating largely from the same cultural source, the

Celts found themselves enmeshed in what is now seen as the West European sexual ethic, an ethic of constraint and guilt.

In that greater sexual freedom of the early Celts is to be found the natural coequal inclusion of women in society. The mother goddess is to be found at the commencement of most civilisations. As Professor Markle has pointed out: 'The oldest myths match the observations of the ethnologists. In the beginning, humanity was convinced that women were mainly responsible for procreation, and the first divine being worshipped was the mother goddess.'

For reasons which can be debated it fell to the cultural lot of the Celts in European society to retain such ideas connected with those early beliefs longer than most other societies. It is true that when the Celtic world emerged into recorded history it was already, as Mary Condren asserts, going through a state of change. The male had asserted that he was essential to fertilisation and began to claim a more than equal role in the previous equitable social partnership. A patriarchal society was undoubtedly evolving. The 'hero cult' was emerging. But it had not completely dominated Celtic society when that society came into collision with Rome. The Romans, as we have seen, were horrified by the status of women in Celtic society, which shattered their materialistic orthodoxy. Women were surely the bearers of children and objects of pleasure; simply domestic slaves? The status of Celtic women was subversive to the patriarchal paradigms of Greece and Rome. Therefore, it had to be destroyed. The destructive influence of the Roman empire, then of Christianity coupled with the cultures of the Anglo-Saxons and the Franks, certainly bludgeoned the Celts into change.

But it is a human condition that the more someone bludgeons, the more resistant the victim becomes. The internal dynamics within Celtic society, in which the role of women was undergoing a natural change, now faced an external force. The internal change was halted and Celtic society became more conservative in the face of this external threat. Thus the Celts clung to the old ways for a considerably longer time than they otherwise would have done. Instead of following other Indo-European societies into patriarchy they, for a while, balanced between the original coequal society and male dominance.

To draw a parallel: would Ireland have clung so fiercely to Roman Catholicism in the period following the Reformation had not its conquerors, England, been Protestant? Until the nineteenth century, when England tried to bludgeon the Welsh language out of existence,

Wales remained predominantly Welsh-speaking. From the turn of
the twentieth century, as constraints were slowly lifted, the Welsh
language began to recede like an ebb-tide. Once again, I do not argue
the moral values, simply make an empirical observation.

According to Professor Markle:

> Here it is necessary to observe that the Celts, as inheritors of
> non-patriarchal societies, stood halfway between these and the
> patriarchal Indo-European societies other than their own. This
> fundamental observation is based on the well-documented know-
> ledge we have of Celtic law, where women enjoyed privileges that
> would have made the Roman women of the same period green
> with envy. Here was a harmony between the roles of men and
> women that was not dependent on the superiority of one sex over
> the other, but on an equality in which each could feel comfortable.

The conclusion is that we are not claiming Celtic society was
advanced but rather retarded in the natural social processes of the
period. The argument as to whether these processes were bad and
regressive, when interpreted with our more enlightened attitudes of
today, is another debating point. Obviously, my personal view is
that Celtic society was more progressive than its modern-day
inheritors and that the feminist concept of a 'descent into [modern]
civilisation' is a reasonable one.

At the conclusion of our examination of the role of women in
Celtic society, we can simply confirm those proposals we outlined
in the introduction. Women had a position in early Celtic society
which their sisters in the majority of other contemporary European
societies did not have. They were able to govern; they played an
active part in political, social and religious life. They could be warriors, doctors, physicians, judges and poets. They could own property
and they remained the owner of that property even when married.
They could freely choose their partners, they could divorce, and if
they were deserted, molested or maltreated then they had the right
to claim considerable damages.

In examining the role of women in early Celtic society we should
not forget the main purpose of the exercise. It is not to substitute
the history of the female for that of the male nor simply to challenge
historical interpretation. In the words of Elizabeth Fox-Genovese, in
her thought-provoking article 'Placing Women's History in History'

(*New Left Review*, May/June, 1982), the object is 'rather to restore conflict, ambiguity and tragedy to the centre of historical process; to explore the varied and unequal terms upon which genders, classes and races participate in the forging of a common destiny.' Above all, with an understanding of the past in terms of how the role of women has changed in history, we can consider the harmony of the roles of men and women in a society based on a comfortable equality which does not rely on the superiority of one sex over another, and then expend our constructive energies in the pursuit of recreating a society that would return to a coequal balance.

Acknowledgements

The Chinese have a curse: 'May you live in interesting times.' August 1969 was certainly an interesting time to be in Ireland. I was in Dublin giving a talk about the Celts. At the entrance to the lecture hall I met Bernadette Devlin (now McAliskey), then newly elected Member of the Westminster Parliament for Mid-Ulster, the youngest Member of Parliament to be elected. It seemed it was Bernadette who personified the changing state of women in Ireland. There was a dynamic and vibrant atmosphere about the place. The revolutionary political attitudes of the time also meant the rise of an exuberant and electrifying feminist mood which had lain dormant in Ireland for a while.

Women had begun a new campaign not be to excluded from history. In the words of Margaret Ward in *The Missing Sex*: 'Men have written women out of history, that is an undeniable truth . . .'

The new self-awareness and self-confidence of the women of Ireland in 1969 marked the start of a justified criticism of professional historians, most of whose awareness of the contribution of women to politics and society was truly scandalous. I was, as a male, perhaps in a more privileged position than some, growing up in a household where few of the prejudices and 'hang-ups' of sexism prevailed. My mother, for example, had been sixteen years old when she joined the Women's Suffrage Society in 1913, quickly passing on to Emmeline Pankhurst's more militant Women's Social and Political Union. When she died in 1991, one month short of her ninety-fifth birthday, I discovered that she had kept her 1926 trade union card, the year of the General Strike, as a symbolic keepsake. There was no room for sexist attitudes in our home.

The elderly male speaker who had preceded me had received something of a grilling from the audience and, in particular, from a fiery and very personable young woman. Her dark hair a-tumble, her blue eyes flashing and with dynamic body language, she reminded me of one of those personifications of the spirit of the French Revolution, the woman at the barricades. She led the way in demolishing the speaker's conditioned sexist attitudes. I therefore approached my talk in some nervousness. But at the end of my address I found that I had won her support for my views. We became friends and colleagues in the same movement for a while.

Her name was Caitlín Maude (1941–81), born in Ros Muc, in the Conamara Gaeltacht. She was a poet and playwright in her native Irish. A graduate of University College Galway, she had become a teacher, an actress and a singer. Her poetry was highly regarded by critics, and was published in a wide variety of journals and anthologies. Only after her death was a collection, *Dánta* (Poems), published in Dublin in 1984. Her poetry was studied in the courses for the old GCE in the North and the Leaving Certificate in the Republic. An LP record of her poetry was issued by Gael Linn some years before her death. She co-authored a play, *An Lasair Choille* (The Blazing Forest), with Micheál Ó hAirtnéide, the bilingual Irish author Michael Hartnett. She was a leading advocate of women's rights and Irish reunification. The tragedy was her early death, on 6 June 1981, before she had come to her full potential as a writer.

The seeds of the idea for this book were sown by her and, therefore, it is to her memory and her values that it is dedicated. *Suaimhneas agus sonas siorraí dá h-anam uasal.*

I would also like to especially thank several who helped guide me along the way but would stress that they might not necessarily share my conclusions. My thanks and appreciation, therefore, go to Liz Curtis, Margaret Ward, Aidín Ní Chaoimh, Sibán Ní Cuinn, Pádraig Ó Conchúir, Professor Wendy Davies, Professor Fergus Kelly, Cristl Jerry, Dr Janig Stephens, Janice Williams, Gráinne Ní Fathaigh and Patricia Bridson; to Ifan Lloyd, for his much-needed guidance through Welsh law, and to the indefatigable Father Joe McVeigh of Fermanagh for his enthusiasm. Part of this book owes its origins to our public debate on the virtues of Celtic Christianity at the Irish Book Fair, at the Camden Town Irish Centre, London, on 20 March 1994. Finally, my love and appreciation go to my wife Dorothea for reminding me over the years that I ought to tackle this subject, and to the memory of my mother for her steadfast social guidance, and revelations of her own youthful battles in the cause of female suffrage which enriched my perceptions and understanding of the world.

Bibliography

As in my previous works, my purpose is to present a work for the general reader. Where sources obviously need crediting, I have made this clear within the body of the text. The following bibliography comprises a selection of 'secondary source' material. Primary sources, that is texts and translations of Greek, Latin, Irish, Welsh or other insular Celtic sources, have not generally been listed here. I would stress that the bibliography here is a *selective* one, bearing in mind that most of the works listed contain extensive bibliographies and footnotes of their own which will allow those readers so inclined to explore further. The purpose of this volume has been no more than to present an argument, a polemic, or an introduction, if you like, on the place of women in Celtic society.

Ancient Laws of Ireland, Vols. 1–6, Commissioners for Publishing the Ancient Laws and Institutions of Ireland, Dublin, 1865–1901.

ANDERSON, M.O., *Kings and Kingship in Early Scotland*, Scottish Academic Press, Edinburgh, 1980.

BAMFORD, CHRISTOPHER, and MARSH, WILLIAM P., *Celtic Christianity, Ecology and Holiness*, Lindisfarne Press, New York, 1982.

BANNERMAN, JOHN, *Studies in the History of Dalriada*, Scottish Academic Press, Edinburgh, 1974.

BERGIN, OSCAR, *Irish Bardic Poetry*, Dublin Institute for Advanced Studies, Dublin, 1970.

BIELER, LUDWIG, *The Irish Penitentials* (Appendix D.A. Binchey), Scriptores Latini Hiberniae, Vol. 5, Dublin, 1963.

BINCHEY, D.A. (ed.), *Studies in Early Irish Law*, Royal Irish Academy, Dublin, 1936.

BLAMIRES, ALCUIN (ed.), *Women Defamed and Women Defended*, Rhyychen, 1992.

Brut Y Tywysogyon (Chronicle of the Princes, Red Book of Hergest

Version), trs., ed., intro. by Thomas Jones, Board of Celtic Studies, History and Law Series No. 16, University of Wales Press, 1955.

BRYANT, SOPHIE, *Liberty, Law and Order Under Native Irish Rule*, Harding and Moore, London, 1923.

BYRNE, JOHN FRANCIS, *Irish Kings and High-Kings*, B.T. Batsford, London, 1973.

BULLOUGH, VERN and BONNIE, *Sin, Sex and Sanity: A History of Sexual Attitudes*, New American Library, New York, 1977.

CALDECOTT, MOYRA, *Women in Celtic Myth*, Arrow Books, London, 1988.

CAMPBELL, J.F., *Popular Tales of the West Highlands*, 4 vols., Edinburgh, 1860–62.

CARMICHAEL, ALEXANDER, *Carmina Gadelica*, 2 vols., Constable, Edinburgh, 1900.

CHADWICK, NORA, *The Druids*, University of Wales Press, Cardiff, 1966.

CHADWICK, NORA, *The Celts*, Pelican, London, 1970.

CHAMBERS, ANNE, *Granuaile. The Life and Times of Grace O'Malley c. 1530–1603*, Wolfhound Press, Dublin, 1979.

CHERICI, PETER R., *Celtic Sexuality: Power, Paradigms and Passages*, Tyrone Press, Connecticut, USA, 1994.

COMYN, DAVID (ed.), *Foras Feasa ar Éirinn by Geoffrey Keating*, 4 vols., Irish Text Society, London, 1901–14.

CONRAN, ANTHONY (ed.), *The Penguin Book of Welsh Verse*, Penguin, London, 1967.

CONDREN, MARY, *The Serpent and the Goddess: Women, Religion and Power in Celtic Ireland*, Harper and Row, San Francisco, 1989.

CORKERY, DANIEL, *The Hidden Ireland*, M.H. Gill, Dublin, 1924.

COSGROVE, ART, *Marriage in Ireland*, Dublin, 1985. (See also 'Marriage in Medieval Ireland', *History Ireland*, Vol. 2, No. 3, Autumn, 1994.)

DAVIES, SIONED, 'Y Ferch yng nGhymru yn yr Oesoedd Canol' (Women in Wales in the Middle Ages) in *Cof Cenedl IX: Ysgnfau ar Hanes Cymru*, ed. Geraint H. Jenkins, Gomer, 1994.

DAVIES, WENDY, 'Celtic Women in the Middle Ages' in *Images of Women in Antiquity*, ed. A. Cameron and A. Kurt, Croom Helm, London, 1983, revised ed. Routledge, 1993.

DE PAOR, LIAM, *Saint Patrick's World*, Four Courts Press, Dublin, 1993.

DILLON, MYLES and CHADWICK, NORA K., *The Celtic Realms*, Weidenfeld and Nicolson, London, 1967.

ELLIS, PETER BERRESFORD, *Celtic Inheritance*, Muller, London, 1985.

ELLIS, PETER BERRESFORD, *A Dictionary of Irish Mythology*, Constable, London, 1987.

ELLIS, PETER BERRESFORD, *The Celtic Empire: The First Millennium of Celtic History 1000 BC–AD 51*, Constable, London, 1990.

ELLIS, PETER BERRESFORD, *A Dictionary of Celtic Mythology*, Constable, London, 1992.

ELLIS, PETER BERRESFORD, *Celt and Saxon: The Struggle for the Supremacy of Britain 410–937*, Constable, London, 1993.

ELLIS, PETER BERRESFORD, *The Druids*, Constable, London, 1994.

ELLIS, T. P., *Welsh Tribal Law and Custom in the Middle Ages*, Oxford, 1926 (reprinted Aaelen, 1982).

EVANS-WENTZ, W.Y., *The Fairy Faith in Celtic Countries*, Oxford University Press, 1911.

FANTHAM, ELAINE; PEET FOLEY, HELEN; BOYMEL KEMPEN, NATALIE; POMEROY, SARAH B. and SHAPIRO, H. ALAN. *Women in the Classical World*, Oxford University Press, Oxford, 1994.

FELL, CHRISTINE, *Women in Anglo-Saxon England*, Oxford University Press, Oxford, 1984.

FOUCAULT, MICHEL, 'The Battle for Chastity' in *Western Sexuality*, ed. P. Aries and A. Bejin, Basil Blackwell, Oxford, 1985.

FUNCK-BRENTANO, F., *A History of Gaul, Celtic, Roman and Frankish Rule*, trs. E.F. Buckley, Barnes and Noble, New York, 1993.

FURLONG, NICHOLAS, *Dermot: King of Leinster and the Foreigners*, Anvil Books, Tralee, 1973.

GALLIOU, PATRICK, and JONES, MICHAEL, *The Bretons*, Basil Blackwell, Oxford, 1991.

GINNELL, LAURENCE, *The Brehon Laws: A Legal Handbook*, T. Fisher Unwin, London, 1894.

GOUGARD, LOUIS, *Christianity in Celtic Lands*, Sheed and Ward, London, 1932.

GREEN, MIRANDA, *Symbol and Image in Celtic Religious Art*, Routledge, London, 1992.

GREEN, MIRANDA, *Dictionary of Celtic Myth and Legend*, Thames and Hudson, London, 1992.

HENNESSY, WILLIAM, 'The Ancient Irish Goddess of War', *Revue Celtique* (1870).

HENNESSY, WILLIAM, and MACCARTHY, B., *Annals of Ulster*, 4 vols., Dublin, 1887–1901.

HENNESSY, WILLIAM, *Annals of Loch Cé: A Chronicle of Irish Affairs 1014–1590*, Irish Manuscripts Commission, ed. 1939.

HUBERT, HENRI, *The Rise of the Celts*, Kegan Paul, Trench and Trubner, London, 1934.

HUBERT, HENRI, *The Greatness and Decline of the Celts*, Kegan Paul, Trench and Trubner, London, 1934.

JAMES, SIMON, *Exploring the World of the Celts*, Thames and Hudson, 1993.

JENKINS, DAFYDD, and OWEN, MORFYDD E., *The Welsh Law of Women*, University of Wales Press, Cardiff, 1980.

JENKINS, DAFYDD, *The Laws of Hywel Dda; Law Texts from Medieval Wales Translated and Edited by* ... Gomer Press, Wales, 1990.

JOHNSTON, DAFYDD, *Iolo Goch: Poems*, Gomer, Llandysul, Dyfed, Wales, 1993.

JOHNSTON, DAFYDD, *Canu Maswedd yr Oesoedd Canol (Medieval Welsh Erotic Poetry)*, Tafol, Cardiff, Wales, 1991.

JOYCE, P.W., *A Social History of Ancient Ireland*, Longman, Green and Co., London, 1903 (2 vols.).

KELLY, FERGUS, *A Guide to Early Irish Law*, Dublin Institute for Advanced Studies, Dublin, 1988.

KIEFER, OTTO, *Sexual Life in Ancient Rome*, Dorset, New York, 1993.

KINSELLA, THOMAS, *The Táin*, Oxford University Press, 1970.

LEHANE, BRENDAN, *Early Celtic Christianity*, Constable, London, 1994 (orig. ed. 1968).

LLOYD, IFAN, 'The Social Status of Women in Wales', *Carn* No. 28, Spring, 1980.

LUCY, SEÁN, *Love Poems of the Irish*, Mercier, Cork, 1967.

MACALISTER, R.A.S. (ed.), *Lebor Gabála Érenn (Leabhar Gabhála, Book of Invasions)*, Dublin, 1938–56.

MACCULLOCH, JOHN ARNOTT, *The Religion of the Ancient Celts*, T. & T. Clark, Edinburgh, 1911.

MACCULLOCH, JOHN ARNOTT, *Celtic Mythology* (first published as Vol. III of *The Mythology of All Races*, Marshal Jones, Boston, USA, 1918) reissued Constable, London, 1992.

MACCURTAIN, MARGARET, and Ó CORRAIN, DONNCHA (eds.), *Women in Irish Society: The Historical Dimension*, Arlen House, 1978.

MACCURTAIN, MARGARET, and O'DOWD, MARY (eds.), *Women in Early Modern Ireland*, Wolfhound Press, Dublin, 1991.

MACKEY, J.P., *An Introduction to Celtic Christianity*, Edinburgh, 1989.

MACNEILL, EOIN, *Early Irish Laws and Institutions*, Burns Oates and Washbourne, Dublin, 1935.

MARKLE, JEAN, *Women of the Celts*, Cremonesi, London, 1975 (orig. *La Femme Celte*, Editions Payot, Paris, 1972).

MEEKS, WAYNE A., *The Origins of Christian Morality: The First Two Centuries*, Yale University Press, New Haven, Connecticut, USA, 1993.

MEGAN, SION, *Gwaith Ann Griffith*, Gwasg Christopher Davies, Llandybie, 1982.

MELLETT, M., *Warrior Queen*, Pan Books, London, 1978.

MERRIMAN, BRYAN, *Cúirt an Mheadhon Oídhe*, trs. as *The Midnight Court* by David Marcus, Dolmen Press, Dublin, 1953.

MESSENGER, JOHN C., 'Sex and Repression in an Irish Folk Community', in *Human Sexual Behaviour*, eds. Donald Marshall and Robert Suggs, Basic Books, New York, 1971.

MEYER, KUNO, *Ancient Irish Poetry*, Constable, London, 1913.

MURPHY, CLIONA, *The Women's Suffrage Movement and Irish Society in the Early Twentieth Century*, Harvester Wheatsheaf, 1989.

MURPHY, GERARD, *Early Irish Lyrics*, Oxford, Clarendon Press, 1962.

NI BHROLCHAIN, MUIREANN, 'The Manuscript Tradition of the *Banshenchas*', *Eriu* xxxiii (1987).

Ó CUÍV, BRIAN, *Párliament na mBan (The Parliament of Women)*, Dublin Institute for Advanced Studies, Dublin, 1970.

O'CURRY, EUGENE, *On the Manners and Customs of the Ancient Irish*, ed. W.K. Sullivan, 3 vols., William Norgate, Dublin, 1878.

Ó HAODHA, DONNCHA, *Bethu Brigte*, Dublin Institute for Advanced Studies, Dublin, 1978.

Ó HÓGÁIN, DÁITHÍ, *Myth, Legend and Romance: An Encyclopaedia of the Irish Folk Tradition*, Ryan Publishing, London, 1990.

O'HARA, MARGARET, and BULFIN, BERNADETTE, 'Descent into Civilisation', *Carn*, No. 26, Summer, 1979.

O'HARA, MARGARET, 'Women of Equal Dignity', *Carn*, No. 34, Summer, 1981.

O'LEARY, PHILIP, 'The Honour of Women in Early Irish Literature', *Eriu* xxxviii (1987).

O'RAHILLY, THOMAS F., *Early Irish History and Mythology*, Dublin Institute for Advanced Studies, Dublin, 1946.

OWEN, ANEURIN, *Ancient Laws and Institutes of Wales*, English Records Commission, London, 1941.

PIGGOT, STUART, *The Druids*, Thames and Hudson, London, 1968.

PLUMMER, CHARLES, *Bethada Náem nÉrenn: Lives of Irish Saints*, Oxford University Press, 1922.

POWER, PATRICK C., *Sex and Marriage in Ancient Ireland*, Mercier Press, Dublin, 1976.

PRESTON, J., *Mother Worship*, University of North Carolina Press, USA, 1982.

RAFTERY, BARRY, *Pagan Celtic Ireland*, Thames and Hudson, London, 1994.

RANKIN, H. D., *Celts and the Classical World*, Croom Helm, London, 1987.

REES, ALWYN and BRINLEY, *Celtic Heritage*, Thames and Hudson, London, 1961.

RICHARDS, MELVILLE, *The Laws of Hywel Dda*, Liverpool University Press, Liverpool, 1954.

RICHTER, MICHAEL, *Medieval Ireland: The Enduring Tradition*, Gill and Macmillan, Dublin, 1983.

ROCHE, RICHARD, *The Norman Invasion of Ireland*, Anvil Books, Tralee, 1970.

ROSS, ANNE, *The Pagan Celts*, Routledge and Kegan Paul, London, 1967.

SEYMOUR, ST JOHN D., *Irish Witchcraft and Demonology*, Dorset, New York, 1992.

SIMMS, KATHLEEN, 'The legal position of Irish women in the later middle ages', *Irish Jurist*, New Series X (1975).

STENTON, SIR FRANK, *Anglo-Saxon England*, Clarendon Press, Oxford, 1943 (revised ed. 1971).

STEPHENS, MEIC, *The Oxford Companion to the Literature of Wales*, Oxford University Press, Oxford, 1986.

STOKES, WHITLEY (ed.), *The Calendar of Oengus*, Transactions of the Royal Irish Academy, Dublin (Vol. 1), 1880.

STOKES, WHITLEY, *The Prose Tales in the Rennes Dindschenchas*, *Revue Celtique*, Nos. 15 and 16 (1894 and 1895).

STOKES, WHITLEY (ed.), *Félire Oengusso: The Martyrology of Oengus the Culdee*, Henry Bradshaw Society, London, 1905.

TANNAHILL, REAY, *Sex in History*, Scarborough House, New York, 1992.

THOMAS, CHARLES, *Christianity in Roman Britain to 500*, B.T. Batsford, London, 1981.

WALKER, DAVID, *Medieval Wales*, Cambridge Medieval Textbooks, Cambridge University Press, 1990.

WARD, MARGARET, *Unmanageable Revolutionaries: Women and Irish Nationalism*, Pluto Press, London, 1983.

WARD, MARGARET, *The Missing Sex: Putting Women into Irish History*, Attic Press, Dublin, 1991.

WEBSTER, G., *Boudicca: The British Revolt Against Rome 60*, B.T. Batsford, London, 1978.

Index

MP10BB